808.3
RAY

Ray, Robert J.

Weekend Novelist Rewrites the Novel: A Step-By-Step Guide to Perfecting Your Work

Robert J. Ray

the
Weekend
Novelist
Re-
wr**i**tes
the
Novel

A STEP-BY-STEP GUIDE TO PERFECTING YOUR WORK

WATSON-GUPTILL PUBLICATIONS
NEW YORK

This book is for Margot, who came back from a long way to help me through

Originally published in Great Britain as *The Weekend Novelist Redrafts the Novel* by
A&C Black Publishers Ltd, London, in 2007.

Library of Congress Cataloging-in-Publication Data

Ray, Robert J. (Robert Joseph), 1935-
  The weekend novelist rewrites the novel / by Robert J. Ray.
      p. cm.
  Includes bibliographical references and index.
  ISBN 978-0-8230-8443-2 (pbk. : alk. paper)
1. Fiction–Technique. I. Title.
  PN3365.R383 2010
  808.3–dc22

                              2009033869

ISBN 978-0-8230-8443-2

Printed in the United States

Design by Dominika Dmytrowski

10 9 8 7 6 5 4 3 2 1

First American Edition

Contents

Acknowledgments

Thanks to Jack Remick, my teaching buddy, for reading and re-reading, for re-structuring and forcing me to rethink. Thanks to my wife Margot for reading and feedback. Thanks to the writers at Louisa's Bakery and Cafe for readings and feedback: Melissa Morse, Geri Gale, Richard "Max" Detrano, Don Harmon, Stacy Lawson, Anne Herman, Marianne Ray, Sondra Kornblatt, Joel Chafetz, Soulaika Mar, Jonathan Locke. Thanks to Valerie Ryan, sage bookseller, for focus.

Thanks to my London agent, Lorella Belli, for finding a home for this book.

Thanks to Katie Taylor and the editors at A & C Black, London. They do magic with words on the page.

Introduction

Your three-hundred-page manuscript needs a rewrite.

You start on Page One, line one.

Your strategy is to cut and replace.

Cut a bad word. Replace it with a good word.

Your tool is line editing.

That strategy, cutting and replacing words, works for three pages.

On page four, however, your line edit unearths a bad paragraph.

The bad paragraph reveals a hole in your story.

Revising that paragraph, turning it from bad to good, widens the hole.

Fixing that hole takes all afternoon.

You read over your work.

Four pages edited, weekend slipping away.

That means 296 pages left to rewrite.

At four pages a weekend, your line edit will take seventy-four weekends.

To rewrite faster, fix your subplots.

Subplot is the secondary story running under the plot. You work the subplots to get at *subtext*, the unsaid, the not-said, the semivisible, very powerful secret stuff working under the text. Here's an example:

- **Character A says:** Where were you last night?
- **Character B says:** Had to work late, honey-bunch.
- **But the subtext says:** Character B is lying. He spent last night making motel-music with Character C.

Subtext is the repressed, drama-packed, *unspoken* thing—the anger, the desperation, the twisted lie, the secret that pops out when you need to create a plot twist. Secrets lurk in the subtext.

TIP FOR YOUR REWRITE

You are heading up the wrong path. The key to rewriting your novel is not line editing; the key is fixing the subplots. If you fix the subplots, the manuscript will shape up.

The easy way to get at secrets in the subtext is to work your subplots. To work your subplots, you need special tools. But before we raid the tool storehouse, let's look at subplot and secret in *Jane Eyre*.

Written in longhand by Charlotte Brontë, *Jane Eyre* was first published in 1847. The novel is a Rags to Riches tale about a Victorian

Cinderella who scrambles up the economic ladder, battling nasty antagonists, to land a rich man of property. The Cinderella character is Jane. The man of property is Mr. Edward Fairfax Rochester, master of Thornfield Hall. At Midpoint in the novel, Mr. Rochester proposes. Jane says yes. Near the end of Act Two, however, Rochester's ugly secret pops out: He already has a wife. Her name is Bertha Mason Rochester. She's a crazy woman locked away in a tower at Thornfield Hall, where Jane has been working as a governess for several months.

The secret is out and now Rochester confesses to Jane: how Bertha's greedy father bribed Rochester's father to take the girl away; how Rochester's father shoved his youngest son, Edward, into a forced marriage with crazy Bertha; how Edward could not lock her away in a madhouse; how he locked her in the tower at Thornfield instead; how he sought female companionship among the courtesans of Europe. The motive is clear. Rochester preys on Jane's sympathy. He wants to persuade her to stay at Thornfield, not as his lawful wife, but as his convenient (and temporary) mistress. In the subtext, we hear the drumbeat of biology: An older man with good resources and no children wants to mate with a young woman and use her to achieve genetic success.

The ugly secret of crazy Bertha has lurked in Rochester's subplot all the way through Act Two. Now the secret explodes to shatter Jane's wedding hopes. Jane is so shocked by the eruption that she leaves Thornfield. In leaving, she almost dies on the heath.

Jane has the plot.

Rochester has Subplot One.

The secret in Rochester's subplot provides a plot twist that forces Jane to leave Thornfield. Jane's departure marks the end of Act Two. The setting changes from the safety of a warm house to the dangers on the lonely heath.

> **TIP FOR YOUR REWRITE**
>
> When you position a confession scene near the end of Act Two, you are making a *structural* decision that affects dramatic conflict in your story. Before you line edit, you must fix story and structure.

Plot Vs. Subplot

When you wrote your rough draft, there's a high probability that you spent most of your writing energy developing the plot, the path of your protagonist. If you're like most novelists, you paid scant attention to subplots because you were busy with the elements of fiction: setting, character description, objects, dialogue, and scene-building.

If you're like most novelists starting out, you reached the last page of your manuscript with a handful of major characters—the protagonist, an antagonist or two, a helper—and a horde of minor characters. Now, in the rewrite, as you work your subplots, you have a chance to add muscle and brains and motivation to your antagonists.

Antagonists hold the key to dramatic tension, entertainment, retellings, book sales, film rights. Jane's fierce struggle with seven antagonists has spawned fourteen feature films (eight on the silent screen from 1910–26; eight on the big screen from 1926–96); six television versions; and spin-off novels like *Wide Sargasso Sea* (1966), in which Jean Rhys rechristened Bertha, naming her Antoinette, and then wrote the story of her arranged marriage to Rochester.

If you've already created half a dozen bad guys (male or female), make them deeper now as you work those subplots. If you can't find a single antagonist in your horde of characters, you have work to do. Often, writers come into a fiction workshop with no visible antagonist. They wrestle with large abstractions—evil, antagonism, political correctness—and then it's time to wheel out Charlotte Brontë's opus.

Jane Eyre has lasted over 150 years.

Jane Eyre has seven antagonists.

There is a connection here.

Checklist for Your Rewrite

To get the most out of this rewrite, you need a substantial body of work:

- [ ] a manuscript measuring some three hundred pages

- [ ] a cast of rowdy characters (protagonist, antagonist, helper, etc.)

- [ ] a time frame

- [ ] a virtual warehouse of objects (cars, suitcases, jewelry, keys, clothes, weapons, office supplies, boats, sleighs, mobile telephones, paintings, statues, etc.)

- [ ] forty to sixty named scenes

- [ ] a plot and three or more subplots

- [ ] a visible *resource base* (think Thornfield Hall in *Jane Eyre*, Manderley in *Rebecca*, East Egg in *The Great Gatsby*, the vice president's house that was occupied by terrorists in *Bel Canto*, the royal castle in *Cinderella*); resource base means object of desire

- [ ] one hundred pages of *back story*—personal histories on your main characters

The Secret of Rewriting

This is the secret: You can't rewrite a whole novel all at once. *You can rewrite a novel one piece at a time, one exercise at a time, one startline at a time.* The exercises in this book combine *timed writing*—writing under the clock, keeping the hand moving, no crossing out—with tools borrowed from screenwriters: list of scenes, character arc, the CUT TO, and more.

Timed Writing

To do timed writing, you grab a *startline* (a phrase that triggers your writing: "I am writing a story about . . ."; "My protagonist wants . . ."; "At plot point one, my protagonist does not know . . ."), set your kitchen timer, and write until the timer beeps. You can write alone, but you generate more energy (and often more insights) with a writing group. I practice my timed writing twice a week, working with a group of writer-friends in a local coffee house. We write for half an hour; then we read around the table. There is no critique; there is only practice. In thirty minutes of writing practice, I produce three scrawled pages. Rough, strange, hard to read. Sometimes the writing leads nowhere. Other times it bristles with insight. I learned the discipline of timed writing from Natalie Goldberg in Taos, New Mexico. It changed my life.

Writing practice can change your life, too.

If you do the writing.

Secrets of
Rewriting:
Story Structure Style

When you rewrite, you work story and structure first. *Story* is a competition for a resource base; *structure* is an arrangement of parts. When your story hums and your structure runs smooth, then you fix the style. *Style* is the words chosen for a page.

Story

Story in fiction means characters struggling to control a scarce resource. Example: Two strong characters—one Virgin and one Death Crone—compete for access to a royal castle. The castle represents the good life. Safety, warmth, hot water, plenty of food, servants to wait on your person, a closed circle that increases the chance of genetic success: a baby to carry the bloodline into the future.

> **TIP FOR YOUR REWRITE**
>
> Some professionals write novels with two protagonists and two plots. Mary McCarthy gained fame with *The Group*, which had seven protagonists. Advice: Keep your rewrite simple. One protagonist, three to four subplots.

The castle sits on a hill above the village. The village is growing into a town, the population swollen by pilgrims, treasure hunters, thieves, ruffians, refugees, characters fleeing their sordid back stories. If the Virgin wins the competition, her baby will have access to the royal resources—education, training, influence, power—to help it prosper in the future. If the Death Crone wins, one of her daughters could produce a baby with the same access to resources. Biology drives both characters. Story tells us who wins.

Structure

The main parts of the novel are a plot and two or more subplots. One character follows the plot; different characters follow their own subplots.

In a story, both plot and subplot follow a path from the beginning through the middle to the end of the story. For structural purposes, your novel begins in Act One, progresses through Act Two (middle), and climaxes in Act Three (the end).

Acts have parts called *scenes*. Scenes have parts: setting (time, place, temperature, lighting, objects), character, action, dialogue, and climax. Characters have interiors (agendas driven by motives created by traumas) and exteriors (body parts, action to carry out the agenda). Action (strong verbs, concrete nouns) and dialogue (short lines controlled by rules) take you out of structure into style.

The scene is the little engine of drama in which characters work their agendas:

- The Virgin tries on a shoe; the shoe fits.
- Enraged, the Death Crone cuts off her daughter's big toe.

Style

When you write a sentence, what do you think about? Do you think about word choice and word order? Or do you think about what the sentence says? What kind of information it delivers? Do you use weak verbs like *"could have been observed remembering* what she *might have thought had been* actually *seen"*? Or do you use strong verbs like *slam, slap, spring, scream, charge*?

Style is word choice. Choices about words and word order.

Style is in your hands.

Choosing words is a full-time job, no time for story, no muscle for structure.

That knowledge—style is a full-time job—dictates a plan for your rewrite.

Story and structure come first in your rewrite because you don't have the

> **TIP FOR YOUR REWRITE**
>
> Style in fiction is word pictures. To make word pictures, you need concrete nouns and strong verbs.

head-room to worry about word choice and word order. Style is the last step in the rewrite process. That's when you put your eye close to the page. That's when you analyze your syntax (word order). That's when you count your nouns and your verbs in selected paragraphs. That's when you analyze your ratios of weak verbs (*could have been observed remembering*) to strong verbs like *slam, slap, scream,* etc. That's when you compare the mushy feel of abstract nouns like *administration* and *frustration* and *culmination* to the solid weight of concrete nouns like *arrow* and *fire* and *teeth*.

Weekend ✓: Planning

Overview: A Plan for Your Rewrite

The plan for your rewrite is based on the invisible hierarchy of story, structure, and style. When you open a novel to Page One, you see style—the words on the page—but you don't see story and structure. They are invisible to the reader.

Not to the writer.

When you rewrite, you must be aware of story and structure. Readers want to be entertained. Entertainment means drama and suspense. Drama comes from conflict—Character A wants the castle; Character B blocks the road, the path, the outer gate, the wide staircase leading up to the royal portals. Character A is the protagonist; she has the plot. Character B is the antagonist; he has Subplot One. If your antagonist comes on late, if he does not enter the story until the middle of your novel, then your story will lack conflict. You have just made a structural decision—bringing on a latecomer-antagonist—with dramatic consequences.

A large part of your rewrite is making structural decisions.

The efficient rewrite starts with a reading of your manuscript. You hold off on the line editing, save it until later. You make notes and lists. A list of subplots, for example, gives you a look at texture and places to park secrets. Make a note and keep moving. A list of flashbacks alerts you to the weight of your back story.

The diagram on the following page shows how your rewrite starts with reading and lists and rethinking the structure. That's the first step, represented by the

TIP FOR YOUR REWRITE

If a big chunk of your manuscript takes place in the back story—in the past before Page One—then you must rethink your structure before you tackle the subplots.

big number 1 inside the first circle. It's the thinking phase of the rewrite. Planning and design, tools and techniques. Once you have the structure that you need to contain the back story, you rewrite subplots (the big number 2); then you rewrite the key scenes (the big number 3); and then you tackle the style (the big number 4).

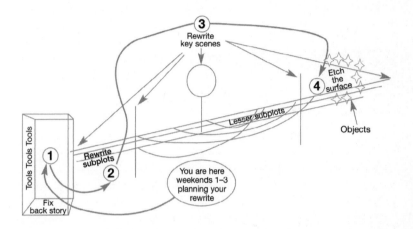

You're in phase 1 now. Reading, fretting, taking notes, burning to get started. To sharpen your focus on the rewrite, you make five lists: character, subplot, scene, flashback, and object. The *character list* is a cast roster; it tells you who's onstage, who's doing the work, who needs to be cut. The *subplot list* takes five or six important characters—those at the top of the list—and packs them into their own special grid. There's a model for the grid in the next chapter, "Weekend 2: Tools." Each of these subplot characters has an arc that stretches from the entry point (the place where they enter the story) to the exit (gone, to be seen no more). Each of these characters has a solid connection to the protagonist. The subplot list gives you a head count of your antagonists.

The *scene list* is your first look at sequence and structure. You need forty to sixty scenes for a novel. To mark the three-act structure, you'll have six key scenes and a First Encounter that floats. When you rewrite your subplots, you will have separate scene lists for each one.

The *flashback list* gives you a glimpse of back story: how much, how deep, how useful. *The object list* gathers recurring objects—weapons, vehicles, money, jewelry, statues, furniture, wardrobe items—concrete nouns aching to become symbols. Objects tell your story. What would happen to the Cinderella fairy tale without those slippers? What would

TIP FOR YOUR REWRITE

If you make these lists now, your rewrite will go smoother. Lists force you to look at structure—how the manuscript is built—and content. *Content* means place, character, time span, objects, body parts. Super Tip: No objects, no story. Clue: How would the fairy tale universe fare without those glass slippers?

happen to the story of the quest for the White Whale without Ahab's harpoon?

With your brain filled by the details on the lists, you use your new tools to fix the back story. You're still in phase 1 on the diagram, heading for phase 2, when you rewrite those subplots. You work with back story now because the fictional past is huge. It can gobble up your story. For example, if you're rewriting a book like Michael Ondaatje's *The English Patient*, with time trips starting on the second page of your manuscript, you have a decision: Either create a zigzag structure to control the time trips or restructure the book in chronological order. If you saw the Oscar-winning film, but did not read the book, you might not know that over half of *The English Patient* in novel form is back story. When he made the film, director Anthony Minghella cut out the back story on Kip, the Sikh sapper, to make room for the heated story of twisted, desert love between Almásy, the scholarly explorer, and Katharine Clifton, the bored young British wife. Back story forces big decisions.

When your back story is stabilized, you rewrite the subplots (now you're in phase 2 on the diagram). Subplot One comes first. It's the path of your antagonist. Keep it simple. When you finish Subplot One, you fix Subplot Two. Then you work the lesser subplots—Three, Four, Five, maybe even Six. *Jane Eyre*, which has seven subplots, was published in 1847—that's a shelf life of a century and a half. Contrast that with today's hurly-burly marketplace, where a long shelf life for a novel is two months. We can all learn from a great classic.

When you finish rewriting the subplots, take time to reread the manuscript. If it feels solid, you can work the style. If the structure needs more work, then you rewrite key scenes (phase 3 on the diagram). If your First Encounter (where the protagonist meets the antagonist) starts on Page One or Plot Point One, you have six key scenes. If your First Encounter floats, landing somewhere in between two key scenes, you have seven: the floating First Encounter, Page One, Plot Point One, Midpoint, Plot Point Two, climax, and the ending. Plot points come from the world of screenwriting.

Rewriting key scenes locks down your three-act structure. With the structure in place, you can work the surface (phase 4 of the diagram).

Surface means what you can see on the page. You see recurring objects; you see opportunities for more suspense; you see word pictures that need fixing. Now, at last, you have the time—and the head space—for style.

TIMED WRITING FOR YOUR REWRITE

The efficient way to rewrite is to do timed writing. Set your kitchen timer. Use a startline like "This scene needs rewriting because . . ." or "My protagonist wants . . ." and write, keeping the hand moving, until the timer dings. Dedicate every weekend to the exercises. During the week, snatch minutes from your day. Five minutes, ten minutes, half an hour of timed writing. For discipline and support, form a writing group, find a place to write, set a designated hour for your writing. Write and read aloud and do not critique unless you want blood on the floor. Critique too early in the writing process snuffs the small blue flame of creativity. Natalie Goldberg, author of *Writing Down the Bones*, gives this advice: "Don't stop writing to think and don't cross out and go deep with your writing." Timed writing will take you deep into plot, subplot, texture, subtext, and core story—all the layers that make up the deep structure of your novel. The key to timed writing is to keep the hand moving. Lose yourself in the words, the flow of language, the ancient river of story.

Exercises for Planning

1. READING

Read the manuscript. Take notes on character, motive, agenda, action, object, sexual attraction, blood connections, loves and hates, betrayals, fake-outs—anything that stops the smooth flow of your story. Take notes on dialogue, setting, pacing (turgid vs. lightning fast), flashbacks. If your notes overwhelm your margins, dedicate a spiral notebook to your rewrite.

2. MAKE LISTS

To prepare for the rewrite, you make lists. A list works two ways: While it helps you create an overview, it also sorts out tasks, unearths problems, and organizes the work of rebuilding into categories. For example, if your character grid has sixty names and your object list has only three objects, and none of those objects is attached to a specific character, then you have work to do. Gather more objects and reduce the size of your cast of characters. Close your eyes and imagine your novel as a feature film streaming by on the screen. Which characters do not have objects? Which characters refuse the object they are offered? You have a choice: a simple list of names (Jane, Helen, Aunt, Mr. B, Mrs. F, Bessie, Mr. R, Grace Poole) or a list that starts a grid. Suggestions for expanding your lists:

- **Character List/Grid.** Play with these categories: name, role (protagonist, antagonist, etc.), object, entrance and exit, strength, weakness, fate.
- **Subplot List/Grid.** Pick the six characters at the top of the list (exclude the protagonist) and isolate six subplots. Track the arc from entrance to exit. Attach an object to each character. Connect each character to the protagonist: blood, money, power, work, school, church, organization, back story.
- **Scene List/Grid.** You're tracking the plot: scene name, setting, who's in the scene, objects in the scene, action, time of day, weather.
- **Flashback List.** Location (act, scene), character, trigger, setting, purpose. Flashbacks have the power to stop the story, to kill the forward momentum. While writers love flashbacks, readers often find them confusing. A list can save your book from oblivion by alerting you to your flashbacks. Bury your flashbacks in Act Two. That's where they're needed most.
- **Object List.** Tracking objects in your prose, you discover the power of repetition. An object that surfaces three or more times (Almásy's book of Herodotus in *The English Patient*, for example), while it aches to become a symbol, also helps to tighten the story. So on your object list, you're seeking helpful objects from these categories: jewelry, vehicles, weapons, wardrobe items, foods, drinks, tools, money.

TIP FOR YOUR REWRITE

Working against the clock will help you focus. Starting the lists now is important because you need to get moving. You can add to the lists when something new turns up. Don't wear yourself out. Be disciplined but not compulsive. Set your timer. Go.

Writing time: Character list, thirty minutes. Subplot list, thirty minutes. Scene list, two hours. Flashback list, forty-five minutes. Object tracker, twenty minutes.

3. PROBING YOUR REWRITE

Explore the reasons for your rewrite. Was it requested by an editor? Was it a suggestion from friends? How did you come up with the idea of rewriting? How much line editing have you already done?

Startline: "I know that my novel needs rewriting because . . ."

Writing time: twenty minutes

4. STRUCTURE OF THE NOVEL

Use a structural diagram to develop a sense of the novel's architecture. The larger units in this structure are acts; the smaller units are dramatic scenes. Locate the First Encounter first, and then locate the other six key scenes: opening, end of Act One, Midpoint, end of Act Two, climax, and the final scene. Mark the entrances and exits for the main characters. Who enters in Act One? Who exits before Act Three? Entrances and exits mark character arcs; character arcs help you chart subplots. There's a model diagram below; another one appears in "Weekend 2: Tools."

Time for the diagram: thirty minutes

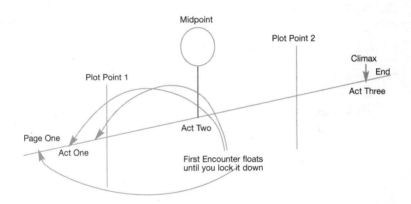

5. RHYTHM IN YOUR REWRITE

A paragraph is a cluster of words defined by white space. First line indented, margins on the sides, end with a period. Paragraphs eat your writing time. Step outside the paragraph. Let your writing breathe. When I do timed writing, the lines spill down the page:

I list scenes down the page

then I do index cards on the lists

then I do CUT TO's on the index cards

and when a scene crashes

I rewrite that scene in the notebook

writing down the page
and then I rewrite the scene before
and the scene after
because the scene sandwich creates a solid block in the structure
a place to stand while you connect with other scenes
not wasting energy on
paragraphs and quote marks and caps
which is so final draft
and after enough writing
down the page
the scenes flow out in proper paragraphs
and there is less rewriting
because lists and index cards and CUT TO's
smooth the way
because when you write a novel
there's always something to rewrite
but the work goes faster if you evade
the paragraph by
writing down the page for ten minutes go

Meet Writer X, Weekend Novelist

To guide you through your rewrite, I'm including a *work-in-progress*, a model novel that will appear in each chapter following the exercises. The novelist is Writer X, male, thirtysomething, a savvy California computer technician who reads lots of novels. Like most writers, X is left-brain heavy. He writes a page, prints it out, and plunges into a serious line edit. X loves the precision of cutting, replacing, adding text. Like magic, one page becomes three pages. Line editing turns him on. Let's have a look at X's progress.

Writer X has this manuscript.

A massive novel, with seven drafts completed.

Seven years of writing and rewriting, eight-hundred double-spaced pages.

The novel weighs five pounds and stacks up seven inches on X's desk.

X's working title is *The Wasteland Odyssey of Marvin Krypton*. The plot, alluded to in the title, is a quest. The protagonist is Marvin Krypton, a lonely and sensitive Gen-X software engineer who seeks true love in a wasteland of rubbish, old tires, wornout computers, decaying cities, and gutted political infrastructures. At the climax of the novel, unable to find true love, Marvin enters the hospital for a heart transplant. The operation fails and Marvin's wasteland odyssey climaxes with our hero lying supine on a silver-white gurney staring up at two biker babes, blondes in black leather, with matching silver nose rings. Because Writer X loves ironic endings, he has the blonde biker babes roll the gurney to a deserted beach, where a barefoot woman, a walk-on character, shoots Marvin's picture. The woman looks familiar, someone he knows, with intelligent eyes and strong brown forearms. She wears faded blue jeans and an old sweatshirt that belonged to X's mother. Marvin reaches out. Who is this barefoot woman? Why didn't she show up sooner? The woman smiles, showing strong white teeth. The camera clicks. The biker babes vanish. End of story.

A practicing weekend novelist, X writes on Saturdays, Sundays, nights, holidays, and coffee breaks at work. Like his protagonist, Marvin Krypton, Writer X is a computer techie who loves books and writing; his life outside work is his writing group. The group helps X trim the Marvin manuscript down to 692 pages. With fame in his eyes, X sends the tome to agents and publishers. Rejected. Bleeding with every lost word, X cuts, reducing the book to 551 pages. Rejected. Rejected. Rejected. When X returns to the group, wounded, bearing his crippled manuscript, there is a new face. Her name is Rhoda Belgrave.

Rhoda has red hair and blue eyes. Born in Scotland, Rhoda grew up in London. She majored in biology in college. She's worked as a waitress, a tour guide, a restaurant chef, and a gofer on two low-budget films. She joins the writing group to get feedback on a screenplay. Writer X gets lost in the wonder of Rhoda's blue eyes. Over coffee, he tells Rhoda the sad tale of his many rejections.

On their first real date, X surrenders his manuscript to Rhoda. It has grown larger again, to 675 pages. She glances at Page One, then flips to the last page. Nods, jots a note. Scans the last ten pages, jotting notes, nodding, humming to herself, smiling up at X. She jumps to the middle of the manuscript, scans pages, makes more notes. Moves at last to the beginning, where she flips through the front pages, jots more notes.

"There's a love story buried in there," Rhoda says. "With a bit of work, it might just make a film."

Rhoda agrees to work with X if he will do a rewrite. X is dazzled by Rhoda, not only the fire-red hair, not only the piercing blue eyes, but also her steel-trap analytical brain. X is under Rhoda's spell; he says okay.

Rhoda's Analysis—Story, Structure, Style

Rhoda is a screenwriter. She has a screenwriter's perspective on story, structure, and style. That means no waste and a tight focus on subplots and texture and character motivation. That also means screenwriter tools—scene list, cast roster, character arc, structural diagram, scene profile, archetype, core story—applied to the novel. "Marvin's core story," Rhoda says, "is a Grail Quest. His Holy Grail is true love and because Marvin dies before finding true love, the quest is unsuccessful, a downer ending." For films, Rhoda prefers an upbeat ending. That means a Rags to Riches core story replaces the Grail Quest. Rhoda's example for Rags to Riches is *Working Girl*, a film that gave her the courage to try screenwriting. X makes a note to watch *Working Girl*.

"Except for Marvin the protagonist," Rhoda says, "the characters who make it to the end of the novel are not present at the beginning. That's a pity, because the two biker women are excellent antagonist material. They need longer arcs; they need their own subplots. A character arc," Rhoda explains, "starts when the character enters the story; it ends when the character exits." When Rhoda asks how many characters inhabit the novel, X shakes his head. "Maybe thirty," he says. "Maybe more." He's not sure about the total. Rhoda gives him an assignment: Make a character list with name, role, entrance, exit, and object.

X asks, "What exactly do you mean by object?"

"Harpoon," Rhoda says. "Like the harpoon your American Captain Ahab sticks in the White Whale in *Moby-Dick*." Writer X remembers a harpoon at the climax of *Moby-Dick*, near the end. Rhoda remembers a harpoon in the opening, when Ishmael meets Queequeg. Rhoda remembers a harpoon at Plot Point One. X jots a note. Reread *Moby-Dick*.

Rhoda asks X, "What is Marvin's object?"

"Harley the Hog," X says.

"What is the object for the biker women?"

"Black leather," X says. "Biker boots with fat soles. Chains and studs."

"And what's in their twin noses?"

"Nose rings," X says, grinning.

"What is the object for the barefoot lady on the beach?" Rhoda asks.

"Camera," X says.

"What sort of camera?" Rhoda asks. "Is it new or old? A digital or a Polaroid? Clumsy or efficient?"

"Old Hasselblad," X says. "It's got this little handle that you crank to advance the film. The camera finish is worn off from years of use."

"Why doesn't she just drive to the mall and purchase a new camera?"

"No money. Hey, wait. No money is code for Rags to Riches."

Rhoda smiles. X smiles back. He takes in a deep breath.

"The woman on the beach is life," Rhoda says. "All that warm sun in her face, the bright welcoming smile, the bare feet. The biker women, clad in leather and chains, are death. Their collective archetype is Death Crone. The archetype for your camera lady"—Rhoda pauses—"is Cinderella Twenty Years After." X's novel, Rhoda says, "needs a dollop of good to balance the evil."

X jots notes. His brain is on tilt. Rhoda looks at her watch. Time to go. She stands up, slings the strap of her purse over her shoulder, and smiles at X. Feeling brave, he invites Rhoda to dinner. Rhoda's smile widens, brightening the room.

Rhoda sits back down. Captures X in her blue gaze.

"One condition before we dine," Rhoda says.

"Shoot," X says.

"Let's move the camera from the last page straight to Page One."

X is stunned. This Rhoda Belgrave is obsessed with work. Is that what it means to be a screenwriter? Taking a page from his manuscript, Rhoda flips the paper over, turns it sideways, and draws a straight line that slants up, rising from left to right. At the end of the rising line, she prints the word *camera*. At the beginning of the line, she prints the word *camera* again. She pushes the page at X, hands him her pen, and instructs him to connect the two cameras with a curved line.

X stares at Rhoda. She stares back. His stomach gurgles.

And we fade.

Weekend 2: Tools

You need tools to fix your subplots. Tools to build texture. Tools to simplify the texture while still keeping it thick. Tools to make your novel multilayered and still easy to read.

Each subplot follows a separate character. Subplot One, for example, follows the main antagonist. Subplot Two follows Antagonist Two or a helper. To get at character, you need back story, the stuff that happened to your character before Page One. To get at back story, you have to build it first. Building back story takes tools like chronology (a list of dates and events) and the personal history—targeted scenes from the character's past. To drop your reader into a character's past, you use flashback. A trapdoor opens and your character drops out of the present into the past. That's why you made a list of flashbacks. Flashbacks are sneaky. Too many flashbacks and your story gets swallowed up by the past.

When you rewrite, take control.

Back story is important for your rewrite because it contains core story, archetype and secret, elements buried deep in the subtext of every good story. *Core story* is a framework of the familiar. For example, a guy in his Chrysler hardtop convertible hunts for his father, who abandoned the family when the Chrysler guy was six years old. The core story is a Grail Quest: A knight in armor hunts for a silver bowl, a golden cup, a miraculous urn that will heal the world. The guy and the knight errant are both archetypal Questers. Archetype reaches beyond the boundaries of the work—novel, film, play, poem. If you name the Chrysler guy Joey or Claude or Ramon, you capture the archetype for your story. Joey is your Quester. To know the reason for Joey's quest—why he chose this time to go hunting for Dad—you must plant a secret in the back story. When Joey stops for a hitchhiker (pretty girl wearing a wedding dress), you have a subplot character with a secret in the back story.

Writer's Toolkit

Once you have back story on a character, you'll use these tools—as many as you need—to rewrite subplots and scenes:

- **The Grid.** A basic table that separates the subplots.
- **List of Scenes.** Naming and scene sequence.
- **Diagram.** A snapshot of your rewrite in progress.
- **Index Cards.** Used for scene compression and capturing sequence.
- **CUT TO.** Zooming from scene to scene.
- **Scene Profile.** A warm-up for a scene rewrite.
- **Thirty-One-Minute Scene Template.** Rewriting the scene in half an hour plus one minute for the warm-up. A tool for moving scenes.

TIP FOR YOUR REWRITE

Tools make the rewrite fast and smooth. Tools help you compress, then expand, then recompress. Tools are hands-on; you learn by using; you get better with practice. When your rewrite stalls, open your toolkit and grab a tool. You won't need all the tools all the time. You're the writer; it's your choice.

GRID

A *grid* is a basic compression tool that separates the plot from your subplots, and the subplots from each other. When you stack your subplots in the grid, you get a hierarchy: Subplot One, Subplot Two, Subplot Three, etc. When you have lots of characters, more than you need for a rewrite, use a grid to get organized.

The grid on the following page gives us a snapshot of characters, roles, objects, entry and exit points in a three-act dramatic structure. The grid lines up the antagonists, sorting them with numbers. Antagonists inhabit subplots.

That's what this book is about—rewriting your novel by focusing on subplots to make room for your small army of antagonists. In the grid on *Jane Eyre*, the main antagonist occupies Row 2, directly under Row 1, the slot for your protagonist. As other antagonists deepen the stack of subplots, they create more trouble for Jane (her chance to grow) and a more dramatic story for the reader.

GRID: FOR JANE EYRE

Name	Role	Plot/Sub-plot (SP)	Object	Entry	Exit	Core Story
Jane	Protag	Plot	Sketch Pad	Act 1	Act 3	Rags to Riches
Mr. Rochester	Antag 1	SP 1	Cloak	Act 2	Act 3	Queen Replacement
Bertha Mason	Antag 2	SP 2	Knife, Fire	Act 2	Act 2	Revenge Quest
Richard Mason	Antag 3	SP 3	Overcoat	Act 2	Act 2	Revenge Quest
Aunt Reed	Antag 4	SP 4	Silk	Act 1	Act 2	Scapegoat Sacrifice
Mr. Brocklehurst	Antag 5	SP 5	Overcoat	Act 1	Act 1	Scapegoat Sacrifice
St. John Rivers	Antag 6	SP 6	Letter/Bible	Act 3	Act 3	King Replacement
Mrs. Fairfax	Helper	SP 7	Apron	Act 2	Act 3	Queen Replacement
Blanche Ingram	Antag 7	SP 8	Party Gown	Act 2	Act 2	Queen Replacement

UNPACKING THE GRID. *Jane Eyre* has seven antagonists—characters who oppose Jane—but they don't crowd the stage all at once. Instead, the writer positions them across the structure for dramatic effect. In Act One, for example, we meet Jane's nasty aunt, her nasty cousins, and a nasty overlord schoolmaster named Mr. Brocklehurst. In Act Two, we meet Mr. Edward Fairfax Rochester; his crazy wife, Bertha; her tubercular brother, Richard; Blanche Ingram, Rochester's fake-out fiancée; and Mrs. Fairfax, the housekeeper who keeps a secret. In Act Three, we meet St. John Rivers, a cousin who wants to marry Jane and take her

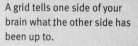

TIP FOR YOUR REWRITE

A grid tells one side of your brain what the other side has been up to.

away to India, not because he loves her, but because a married couple will make a better missionary team. There is not a romantic bone in his body. St. John Rivers's goal—saving the heathen—clashes with Jane's goal, which is finding true love with Mr. Right. In Act Three, Jane replaces St. John Rivers with Mr. Rochester from Act Two.

Each character in the grid has an object attached. Rochester has his cloak, Richard Mason has his overcoat, but Bertha has two objects—knife and fire—that make her more dangerous. She knifes Mason; she sets fire to Rochester's bedsheets. St. John Rivers delivers the letter that gives Jane her inheritance, but his real object is his Bible. When Jane rejects him, St. John Rivers sails to India clutching his Bible.

Each character in the grid has a core story attached. Core story is important for your rewrite because it separates plot from subplot while

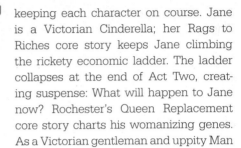

TIP FOR YOUR REWRITE

Once you attach core stories to the two main characters—your protagonist and antagonist— you do the same for each of your subplot characters.

keeping each character on course. Jane is a Victorian Cinderella; her Rags to Riches core story keeps Jane climbing the rickety economic ladder. The ladder collapses at the end of Act Two, creating suspense: What will happen to Jane now? Rochester's Queen Replacement core story charts his womanizing genes. As a Victorian gentleman and uppity Man of Property, he sees nothing wrong with keeping two women (one wife and one mistress) under the same roof. Queen Replacement reflects Rochester's sense of entitlement—in his view, the universe owes him some form of genetic success, a payback for his father's betrayal. Rochester's bald sense of entitlement clashes with Jane's burning need for a proper marriage. Cinderella needs a wedding; it's a reward for her sweaty climb.

- **Revenge Quest.** Bertha Mason and her brother Richard both want revenge. Their own father is beyond their reach, so they go after Rochester. He is handy; he has deep pockets. For his revenge, Richard invokes the bigamy laws in the wedding chapel scene; for hers, Bertha burns down the house.
- **Scapegoat Sacrifice.** Aunt Reed and Mr. Brocklehurst both punish innocent Jane. Aunt Reed is the Wicked Stepmother figure from the Cinderella fairy tale; Mr. Brocklehurst is a monster who preys on children.
- **Failed King Replacement.** Cousin St. John Rivers reveals his core story when he proposes a chaste, biblical marriage to Jane. And when Jane, who still loves Rochester, says no.
- **Ambiguous Queen Replacement.** Mrs. Fairfax likes Jane; she knows about crazy Bertha. She has lots of chances to tell Jane about Rochester's wife. Her loyalty to Rochester forces her to keep the secret. It's a good choice. If Charlotte Brontë had released the secret any sooner, it would have lost power.
- **Failed Queen Replacement.** Because Blanche Ingram is so beautiful, Jane assumes that she will wind up with Mr. Rochester. Just as St. John Rivers fails to replace Rochester, beautiful Blanche Ingram fails to replace Jane in Rochester's heart.

There are seven core stories in storytelling—more if you play the reversal game of Riches to Rags—enough to keep your subplot characters on separate tracks until their trains collide to create scenes. *Jane Eyre* has five of the seven—Rags to Riches, Queen Replacement,

Scapegoat Sacrifice, Revenge Quest, and King Replacement—leaving only two: Grail Quest (a knight errant hunts for treasure) and Coming of Age (a child grows up). An example of Grail Quest is Count Almásy in *The English Patient*. His Grail is the Cave of Swimmers. Examples of Coming of Age include Astrid Magnussen, the plucky teen heroine of *White Oleander;* and Josh Waitzkin, the boy who transforms into a chess warrior in *Searching for Bobby Fischer*.

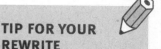

TIP FOR YOUR REWRITE

Watch for core stories not only when you read, but also when you watch films and the evening news. If there's an election or a political coup, watch for King Replacement. If the cops have caught a serial killer, check their faces for the steely look of Revenge Quest, a staple for cop stories. When you watch a romantic comedy like *Working Girl* or *Pretty Woman,* jot down elements of the Rags to Riches/Cinderella fairy tale: orphaned blue collar protagonist, the object left behind, the transforming wardrobe scene, etc.

SCENE LIST

With your subplots separated, you check your scene list for Subplot One. This first scene list has two components: the scene name (First Encounter, First Date, etc.) and then an action for each scene. The scene list starts when your subplot character enters the story; it ends when the same character exits. The scene list gives you sequence—how the scenes for each subplot string together, building toward climax—and relative weight. Are all the scenes the same length? Are some scenes too long? Other scenes too short? The scene list helps you make decisions. If you were listing scenes for Mr. Rochester's subplot, then the first scene in the list would be First Encounter. His horse slips on the ice, tossing Rochester to the cold ground. The second scene is First Interrogation, when Jane rushes to the rescue. There's a full scene list for a subplot in "Weekend 4, Rewriting Subplot One."

DIAGRAM

If the scene list does not cough up insights for your rewrite, then you make a diagram, a line drawing that shows the architecture of your novel—three acts, character arcs, key scenes, and subplots. The diagram gives you a snapshot of your rewrite. On the following page, you'll find a sample sketch for *Jane Eyre*.

Entrances and exits mark character arcs. Jane has the longest arc—it follows the plot—and Rochester has the next longest, even though he does not enter the story until Act Two, when he gallops

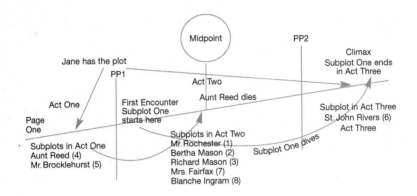

onstage for a historic First Encounter. Each character name is followed by a numbered subplot.

The *Jane Eyre* sketch above has a simple Aristotelian structure— a rising line divided by vertical lines. The rising line represents action rising to the climax. The vertical lines divide the action into acts. Because of its complexity and thickness (back story, subplots colliding), Act Two in most novels is longer than Acts One and Three. The short line with the little bubble on top marks the Midpoint, the center of Act Two in the structure and the point of no return for your characters. In most novels and films, the Midpoint is a sequence of scenes and a' major intertwining of plot and subplot.

When you draw a diagram, make sure you name the scenes. Start with key scenes—Page One, Plot Point One, Midpoint—and then look for first-time scenes. When Rochester enters the story in Act Two, the scene is First Encounter. When he kisses Jane at the Midpoint, that scene is First Kiss, a familiar event in storytelling, an important step in the courtship ritual. The name "First Kiss" opens the door for description, a close-up, and inspired writing. Is the kiss hot? Cold? Wet? Chaste? Sisterly? Disinterested? Do twin tongues probe? Do the teeth click on impact? Is it a kiss of love or the kiss of death? First Kiss connects to First Proposal. First Kiss and First Proposal follow in sequence after First Encounter, when the incipient kissers meet for the first time, where they speak (First Words), shake hands (First Touch), part (First Separation), reconnect (First Phone Call), working up to First Kiss, First Foreplay, and First Sex. (More on First Kiss when we rewrite key scenes.)

Filmmakers think in scenes. So do smart novelists eager for a speedy rewrite. A scene is tight and controlled. It is a container for your drama. A scene has an internal clock, a time limit, a little bell that goes "ding" when the scene is over, when the clock strikes midnight. Time's up, time to split and head back home. When the dramatic machinery shuts down and the scene stops, then you build your way to the next scene. Scenes help you create a tighter rewrite.

INDEX CARDS

This is a tool borrowed from screenwriting. Each scene has its own card. You jot down information like this: setting (time, temperature, season, lighting), characters in the scene, action, dialogue, and high point. Index cards give you flexibility; you can change the scene sequence *before* you cut and paste in the manuscript. Here's a sample card from Subplot One of *Jane Eyre*:

> ### Index Card #1
>
> *Subplot One, Mr. Edward Fairfax Rochester. Name: First Encounter. Setting: the icy causeway. Winter, early evening. The object: boots. Action: the horse slips, Mr. R. falls, pale Jane runs to the rescue. Archetype: Monster. Core story: Queen Replacement.*

Index cards compress information about a single scene. This First Encounter scene, for example, launches Subplot One. The index card contains setting and season, object and action. If you know the archetype—in Rochester's case it's a choice between Hero and Monster—you jot that down on the index card. If you write down Monster, then you project a transformation sequence as Jane transforms Rochester with her love. If Rochester entered the novel as Hero, you would lose a chance for dramatic conflict, not only in this scene but in scenes down the road. Rochester's core story, Queen Replacement, reaches all the way to his Confession Scene near the end of Act Two. Have fun with index cards.

CUT TO

Another tool borrowed from screenwriting, the CUT TO exercise speeds you across your list of scenes. You feel free, you write like the wind. The speed of the writing fires your mind. You grab insights about which scene needs a minor fix and which needs a major rewrite. The CUT TO is flexible. It bends to your need, your will, your immediate writing purpose. If you're

TIP FOR YOUR REWRITE

This box of tools—grid, scene list, diagram, index cards, and the CUT TO—help you make structural changes: reordering your scenes before you spend time rewriting. Once you straighten the structure, you'll be ready to rewrite scenes. When you rewrite a scene, don't forget subtext.

building a scene sequence, for example, then you zip down the page without changing the point of view. The CUT TO lays the groundwork for a scene sequence. Here's an example from Mr. Rochester's subplot, starting at First Encounter in Act Two; Jane has the Point of View:

EXAMPLE: Moving through the CUT TO. We open in Jane's point of view watching Rochester's horse slip on the icy causeway on a dark winter evening and Rochester flying through the air and landing hard.
CUT TO:
Jane on her knees as Rochester opens his eyes and starts his interrogation of where does she come from and where does she work.
CUT TO:
Jane helping Rochester onto his horse.
CUT TO:
Jane alone, watching Rochester ride off, followed by the dog.

SCENE PROFILE

A profile is a warm-up tool for rewriting a single scene. You do the scene profile from memory, using these categories: name of the scene, location in the structure, ritual, setting, characters, action, dialogue, high point, and subtext.

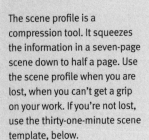

TIP FOR YOUR REWRITE

The scene profile is a compression tool. It squeezes the information in a seven-page scene down to half a page. Use the scene profile when you are lost, when you can't get a grip on your work. If you're not lost, use the thirty-one-minute scene template, below.

NAME OF THE SCENE. Naming the scene gives you control; helps you remember.

LOCATION IN THE STRUCTURE. Place the scene in Act One, Act Two, or Act Three.

RITUAL. The two largest rituals are threshold crossing and barter. Burial of the Dead, a funeral ritual, is a threshold crossing. So is First Kiss.

SETTING. Includes time, temperature, season, weather, lighting, and objects.

CHARACTERS. Includes the point of view and character descriptions.

ACTION. Needs strong verbs. Example: The horse *slips*, Rochester *hits* the ice.

DIALOGUE. Follows the Five Rules: short lines, echo words, object inserted, hook to the future, link to the past.

HIGH POINT. A miniclimax where the action peaks and the scene ends.

SUBTEXT. The unspoken, invisible unsaid thing under the text:

- Intruder and closed circle create instant drama.
- The Three Goods (good genes, good resources, good behavior) provide a biological basis for mate selection.
- Sexual triad can be two females and one male; or two males and one female.
- Secret can be a sexual triad or trauma in the back story.

TIP FOR YOUR REWRITE

Whenever you rewrite a scene, you have a chance to work the subtext. The scene is a *closed circle* waiting for an *intruder*, Character C. Character A's description of Character B is your chance to use the Three Goods. What if Character C's *secret* exposes a *sexual triad*? Let's explore subtext, below.

THIRTY-ONE-MINUTE SCENE TEMPLATE

This is a tool that helps you to rewrite a scene fast, without stalling and fretting. The template gives you one minute for a warm-up ("I am writing a story about . . . "); then thirty minutes for six scene elements: overview, setting, character description (Character A describes Character B), action and dialogue, intruder and closed circle, and climax. Each scene element has its own startline. You write for five minutes on the overview ("This is a scene about . . . "), and then you write for five minutes on setting ("The time was . . ."; "The place smelled of . . ."). The timer keeps you moving through the scene; the startlines help you to focus. By invoking a smell for setting, you lock down the point of view in the scene.

Subtext: Intruder and Closed Circle

Cinderella is an intruder, a character from Lower World who penetrates the closed circle of Upper World seeking sanctuary. She gets lucky. The shoe fits and she's invited in. Jane Eyre, an early Victorian Cinderella, penetrates the closed circle at Thornfield Hall. She wants in because it's cold outside, and dangerous. She's young and fertile. She's poor like Cinderella, but the Handsome Prince is already married. Instead of letting her all the way inside, the writer burns down the closed circle.

TIP FOR YOUR REWRITE

Rewriting opens your writer's brain to secrets of the masters. Although *The Great Gatsby* sold only a few thousand copies during the author's lifetime, today it sells five hundred thousand copies a year. We'll be probing *Gatsby* and other novels that have lasted for secrets of the long shelf life. When you study a master novelist, look deep.

The same pattern of intruder and closed circle drives the action in *The Great Gatsby*, where F. Scott Fitzgerald created two Cinderella figures—the protagonist Jay Gatsby and a minor antagonist named Myrtle Wilson, the blue-collar mistress of womanizer Tom Buchanan. Two intruders, both from Lower World, try to penetrate the closed circle of East Egg. A structural inevitability exists here: the two Rags to Riches characters die without meeting. This shows the isolating power of subplots. Gatsby meets Myrtle for the first time when she runs out from her husband's garage, waving at the yellow car, calling for it to stop. They meet by deadly association when Daisy, behind the wheel of the yellow car, runs Myrtle down. Daisy is Upper World, a Death Crone killer wearing a pure white dress. In a single action, she erases her husband's blue-collar mistress and dooms her own blue-collar lover, Gatsby, to execution. She's at the center of the closed circle of money and power. We'll see more of Miss Daisy in "Weekend 4: Rewriting Subplot 1."

Subtext: The Three Goods and Mate Selection

The Three Goods (good genes, good resources, good behavior) come from evolutionary biology. When Character A meets Character B, biology guides the ritual of mate selection.

Let's imagine a party scene. The guests are thirtysomething, educated, attractive, a mixture of singles, marrieds, and divorced persons. We focus on two characters, a single man named Claude, and a single woman named Eileen. Claude is handsome. He's sporting a Rolex and driving a Mercedes. Eileen is attractive. She has no car; she came to the party with a friend. Claude is witty. He tells a good story. Eileen is reserved, formal. She's attracted to Claude. Her secret in this scene is her borrowed wardrobe. She loves good clothes. Two days before the party, Eileen was laid off. One week before the party, she broke off a relationship. She is polite, well mannered, a lady.

What's going on in the subtext? To find out, we decode the details.

- *Handsome* is code for *good genes*. *Mercedes* and *Rolex* are code for good resources. Claude has two goods out of a possible three. No judgment yet on his behavior.
- *Attractive* is code for *Eileen's good genes*. The term *laid off* is code for *bad resources*. The *borrowed wardrobe* suggests that Eileen is pinching her pennies. Another clue to bad resources. Eileen is a *lady*, which suggests good behavior.

Action: Claude flirts with Eileen, heats her blood. Claude offers to take her home after the party and, even though his eyes are wild, she accepts. She only sees a very good-looking man. A short time later, Claude gets into a loud argument. His face turns red. He breaks an expensive table lamp. He laughs, stumbles, touches Eileen, and says, "Let's split, baby."

TIP FOR YOUR REWRITE

The Three Goods help you peel back the veil of appearance—what we see on the surface—so that you can work the subtext.

Line up the actions: *loud argument, face turns red, breaks a lamp, touches Eileen*. All codes for bad behavior. Seeing this behavior, Eileen has a decision to make: Do Claude's good looks and impressive resources outweigh his bad behavior? Is this guy trainable? Will she still go home with him?

The same question—Is this lout trainable?—is the big theme in the Oscar-winning film *As Good as It Gets*. (Rewrite mantra: To find story secrets, study good films.) There are three main characters in this film. A writer named Melvin, played by Jack Nicholson. A waitress named Carol, played by Helen Hunt. And a painter named Simon, played by Greg Kinnear. Melvin is crazy. Simon is gay. Carol has a sick child. Let's use a grid to nail down the Three Goods.

GRID: THE THREE GOODS—*AS GOOD AS IT GETS*

Character	Genes	Resources	Behavior	Archetype	Core Story
Melvin	Good	Good	Bad	Monster	Coming of Age
Carol	Good	Bad	Good	Cinderella	Rags to Riches
Simon	Good	Bad	Good	Wounded Knight	Grail Quest

In Act One of the film, two bad boys put Simon in the hospital, where he can't paint. Simon is broke. Melvin, the next-door neighbor, has money.

Melvin is a nasty child in a man's body. He is selfish and half-crazy. Melvin eats the same breakfast every day at the same neighborhood restaurant, where he demands service from Carol.

Carol the waitress is Cinderella twenty years after the ball. She is mature, solid, maternal. Carol works hard, but she lacks the financial resources to care for her sick child. Carol's appearance—she's pretty, shapely, quick-witted, and she serves a hearty breakfast to Melvin— verifies good genes. When she misses work because of her sick child, Melvin sends help from Upper World, a high-powered doctor on a house call to her home. Now Carol owes Melvin. Like Cinderella, Carol is trapped in Lower World, but she shows her *Jane Eyre* ethics when she runs through the rain to confront Melvin, saying she won't sleep with him. Melvin, the monster of suppression, denies his sexual attraction to Carol, but uses his medical leverage to force Carol to play chaperone when Melvin drives Simon the artist to Baltimore to see his parents. Simon's archetype is Wounded Knight. He makes a Grail Quest to Baltimore to seek acceptance from his parents, who ejected him because he's gay. Simon's parents believe that homosexuality is bad behavior.

The trip to Baltimore is a pilgrimage that brings out the worst in Melvin. When he displays bad behavior, Carol avoids him. She poses for Simon. Drawing Carol in the nude triggers a rebirth for Simon's art.

Subtext: The Sexual Triad

When Carol poses for Simon, she creates a sexual triad: two males and one female. She rejects Melvin the macho man and bonds with Simon the gay artist. Melvin can't utter the word *love*, but they can. The sexual triad connects Carol's Rags to Riches plot with both subplots: Melvin's Coming of Age story in Subplot One; Simon's Grail Quest in Subplot Two.

The sexual triad bristles with biology, mate selection, power, and the dramatic intensity of the intruder penetrating a closed circle. Let's say you have two characters, A and B. They are married; their marriage forms a sacred circle: home, family, trust, resources. Along comes a stranger, Character C, who seduces Character A. A single act changes the balance of power. When Characters A and B were joined, they were a unit. They were two against one until the seduction. Now it's Characters A and C against Character B. Two against one means dramatic conflict.

If Character A happens to be a king, there are resources at stake, perhaps a kingdom. If the king replaces his queen with a stranger, what happens to the queen? If the queen replaces the king with a stranger, what happens to the king? If you keep digging into the subtext, you come to motive and the Three Goods. Is the stranger younger than the queen? Stronger? More beautiful? Is the Queen unable to produce children? Is the king hungry for genetic success verified by a gene carrier?

When you read a novel, pay attention to sexual triads. A sexual triad means danger for the characters, perhaps even death. There is always fear of discovery. In *The English Patient*, the husband finds out he's part of a sexual triad (husband-wife-explorer) and tries to kill the explorer with his yellow airplane. In *The Great Gatsby*, the wronged wife finds out she's part of a sexual triad (wife-husband-mistress) and gets some naughty payback by forming her own sexual triad (lover-wife-husband). The wife is Daisy. The husband is Tom, a king with substantial resources. Daisy's lover happens to be Mr. Jay Gatsby, bootlegger, poor boy, and innocent knight errant. Lured by the blinking green light at the end of Daisy's dock, Gatsby enters Daisy's world and gets executed for trespassing. And for stealing the king's woman. And for not understanding subtext and the power of the sexual triad.

Subtext: Secrets

In *Jane Eyre*, Mr. Rochester has Subplot Two. His secret is the crazy wife in the tower. Rochester wants Jane. His desire for genetic success—a baby with his genes—creates the sexual triad of Jane-Rochester-Bertha that motivates Bertha to set his bed on fire. Like most first-person narrators, Jane is isolated in the plot; while others know the secret of the crazy wife locked up in the tower, Jane does not discover the secret until her wedding day.

Before we leave the subject of subtext, let's decode Jane's connection to Rochester. Protagonist Jane holds onto her virginity until marriage; guarding her sexuality shows good behavior. Jane is plain, not pretty, the code for bad genes. She has no money, the code for bad resources, until she inherits twenty thousand pounds in Act Three. Her good behavior shines in Act Three when she gives fifteen thousand pounds away to the cousins who saved her from death on the heath.

Mr. Rochester has money, servants, a big mansion (code for good resources). Jane finds him handsome (code for good genes). So do the neighbor ladies with daughters lusting for marriage. But from his first entrance onstage, Rochester shows bad behavior. He's nasty to Jane. He makes her feel bad about her music and art—what the Victorians would call her "accomplishments." Rochester forces Jane to attend an Upper World house party, then embarrasses her in front of his guests. More bad behavior. But homeless Jane wants Thornfield Hall—it represents Rochester's resources—and she responds to his power and his dark looks and falls in love. At the end of the story, with Thornfield torched by mad Bertha, leaving Rochester blind and wounded, look what happens. His behavior softens. He needs Jane even more, and Fate has removed the obstacle of his crazy wife. Jane is now rich (good resources) and Rochester is now poor (bad resources). Jane is still young. Through marriage she discovers a resource in her body: Plain Jane is a fertile female. The lovers get married. They produce a baby.

The word *baby*—remember this for your rewrite—is a code for "gene carrier." As *Jane Eyre* draws to a close, Jane looks back at her marriage and the birth of the baby she has created with Mr. Rochester: "When his first-born was put into [Rochester's] arms," Brontë writes, "he could see that the boy had inherited his own eyes, as they once were—large, brilliant, and black." Rochester does not need Darwin (*On the Origin of Species* is a decade away) or any insights from evolutionary biology to see his genes in their gene-carrier. The baby verifies Rochester's genetic success.

Exercises for Tools

1. SYNOPSIS—WARM UP TO THE REWRITE

The startlines below guide you through a three-act synopsis, from the opening of your novel in Act One to the end in Act Three. The startlines work for any genre, any core story. If a startline doesn't get you going, feel free to change the words. The point is to keep going, pushing through to the end. Write longhand first. Use a kitchen timer to distract your internal editor. Follow the guidelines set by Natalie Goldberg in *Writing Down the Bones*: Keep the hand moving, don't stop to think, don't cross out. Writing in longhand pulls your brain away from the computer monitor, from the Age of Screens. Writing in longhand slows you down. Slowing down is good; it gives you a chance to go deep. When the timer dings, stop writing. Type your writing into your computer. Print out the pages. Put them in a folder. Do not edit your work. Give it a chance to sit there and just be. Before you write, get comfortable, take some deep breaths. Remember to exhale. Write from memory. No lists, no crib notes. Give each startline five minutes. When the timer beeps, move to the next startline. Moving, you will push through to the end. Go.

> Startline: My protagonist enters the story on Page One wearing . . .
>   (five minutes)
> Startline: The end of Act One finds my protagonist stumbling . . .
>   (five minutes)

Startline: Act Two opens with the image of . . . (five minutes)
Startline: At the middle of Act Two, my protagonist kills . . .
    (five minutes)
Startline: At the end of Act Two, my protagonist must . . .
    (five minutes)
Startline: Act Three opens as my protagonist faces . . . (five minutes)
Startline: At the climax, my protagonist confronts the Dragon in a
    scene called . . . (five minutes)
Startline: My novel ends in (darkness or light or shadow) as . . .
    (five minutes)

2. THE GRID—SEPARATING THE SUBPLOTS

Follow the model for the character grid in this chapter. Name, role, plot/subplot, object, entry, exit, and core story. It's all right to guess at core story. This is not a test. And you will get better at grid-making. Core story helps you separate the subplots from the plot, and the subplots from each other. For your first grid, you might do a rough sketch in ballpoint, then dress it up using the table function in your favorite software program.

    Time for the grid: thirty minutes

3. TRACKING OBJECTS

Pull two objects from the grid: one for your protagonist, another for your antagonist. Track both objects through the manuscript. Each time the object surfaces, jot down the scene name (naming scenes is fun) and page number. On your object list, note whether the object is in narration, exposition, description, or dialogue. Tracking objects trains your brain. A trained brain rewrites faster and better.

    Tracking time: sixty minutes

4. PROBE YOUR SUBTEXT

With the right tools (the Three Goods, intruder and closed circle, sexual triad, and secret), you nail the subtext in your novel. Suggestions:

- **The Three Goods:** Describe two characters, A (female) and B (male). Give good genes and good resources to A; give good genes and good behavior to B. Give the point of view to Character A and have her describe Character B.

- **Intruder and Closed Circle:** Write some dialogue for Characters A and B. When they are talking like old friends—they have formed a closed circle—then bring on the intruder. What happens? Do they welcome the intruder? Do they eject the intruder? Do they assimilate the intruder?
- **Sexual Triad:** Connect the intruder to one of the characters. Make the connection sexual. Keep writing dialogue.
- **Secret:** The intruder has an object that belongs to either Character A or Character B. The object is a secret. What happens when it pops out, exploding from the subtext?

5. FEED YOUR BRAIN—THE BIOLOGY OF MATE SELECTION

The quick way to character in fiction is biology. There are three books to look at: *Madame Bovary's Ovaries* (David Barash and Nanelle Barash; check the chapter on Jane Austen); *The Selfish Gene* (Richard Dawkins; check the index for "sexual selection"); and *The Red Queen* (Matt Ridley; read the chapters on male polygamy and female monogamy). Knowing just a smidgen about the biology of mate selection will deepen your characters and make them more real. You'll still have to work, packing in the right details for good genes and good resources. You'll still have to write action to show behavior. But biology takes the guesswork out of motives, survivors, and witnesses.

Startline: Lover A meets Lover B when . . .

Writing time: thirty minutes. (Have fun.)

The Rewrite: Writer X Uses the Tools

Following Rhoda's advice, Writer X moves the camera from page 675 back across the structure to Page One. When he moves the camera, the Camera Lady tags along. As she moves, Camera Lady grows. X jots notes: Camera Lady is a mature female, thirtysomething, lonely and attractive, wearing faded jeans and a baggy sweatshirt. She has energy as she enters the story shooting photos of a deserted beach. Why is the beach empty? What if the setting changed to a town? What if the time changed from dusk on the beach to early morning? X draws a diagram:

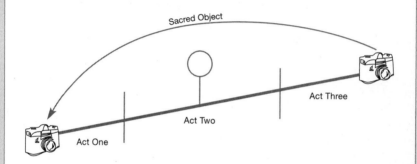

Typing his notes, X sees a way to transform characters from the old Marvin manuscript. Camera Lady needs a husband. Make him an older man, a man of wealth and property. Turn the husband's mother into an enemy for Camera Lady, adding another antagonist. If the husband is mean to Camera Lady, the door opens for a lover named Marvin.

A week passes. On their next date, Rhoda coaches X on using the Three Goods for the ritual of mate selection. The Three Goods, Rhoda explains, are good genes, good resources, and good behavior. X takes notes. He grins.

Rhoda continues: "Take your Quester protagonist, for example. Marvin Krypton is educated and quite well read—all those quotations from the poets—and he's attractive enough to attract various females as he motors down the road astride his macho machine. Attractive," Rhoda explains, "is shorthand for good genes. He has money and no visible employment. He has an expensive motorcycle. He buys flowers and expensive trinkets with which to woo the ladies. Having enough money means good resources.

"Now to behavior. When he starts his quest, Marvin's behavior is neutral. When he allows himself to be seduced by the biker women, however, he shows bad behavior. They are evil. Marvin snuggles close to evil and becomes tainted. The barefoot woman is his chance for redemption."

Rhoda switches to the Camera Lady. "A beautiful woman," she says, "with connections to the earth. Bare feet, tanned skin, a strong smile that goes with a strong body—all indicate good genes. As she shoots Marvin's picture, Camera Lady captures his image, taking him into her camera. There is symbolism here. What if the camera is her way of connecting to the world? An eye, a hand reaching out, a heart yearning? She captures Marvin, takes him into her camera-heart. Into her closed circle. Perhaps she becomes aware of her action when she develops her film and Marvin appears in the developing fluid. The Camera Lady exhibits good genes and good behavior. What of her resources?"

X answers with a "what if": "What if she's driving an old beater car? A paint-faded Subaru wagon with ripped upholstery and a crack in the windshield?"

Rhoda keeps the what-ifs going: "What if," Rhoda asks, "she married at a young age? She was poor; the man was older and he had money. She was Cinderella and he was her handsome prince. Now what if we fast-forward twenty years? What if the husband is stingy with spending money? What if he puts a spending limit on her credit cards? What if he destroys all her credit cards? Camera Lady is Cinderella locked in a cage. A princess in a cage needs a knight in shining armor to let her out. Biology and the Three Goods—good genes balanced by bad resources—point to a Rags to Riches core story. She meets a man on the beach. She's lonely and the man needs saving." Triggered by the fire in Rhoda's blue eyes, X builds his first grid:

X'S FIRST GRID

Name	Archetype	Core Story	Object	Entry	Exit
Marvin	Quester	King Replacement	Harley	Act 1	Act 3
Camera Lady	Cinderella	Rags to Riches	Camera	Act 1	Act 3
Husband	Monster	Queen Replacement	Wallet	Act 1	Act 3
Child	Wonder Boy	Coming of Age	Racquet	Act 2	Act 2
Babe One	Death Crone	Scapegoat Sacrifice	Ring	Act 1	Act 3
Babe Two	Death Crone	Scapegoat Sacrifice	Ring	Act 1	Act 3

As he fills in the grid, X makes story discoveries about archetype and core story. The husband is a Monster with a Queen Replacement core story because he cheats on Camera Lady. The same core story, Rhoda points out, as Mr. Rochester in *Jane Eyre*. X makes a note: Read *Jane Eyre*. What if the husband's mother hates Camera Lady? What if the child is a prodigy? What if the child grabs for an object and comes up with a tennis racquet? What if the husband is French and Camera Lady is American? What if the French husband has a house in France? Two Americans, drawn together: Camera Lady hooks up with Marvin. What if the biker babes want the house in France?

Working through the what-ifs, X remembers a trip to Provence from his college days. He digs out some old photos. Vineyards, narrow twisting roads, a sidewalk café, a pretty girl in a short dress. He remembers the Palace of the Popes, the square in Avignon. It's insight time. What would happen if X moved the scene on the beach in California to the square in Avignon?

LEARNING CURVE

Writer X's rewriting experience takes him deep. His protagonist changes; his antagonists multiply; and his subplots get stronger. With help from Rhoda the Muse, X realizes that his Marvin manuscript is veiled autobiography. X is Marvin, and Marvin is X on a Harley motorcycle. In this powerful rewrite, Writer X transforms the stuff of autobiography into a novel with a better chance of survival in the marketplace. When X gets famous, he plans to rebuild Marvin Krypton. (Don't tell Rhoda.)

Weekend 3: Flashback and Back Story

When Mr. Rochester confesses to Jane at the end of Act Two, he's digging up the past. It's messy back there: betrayal, greed, madness. When Arkady Renko, the sleuth of *Gorky Park*, needs to catch a killer, he digs up the killer's past. When Almásy, the Burned Man in *The English Patient,* touches his Herodotus—a magic book that makes it through an airplane fire—he slides away from his bed of pain in Italy in 1944, slides down the scales of time into a back story of heat, sex, betrayal, twisted love, and death. The book is the gateway to back story.

Back story is the trauma that burns your characters before Page One. Back story holds the secrets that create the subtext that makes your subplots throb. There are two kinds of back story: visible and invisible.

- *Visible back story* is what the reader reads on the page.
- *Invisible back story* is for your eyes only.

If you have lots of visible back story—over 50 percent of *The English Patient*, for example, takes place in the past—then you'll need to build a contrapuntal structure that zigzags between the present and the past. If most of your back story is invisible, you pack the visible stuff into Act Two and then you use assorted techniques—document, dialogue, monologue, flashback triggers—to present choice slivers of the past to the reader. In *Jane Eyre*, as we have seen, Brontë uses Rochester's confession to pull back story into the present. He takes the floor; he talks while Jane listens. The technique here, borrowed from the theatre, is external monologue.

The cleanest way to bring back story to the reader is a line of dialogue. Early in Hemingway's landmark book, *The Sun Also Rises*, the protagonist buys a drink for a Paris *poule*, a lady of the evening. The protagonist is attractive (good genes). He has money (good resources) and manners (good behavior), so she assumes he wants to party.

He says no. "What's wrong," she asks, "are you sick?" To answer her, Hemingway creates a dialogue line that hums with understatement: "I got hurt in the war." Subtext cracks through the crust: the protagonist was wounded in the past. The back story appears, then disappears. The story moves on.

Before you start fixing your subplots, you need to weigh your back story. Study it, measure it, poke it for secrets.

How much back story do you have?

How much back story does the reader see?

How much detail from the past does the reader *need* to see?

Back story holds the secrets of your characters. Back story gives the characters weight and heft and purpose. Whether it's pain or betrayal or murder or being left at the altar, you need back stories on your protagonist, your antagonist, and your other characters. The bigger the character, the more back story you need. Invisible back story is better when it's written down. You can write the back story in paragraphs or lists or scenes or dialogue.

Tools for Working Back Story

- **List of Flashbacks.** You made this list on Weekend 1. Review it now. How many flashbacks? How much room do they grab? How many sentences? Paragraphs? Pages? Where do the flashbacks cluster together?
- **Chronology.** Turn the list of flashbacks into a chronology of events by attaching dates, times, and places.
- **Document.** Introduce a photo; describe the photo. Introduce a diary, a journal, a videotape.
- **Object.** A wardrobe item can trigger a flashback. The pretty dress does not fit. The coat is out of style. The trousers have bell bottoms. Coins are excellent objects because they have dates stamped on them. The Maltese Falcon, a black bird statuette, carries a long history of murder and blood. (More on this object later.)
- **Dialogue.** Characters talk about the past. One character knows more than the other.
- **Monologue.** One character talks about the past while the other character listens.
- **One Hour Before.** A back-story builder that starts one hour before Page One, and then keeps moving backward in time, taking measured leaps.

Tools for Control: The Grid

If you study the time patterns in *The English Patient*, you can see the zigzag structure at work. The Burned Man lies on his bed in Italy in 1944. Then he is a bird, floating down the circles of time, back to the African desert between the wars. This is a tricky structure, but lots of writers enjoy fooling with time. If you're one of those, use a grid like this one, which tracks the time changes for the first three chapters of *The English Patient*.

GRID: *THE ENGLISH PATIENT*, CHAPTERS 1–3

POV	Place	Time	Object
Nurse	villa, garden, bedroom	present	water
Patient	desert, Sand Sea	past	fire, kiss
Nurse	villa, bedroom	present	candle
Patient	oasis, desert	past	oil
Nurse	villa, library	present	book
Patient	desert, oasis	past	glass, oils
Nurse	villa	present	sink
Thief	hospital, Pisa	past	bandaged hands
Nurse	villa, garden	present	headless statue
Thief	villa, Milan	past	photo, camera
Nurse	hospital, Pisa	past	lion, plums, hammock
Thief	chamber, Milan	past	blood, thumbs
Nurse	villa, library	present	piano, bomb
Author	Italy	past	crossbow, hot oil
Sapper	Italy, rivers, Arezzo	past	mud, motorbike, frescoes

Objects tell the story as the point of view slides from character to character, as the story zigzags between past and present. The recurring object in *The English Patient*—both the novel and the film adaptation—is a book, the Patient's copy of Herodotus's *The Histories*, which enters the story in the Nurse's hands in her third flashback on page 16. The first thing she reads from the Herodotus history is a description of wind and sandstorms. Two objects—*glass* and *oils*—take us back to the desert. When the Patient's plane falls burning into the sand, he is rescued by Bedouins. In the back story, a Bedouin healer anoints the Patient's body with oils from glass bottles. The *bandaged hands* identify the Thief's back story. Objects like *piano* and *bomb* in the grid mark the entrance of the Sikh Sapper, and the story is back in the present. When you pull the past into the present in your novel, make sure you mark the reader's path with objects.

The grid for the first three chapters illustrates the page-gobbling power of four protagonists (Patient, Nurse, Thief, Sapper) and their back stories. The novel is only three hundred pages long and the antagonist—Katharine Clifton—has not made her entrance yet. In the novel, Katharine shows up late, on page 141, to mark the Midpoint. In Anthony Minghella's film adaptation, she enters the story in minute number ten, bringing with her the dangerous flame of twisted love.

Using the CUT TO for Control

Whether you are digging up scenes from the past or trying to merge the past with the present, you can use a series of CUT TO's for control. Each CUT TO is a compressed scene, easy to move. If you were trying to sequence flashbacks in a complex novel like *The English Patient,* you could use some CUT TO's starting with the Patient's first memory of Katharine Clifton. Katharine is Lover B.

CUT TO:

A memory of Lover B leaning her naked body out a window in Cairo, wet with rain.

CUT TO:

A memory of going crazy when Lover B turns away, ending the affair.

CUT TO:

A memory of the husband's yellow airplane diving at him, the pilot intent on murder.

CUT TO:

A memory of Lover B, the pilot's wife, broken when the yellow plane crashes.

CUT TO:

A memory of leaving Lover B in the Cave of Swimmers while he hikes into the desert, in search of help.

CUT TO:

A memory of returning to the Cave of Swimmers to find Lover B dead.

CUT TO:

A memory of the plane burning, a Burned Man falling to earth.

The Burned Man winds up in bed in a ruined villa in wartime Italy, remembering the steps of his affair that brought him to this place. Steps in the past contain a sexual triad—the wife, her husband, her lover—that kills two people and gives the third a mortal wound.

Secrets in the Subtext—The Sexual Triad

When you examine the back story, look for a sexual triad—two men and one woman; two women and one man—because the sexual triad shows the Three Goods (genes, resources, behavior) at work, and biology makes the subtext hum with life. *The English Patient* has two sexual triads. One in ancient Lydia stars a King, his Queen, and her Lover. The other in the desert before the war stars an Explorer, a Wife, and her Husband. The Explorer is Lover A, a Hungarian Count named Almásy, before he becomes the Burned Man. The Wife is Lover B. Her name is Katharine Clifton. She is married to a spy named Geoffrey when she initiates an affair with Almásy. To ignite this affair, Katharine tells the story of King Replacement in ancient Lydia, a story built on a sexual triad. She uses the story of love in ancient Lydia to seduce Almásy the Explorer in the African desert.

Both sexual triads bristle with biology. Lover A is smart (good genes). Lover B is beautiful (good genes). Both lovers come from money (good resources). Lover B's invitation to love is bad behavior, but once the affair starts, Lover A goes crazy. His bad behavior alerts the husband, who fires up his yellow airplane, turning a spy plane into a murder weapon.

In the sexual triad from Herodotus, King Candaules (good resources) invites a handsome spear-carrier (good genes) to verify the queen's beauty (perfect genes) by viewing her naked. The Queen regards spying as bad behavior, but the King is old and the spear-carrier is handsome, so she forces him to a decision: either kill the King or be killed yourself. The spear-carrier kills the King, passes the character test, marries the queen, and rules the land (resource base) for many years.

Checklist for Handling Back Story

- [ ] How much back story?
- [ ] How much back story does the reader see?
- [ ] Where is it positioned in the structure?
- [ ] Are you working a zigzag structure?

☐ Where is the first flashback? The last flashback? (If you have a whopper of a flashback in Act Three, move it to Act Two now.)

☐ Does your back story contain murder?

☐ Does it contain a sexual triad?

☐ What core stories are working in the sexual triad?

☐ How are the Three Goods distributed?

☐ Is your time span wide enough to require a chronology?

☐ What secrets lurk in the back story? Where in the book do you release the secrets?

☐ What objects start in the back story?

☐ Do your characters make connections in the back story?

☐ How many character histories have you written?

☐ How many do you have left to write?

Exercises for Back Story

1. TAKING INVENTORY

Check your list of scenes and your list of flashbacks. How many flashbacks do you have? Where are they located in the structure? How long is the longest flashback? Long enough to make a scene? A chapter? Name each flashback, and then add a date. In the rough draft, the novelist uses flashbacks to probe the back story that is not yet written. In the rewrite, the novelist has a chance to cut.

2. DOES YOUR STRUCTURE NEED REBUILDING?

If you have a large chunk of back story in the body of your novel, you have two choices: 1) You can pack the back story into Act Two. 2) You can develop a smooth zigzag structure, following the example of *December 6*, by Martin Cruz Smith; *The English Patient*, by Michael Ondaatje; *Evening*, by Susan Minot; and *Eye of the Needle*, by Ken Follett. Follett structured *Eye of the Needle* before he started writing. Six sections, each with six chapters or scenes, and a systematic switching of the point of view. Use grids and architectural sketches before you start writing. Lock down every structural change with dates, locations, characters, subplots.

3. ONE HOUR BEFORE

If you need back story on only one character, take the dive into back story using this simple time-ladder. What was your protagonist doing an hour before the book opens on Page One? A week? A year? Five years? What happened to the protagonist ten years ago (ten, fifteen, twenty years?) that drives her in the story starting on Page One? Use detail here. An hour before the book opens, the protagonist tidies up her apartment. It's a shabby place, filled with shadows. The protagonist is a tidy housekeeper, but no matter what she does—cleaning, polishing, sweeping with verve—the place stays shabby. With each backward move in time (one hour, one week, etc.), this One Hour Before exercise takes you deeper into the character's back story. The more you write, the better you'll know your character.

Startline: An hour before the book opens, the protagonist was . . .
Startline: A week before the book opens, the protagonist was . . .
Startline: A year before the book opens, the protagonist was . . .
Startline: Five years before the book opens, the protagonist was . . .
Writing time: five minutes for each startline

4. OBJECTS AND DOCUMENTS

The English Patient has his book. The book contains the sexual triad of King Candaules, Gyges, and Queen Omphale. The book travels through time, from the love story in the desert in 1936 to the Italian villa in 1944. In *All the King's Men*, Jack Burden finds a sexual triad in the journal of Cass Mastern. Dirt from the past creates another sexual triad in the present, with Jack Burden as a part. When you dig into the past, use documents: letters, photos, diaries, journals, videotapes, computer disks, ancient scrolls. If you're going to dig an object up in Act Three, make sure you bury it in Act One.

Startline: The document in my novel is a . . . that contains the secret of . . .
Writing time: twenty minutes

5. CHRONOLOGY

Build a chronology for the major events in your novel. Start with the birth of your protagonist. Record the date of a childhood trauma—death of a parent, divorce, changing homes, living with relatives, violence—and then continue the chronology up through Page One, and all the way to the climax. If your protagonist and antagonist meet in the back story, make sure to date that meeting. Follow the model from Writer X in the back story section.

The Rewrite: Writer X Wrestles with Change

Rhoda enters the room to find Writer X on his back on the floor with his legs up and his heels on the wall, doing his deep breathing exercise. It's Saturday. He should be hard at work. Instead, X is lying there in the Corpse Pose from yoga with his eyes closed. Rhoda says hello. X's answer is muffled. Rhoda senses a change in his mood.

"Something wrong, Mr. X?"

"Can't work today, Miss Rhoda. Can't do this back story stuff."

"And why not?"

"Too much change," he says.

"Tell me," she says. "Please."

"Okay. The changes are overwhelming. My guy is gone. Old Marvin. He was, like, my alter ego, my darker self. The more stuff I change, the more I lose from the original story. Losing all that work makes me crazy, okay? So I need a break, is all. So no work today. I need to reflect, sort things out."

"What else have you lost besides Marvin?" Rhoda asks.

X sighs.

"I've lost the biker babes. And that real estate guy, Charley F., with the gold Mercedes. He was a fun dude. When Charley went, along went his castle, that big rock house. And his Aunt Maggie."

Rhoda says nothing. She leaves her things on the table, enters the kitchen, and heats water for coffee. She rinses out the French press coffee pot. When the water boils, she pours it over fresh coffee grounds, sets the timer for four minutes. When the timer rings, she pours two cups of coffee and returns to the living room. Writer X opens his eyes. "I smell coffee," he says.

"That's a good sign."

Pulling his knees to his chest, Writer X rolls sideways. He pushes himself to a sitting position, his back to the wall. Rhoda hands him a coffee, waits until he takes three sips. Then she sits beside him on the floor, their shoulders almost touching.

"Can we talk, Mr. X?"

"Shoot," he says.

"Your characters—Marvin and Charley and the biker females—will surface in their own subplots. With a name change, Charley F. would make an excellent husband for your Camera Lady. She needs a name, by the way."

"Katharine," X says. "Kate."

"Excellent name," Rhoda says. "With another name change, Charley's Aunt Maggie can become Kate's mother-in-law. What if you gave Kate a child? What if the mother-in-law tried to steal the child away from Kate?"

"Good idea," X says.

"Kate needs some back story," Rhoda says.

"What weekend is it?" X asks.

"It's Weekend 3, Mr. X."

"Back story, right?"

Rhoda nods. She stands up. Looks down at X.

"More coffee?"

X nods yes and Rhoda leaves the room. When she returns with more coffee, Writer X is sitting with his laptop, his back to the wall, typing away on the back story for his Camera Lady protagonist, now named Kate.

ONE HOUR BEFORE. One hour before her First Encounter on Page One, Kate loads her vehicle with camera equipment. Cameras. Tripods. Film bags. Battery-powered lights. An umbrella. Her hooded raincoat. Kate wears hiking boots and faded jeans and the old red sweater. Kate drives the narrow stone driveway that leads from her courtyard down to the main road, and then west toward Avignon. She arrives at her location, the Palace of the Popes. Headlights probe the dark. She parks in her usual spot near Café Faux, where raindrops tickle the windshield. Kate stares through the windshield at the empty dark. Dawn is ten minutes away.

ONE WEEK BEFORE. One week before her First Encounter, Kate argues with her husband about money. The time is Sunday afternoon, leaning toward twilight. Her husband sprawls in a director's chair at the end of the tennis court, where Kate's son (Richard? Robert? Jacques? Raoul?) hits practice balls with a friend from Paris. Her son is seventeen, a tennis prodigy being groomed by French tennis officials. This is a weekly ritual in which Kate begs for money. She owes merchants: the butcher, the baker, the plumber. The stairs need repair. The driveway up to the house is crumbling. Her husband peels off bills, but not enough. Never enough. He wants Kate to cry, so she obliges. As he doles out money, the husband lectures Kate on the virtues of economy. The husband is a lout who drives a new Mercedes and squanders money on pretty girls.

\#

ONE MONTH BEFORE. One month before her First Encounter, Kate shoots pictures of an ancient castle nestled at the foot of Mont Ventoux. The rain has stopped, the stones glisten in a pale yellow light. Half the castle is rubble. The other half is new construction. A local construction firm from Isle-sur-la-Sorgue is turning the castle into a garish tourist hotel and Kate catches the tension of contrasting times on film. The old, the new. Coexisting. Like her marriage to a cheating husband. Kate hates the changes in the Ventoux Valley. All this new construction wiping out history. At least her house is safe. Or is it? Kate shivers at the thought. There is history here: What if the house was occupied by Germans? What if the Germans were driven out by Partisans? What if the Partisans were led by a brave man named Auguste Ventoux? What if Ventoux is the maiden name of Kate's mother-in-law?

LEARNING CURVE

As X probes the past, insights pop: Charley F.'s Aunt Maggie becomes Madeleine Ventoux, Kate's mother-in-law. If Madeleine steals Kate's son away, then Writer X has another worthy antagonist. She is the real owner of Kate's husband's house. The house is Charley F.'s rock castle from the old Marvin manuscript. When he moves the house to Provence, X generates a title: *A House in Provence*? Buzzed by insights, X keeps writing.

\#

ONE YEAR BEFORE. One year before Page One of *A House in Provence*, Kate has a fight with her son. The subject of the fight is his bad behavior, excessive drinking, and reckless driving. The boy wants to live in Paris with his grandmother, Madeleine. Provence is so boring, he says. Driving too fast, the boy smashes his little red Audi into a truck carrying wine barrels. His father rushes home from a meeting in Paris. He spends ten thousand euros to keep the son out of jail. Enough money to run the house in Provence for a year.

FIVE YEARS BEFORE. Five years before Page One of *A House in Provence*, Kate has a tussle with her husband because a woman answered the phone in his hotel room. The husband explains: That woman was the maid, Madame. He slaps Kate and she fights back. She is younger than her husband and she is strong from hiking and garden work. When she throws him off, her husband bangs his head on the headboard of the fancy bed frame. Blood dribbles from a cut on his cheek. Kate drives him to the doctor. His head wound keeps him at home for ten days. He conducts business on the telephone. Kate becomes his caregiver. When Sunday rolls around, her husband gives Kate enough money to run the house for three months.

TWENTY YEARS BEFORE. Twenty years before Page One of *A House in Provence*, Kate Bernardi, age eighteen, marries Mr. Charles D'Amboise, age thirty-two, in the chapel of the church of Saint-Germain-des-Prés on the Rive Gauche in Paris on a spring day of birds and blossoms and honeybees buzzing the church bells clanging and Kate overheated in a heavily lined off-white wedding dress feeling full with love floats through a door with Charles on the other side waiting and aroused the gleam in his eye saying in French yes I do yes I do yes and then the reception at Madeleine's elegant apartment overlooking the River Seine.

TWENTY-FIVE YEARS BEFORE. Twenty-five years before Page One of *A House in Provence*, Kate watches her Uncle Julian Bernard get married to Mrs. Tabitha Smith in Pasadena, California. A week later, Mrs. Smith, now Mrs. Julian Bernard, moves Kate out of her bedroom into a small cramped room upstairs. A week after that, Kate overhears a loud argument between her father and Uncle Julian in the library. The next morning, Kate packs her bags. She is leaving Pasadena. Ejected by her uncle's new wife, she must live in Paris with Mademoiselle Bernardi, her father's older sister. Kate's father is sick. His face is gray. He smokes too much. Smoking makes him cough. A month after leaving Kate in Paris, her father dies in Lyon. Uncle Julian sends money for his funeral. Mademoiselle uses the money to run the house. Mademoiselle opens Kate's mail. When it rains in Paris, Kate longs for the warm sun of California.

Back Story Creates Scenes

Rhoda compliments X on his back story work. After a quick kiss on his cheek, she helps him develop a list of scenes generated by Kate's back story:

- A sidewalk café in Isle-sur-la-Sorgue. Lunch with the Biker.
- Stade Roland Garros in Paris, where Charles and Madeleine watch Raoul play tennis.
- Train station reunion. Kate returns from Paris to find the Biker waiting.
- First Sex. An electric, heated encounter in a small hotel.
- First Betrayals. The Biker confesses his real reason for being in France.
- Auto accident. Raoul's bad driving brings Kate back to California.

"How do you do that?" X asks.

"How do I do what?"

"How do you dig up scenes from that stuff I did on back story?"

"I visualize the scenes," Rhoda says. "Inside my head, in a series of CUT TO's, while I'm reading your words."

X laughs.

"Lady," he says. "I am glad you are on my team."

Rhoda smiles. Her eyes glisten.

"Time for your subplots, Mr. X."

Rewriting:
Subplots

Subplot is the secondary story running under the plot. Subplots, as the name implies, are subsurface, subterranean, slick as eels, tricky to catch, hard to hold. A subplot can surface in Chapter One, then duck down below the surface, and pop up again in Act Two or Three.

When a subplot surfaces, you want to be ready.

Surprise the reader, not the writer.

Being ready means you know the name of the scene where the subplot reappears. Being ready means you know the characters and their agendas, what brings them to this place. You must know time, place, temperature, season, and objects. If it's snowing when the subplot reappears, if the thermometer reads ten below, then your scene needs helpful physical detail: parkas, sweaters, boots, snow tires, tingly fingertips, sleigh bells.

Because a subplot is out of sight a lot, it's a good place to park a secret. And when you stack subplots up (see the stacker grid below, subplots in *The Great Gatsby*), you create texture in the subtext. Subtext means under the surface. Texture is the reader's perception of thickness in the work. Thickness, in turn, translates into value. A thick subtext, when well crafted, makes the reader think of your book in positive terms: deep, rich, good, good fun, good value for the money, and multilayered.

GRID: SUBPLOTS IN THE GREAT GATSBY

Level	Character	Role	Core Story	Fate
Plot	Gatsby	Protagonist	Rags to Riches	Dies
Subplot 1	Daisy	Antagonist 1	King Replacement	Lives
Subplot 2	Tom	Antagonist 2	Queen Replacement	Lives
Subplot 3	Myrtle	Antagonist 3	Rags to Riches	Dies

(Continued on following page)

Subplot 4	George	Antagonist 4	Revenge Quest	Dies
Subplot 5	Jordan	Greek Chorus	Grail Quest	Lives
Subplot 6	Nick	Author's Eye	Coming of Age	Lives

Subplot One is the path of your antagonist. Antagonist means "the one who opposes." If you don't have a worthy antagonist, create one now. If your antagonist enters the story late—Act Two or Act Three—then you send in Antagonists Two and Three to block the protagonist's path to the resource base.

- On Weekend 4, you'll rewrite Subplot One, the path of your antagonist.
- On Weekend 5, you'll rewrite Subplot Two. You could have a helper here; better to have a secondary antagonist.
- On Weekend 6, you'll rewrite Subplots Three, Four, and Five. If you have more than five subplots, you can downsize or cut.

The tools for rewriting—character arc, list of scenes, structural diagram, index cards, and the CUT TO—prepare you for rewriting scenes. On master scenes, you'll need the Thirty-One-Minute Scene Template; on shorter scenes, you can slim down to the Quick Scene Fix. The danger in rewriting subplots comes with Subplot Two: Characters in that position want more scenes, more monologues, more ink, more stature.

· Have fun. Do timed writing to keep the editor at bay. Keep the hand moving. Use the notebook for probing, the computer for editing.

Go.

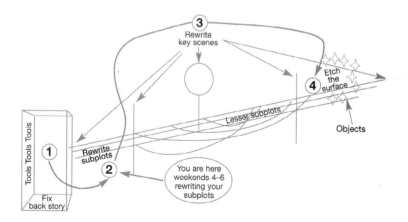

Weekend : Rewriting Subplot One

Subplot One in *Jane Eyre* belongs to Mr. Edward Fairfax Rochester, the sardonic man of property whose ugly secret—the mad wife locked in the tower—burbles up from the subtext near the end of Act Two, driving the protagonist out of Thornfield Hall, away from safety and warmth. The secret pops out in a Confession Scene, where Rochester uses his back story to portray himself as the victim of betrayal and circumstance. He was young and innocent, he says; his father was greedy. Papa Rochester snatched the bridal dowry and left his younger son, Edward, to handle the crazy bride. Rochester's motive in this confession scene is to persuade Jane to stay on at Thornfield as his mistress.

On the scale of the Three Goods, Rochester is hoping that his good resources will wipe out his bad behavior. Jane, the soul of good behavior, says no. If she can't be Mrs. Edward Fairfax Rochester, she can't stay at Thornfield. As Mistress Jane, she would have no stature in society; without the safety net of marriage, she would have no claim on Rochester's resources.

Bring Out the Tools

If you were rewriting a Rags to Riches tale like *Jane Eyre*, you would define Rochester's role, and then you would use tools like archetype and core story and character arc to zoom in on Subplot One.

- **Role.** Rochester is Antagonist One.
- **Archetype.** Rochester's archetype is Monster.
- **Core Story.** Rochester's core story is Queen Replacement.
- **Character Arc.** Rochester's character arc starts in Chapter Twelve, when he gallops into the story and his horse slips on the icy causeway. His character arc ends in the final chapter, when Jane finds him, blind and wounded, at Ferndean.

- **High Point.** Subplot One has two high points: visible (onstage) and invisible (offstage). The visible high point is the Confession Scene. The invisible high point is the fire that destroys Thornfield, that blinds and maims Rochester, and that kills Bertha.
- **Impact on the Structure.** When she discovers the secret in Subplot One, the protagonist leaves Thornfield. Her departure marks the end of Act Two and the beginning of Act Three.

Until the end of Act Two, Rochester has the raw power, driven by ego and a desire for genetic success, to destroy Jane's life. Rochester is a worthy antagonist, a perfect character for Subplot One. He's got money and property. He can buy and sell poor Jane. He teases her, he pushes her around when they talk. To match Rochester's power, Jane must grow.

Protagonist growth is the reason you want a strong antagonist. Rochester's power displays, his insulting magisterial behavior, forces our poor plain pale penniless protagonist to build some muscle. He flexes his power; Jane flexes her ethics. At the same time, she falls in love because she can see through the Monster mask. There is automatic conflict between these two characters. Rochester is rich; Jane is poor. He's older and more experienced, but Jane learns fast. He's a bad boy; she's the perfect virgin. In biological terms, Rochester is the archetypal polygamous male; Jane is the archetypal monogamous female. While the secret of the crazy wife ticks like a time bomb in Rochester's subplot, his yen for Jane is pure biology: Jane is a fertile female and Rochester wants an heir, evidence of genetic success, something mad Bertha cannot supply. If you cut Rochester from Brontë's cast of characters, *Jane Eyre* would not have survived for over 150 years.

TIP FOR YOUR REWRITE

One key to a successful rewrite is a strong antagonist in Subplot One. If you don't have an antagonist in your Subplot One, now is your chance.

Death Crone Antagonist—Tracking Miss Daisy

Plot runs on the surface; subplots run under the plot. The plot is the path of the protagonist. Subplot One is the path of the antagonist. While Subplot One in *Jane Eyre* belongs to Mr. Rochester, Subplot One in *The Great Gatsby* belongs to Miss Daisy Fay Buchanan, a Death

Crone in virginal white. White is Daisy's mask. Her core story is King Replacement. She works this powerful ritual three times:

- In the back story, when Gatsby goes off to war, Daisy replaces him by marrying Tom Buchanan, a rich man from Chicago.

- At Midpoint in the novel, she replaces her husband, Tom, with her lover, Gatsby, who lives in a garish mansion in West Egg, across from Daisy's mansion in East Egg.

- Near the end of the novel, with a murder and Gatsby's execution, Daisy plays her King Replacement card again. Using Gatsby's yellow car as a murder weapon, Daisy kills Myrtle Wilson, her husband's current mistress. A day later, Myrtle's husband—deranged by grief, and directed by Tom to Gatsby's house—executes Gatsby in his swimming pool. With Gatsby and Myrtle dead, Daisy has her true king back.

Tools for Rewriting Subplots

Secrets come from the back story. So does core story. You use core story to separate the plot from the subplots. You need a character grid for sorting and stacking subplots under the plot. The grid gives you control. For this grid, you add a column for *secrets*.

GRID: *THE GREAT GATSBY*

Name	Role	Plot/ Subplot	Core Story	Secret
Gatsby	Protagonist	Plot	Rags to Riches	Dirty Money
Daisy	Antagonist 1	Subplot 1	King Replacement	Protect Resource Base

Daisy's second King Replacement—replacing Tom with Gatsby—is temporary and strategic. It starts at Midpoint, when she reunites with Gatsby; it ends at the climax with Gatsby's execution. Daisy is deadly. She understands that Tom is rich (good resources) and that Gatsby is a crook (bad resources from dirty money). Tom is cruel (bad behavior) and Gatsby is innocent, a dopey romantic (okay behavior), but Tom is the father of Daisy's child (genetic connection). Daisy will have a dalliance with Gatsby, but there's no way she'll leave Tom behind. Too many resources. And Mrs. Thomas Buchanan sounds better in society than Mrs. Jimmy Gatz. Whether your Subplot One character is Rochester

(Queen Replacement) or Daisy (King Replacement) or the killer in *Gorky Park* (Scapegoat Sacrifice), you use core story to keep the subplot on track.

When you use the tools, you're on the hunt for insights. What insight will throw light on your rewriting task? What insight will help you rewrite the scenes for your Subplot One? If you don't get an insight from core story and secret locked in the grid, you keep working through the tools. Here's a quick list: character arc, structural diagram, list of scenes, index cards, and the CUT TO from screenwriting. When you rewrite scenes, you use a scene profile and the Thirty-One-Minute Scene Template. Study the examples from *The Great Gatsby* below.

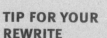

TIP FOR YOUR REWRITE

You generate more drama if you mask your Death Crone. To create Daisy's mask, Fitzgerald dresses her in white. She is the pretty mother of a young child. Her talk is light, bubbly. In the back story, she drives a white roadster and walks with Gatsby in white moonlight. In the back story, she seems innocent and pure. Steal from the masters.

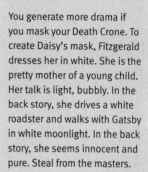

EXAMPLE: CHARACTER ARC

Character arc comes from entrances and exits. Daisy's subplot starts in Act One in the Crimson Room. She's wearing white, floating on a divan, suspended on the soft breeze, a figure from a fairy tale as seen through the innocent eyes of Nick Carraway, the First Person Narrator. The white dress is part of Daisy's mask. She's still wearing white as she drives away with Gatsby in his yellow car, on her way to kill Myrtle. That's the last the reader sees of Daisy, but her character arc does not end until Gatsby's funeral, when she fails to show up. The more Daisy fades, the more deadly she becomes.

EXAMPLE: LIST OF SCENES

The list of scenes fills in the parts of the character arc. When you name a scene, you take control. Practice naming scenes now. Pull your scene names from setting (the Crimson Room in *The Great Gatsby*), from symbolism (Rainbow Shirts), from ritual (Last West Egg Party; Verbal Combat). The kind of name is not as important as the act of naming the scene. If you are a novelist, scene names are your secret. Novels have chapters, but chapters can be any length, one page to fifty pages. And chapters usually contain more than one scene. Scene names are for your own use, in your own private space. So have fun with your naming.

When I jot down a scene list for my fiction, I add bits of information about who's there and what they're doing and the objects they are doing it with. Here's a list of scenes for Daisy's subplot:

- **Crimson Room.** Daisy is shocked when Jordan drops Gatsby's name.
- **First Encounter.** Daisy meets Jay in the back story. When Jay sails away, Daisy marries Tom, a womanizing rich racist.
- **Reunion.** Daisy reunites with Jay in Nick's West Egg cottage.
- **Rainbow Shirts.** Daisy exults watching Gatsby toss colored shirts into the air. (Offstage, the lovers mate.)
- **Last West Egg Party.** Daisy drags Tom to Gatsby's last party.
- **Kiss of Death.** Daisy kisses Gatsby in the Crimson Room.
- **Hot Lunch.** Daisy reveals her affair to Tom with the Look of Love.
- **Car Swap.** Daisy rides with Gatsby; Tom grabs Gatsby's yellow car.
- **Verbal Combat.** Watching Gatsby and Tom do verbal combat, Daisy bursts into tears.
- **Exit Miss Daisy.** Daisy drives off with Gatsby at the wheel of the yellow car.
- **Hit and Run, Offstage.** Daisy hits Myrtle Wilson with the yellow car.
- **Seclusion, Offstage.** Daisy hides inside her house while Gatsby stands vigil outside in the dark.
- **Escape.** Tom tells Nick that he's taking Daisy away.

EXAMPLE: ARCHITECTURAL DIAGRAM

A structural diagram shows the subplot intertwining with the plot. If you don't have enough insights from core story, secret, character arc, and the list of scenes, you compress your information about Subplot One into a line drawing that targets the problem. In this case, the problem is how to rewrite Subplot One. When you draw a diagram, named scenes help you understand sequence. For this exercise, I use Aristotle's action rising to a climax in Act Three. I also like to break Act Two in half at the Midpoint. Study the diagram below; use it as a model for your diagram Subplot One in your rewrite.

The diagram on the following page gives us a snapshot of scenes for Subplot One, Daisy's deadly path. The chapters that contain Daisy's scenes—One, Four, Five, Six, and Seven—hang just below the plot line.

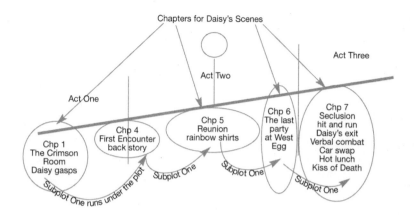

Daisy disappears from the stage in Act Three as Gatsby relates his version of Myrtle's murder, ruled an accident by the police. Daisy's easy exit from the stage verifies her power as a Death Crone. What she has set in motion works like a killing machine: Gatsby dies, Myrtle dies, and Daisy gets her husband back.

If you bristle at the word *antagonist,* remember that you are rewriting a novel that must fight for space in a world of screens (TV, film, computer). You are writing a story about characters who compete for a resource base and rewriting Subplot One—your task for this weekend—can make or break your novel. So if your diagram shows only two scenes for your antagonist, get busy. *The Great Gatsby* did not become a household word because a bootlegger got shot in his swimming pool.

TIP FOR YOUR REWRITE

Writers who take fiction workshops often avoid conflict. Instead, they create two or more protagonists. The result: Only a few writers finish a solid, dramatic draft.

EXAMPLE: INDEX CARDS

Using index cards, a device on loan from screenwriters, is a way to expand scene content while getting a feel for an alternate structure. If you use one index card per scene, you can compress the parts of a scene—character and setting, action and object, dialogue and subtext—and still be free to move scenes around. If your diagram shows you that the sequence is not working, you rearrange the index cards and get more drama.

Index Card #1—Crimson Room

Setting: a magical room where Daisy and Jordan ride a floating couch. Objects: white dresses, telephone. Secrets: Tom has a girl in New York. Bombshell: Jordan drops Gatsby's name.

Index Card #2—First Encounter

Setting: Louisville. Time: during the war. Action: Daisy meets atsby. **Objects:** white dress, white roadster, and romantic white moonlight. King Replacement: Gatsby exits to fight the Great War, Daisy marries Tom. Clues: Tom and the hotel maid. Hook: reunion of the lovers.

Index Card #3—Reunion

Setting: Nick's cottage. Action: Nick smokes, Gatsby woos Daisy. **Object:** the stopped clock. Symbolism: Time stops for the lovers. **Hook:** pathway to Gatsby's house.

Index Card #4—Rainbow Shirts

Setting: Gatsby's bedroom. Action: Gatsby tosses his colored dress shirts into the air. Subtext: money and sex. Nick exits, but the lovers stay behind. Core story: King Replacement, Gatsby for Tom.

EXAMPLE: CUT TO WRITING

If you look at a movie script, you can see the words CUT TO at the end of a shot. CUT TO is fast. It forces you to get moving while your hand develops a rhythm that is different from the pace of writing standard old average-length sentences. If you need momentum in your rewrite, use CUT TO. If you look back at the structural diagram for Daisy's subplot, you can see gaps where Daisy does not surface. She's offstage in Chapters Two and Three. She's offstage again in Chapters Eight and Nine. To tighten Daisy's subplot, we speed through, using the CUT TO, a good way to jump-start the rewrite process.

We open with Daisy in her white virgin dress floating on a divan with Jordan Baker while Tom talks to his girlfriend on the telephone. The scene climaxes when Jordan drops Gatsby's name.
CUT TO:
Jordan Baker telling Nick how Daisy fell in love with Gatsby, how Gatsby left her for the war, how Daisy married Tom, how Tom cheated on Daisy.

CUT TO:

Daisy's tearful reunion with Gatsby in Nick's cottage in the rain with the clock stopped dead for the lovers and then Gatsby ushers Daisy over to his bedroom for the colored shirt scene.

CUT TO:

The bedroom filled with colored shirts floating like the divan and Daisy's eyes bright with love as Nick exits leaving the lovers alone with their twisted love.

Note: A string of CUT TO's speeds up your rewrite. In a half hour or less, you can zip across a whole subplot or a whole scene sequence. (Tools for rewriting scenes—scene profile and the Thirty-One-Minute Template—are waiting for you in Exercises.)

REMINDER—SUBPLOTS HAVE THREE FUNCTIONS IN YOUR NOVEL

- First, subplots isolate the protagonist so you can create dramatic irony. Dramatic irony occurs when the reader sees danger around the bend—a dragon lurking behind a tree, a runaway truck on the road ahead—which the protagonist cannot see. In some films, members of the audience call out warnings about threshold crossings: *Don't go in there!*

- Second, subplots contain secrets. If you plant the secrets deep, you can splash them onto the page when your novel slows down, usually in Act Two. In Act Two, *Jane Eyre* sees Bertha Mason, kept secret by Rochester in his subplot.

- Third, subplots create texture for your novel. Texture is the reader's perception of thickness in the work. Texture is what book reviewers are talking about when they gloat about a book being "multilayered." Texture has its dangers; too much texture makes a book too thick, too multilayered. Gooey texture makes for a slow read.

Character Arcs: Entrances and Exits for Other Subplot Two Inhabitants

There is no substitute for a powerful antagonist. A good antagonist locks the book in your reader's mind. Good antagonists enter the story early and they leave late. Here are some notes on a few antagonists from novels and films:

Hannibal Lecter, who controls Subplot One in *The Silence of the Lambs*, enters the novel in Chapter Three, when Agent Starling (she has the point of view) visits him in his cell in a psycho ward. Lecter exits in the last scene, as he tracks Dr. Chilton, his next victim. Lecter's core story is Revenge Quest.

John Osborne, the antagonist of *Gorky Park*, enters the novel in Chapter Nine. He is naked except for a gold wristwatch. Like Lecter, Osborne exits in the last scene, when he is executed by the sleuth. Osborne's core story is Scapegoat Sacrifice.

Ingrid Magnussen, the murderous mother of Astrid in *White Oleander* (novel and film adaptation), enters in Chapter One and exits in the last chapter. This mother, who goes to jail for murder, exists through visits to the prison and letters to her daughter, Astrid. Her core story is Revenge Quest.

The Wicked Stepmom in the Cinderella fairy tale enters early in Act One and exits at the trying-on scene. The Stepmom's core story is Scapegoat Sacrifice. Katharine Parker, the Wicked Stepmom role in *Working Girl*, is played by Sigourney Weaver. Her entrance in Act One focuses the dramatic conflict, which climaxes in Act Three when the protagonist wins with a chronology of ideas. Katherine Parker has the same core story as the Wicked Stepmom, Scapegoat Sacrifice.

Melvin Udall, played by Jack Nicholson in *As Good as It Gets*, is a child trapped in the body of a grown man. Melvin opens the story when he tosses Verdell the Dog down a laundry chute. He ends the film taking a behavior lesson from Carol, played by Helen Hunt. Melvin's core story is Coming of Age.

Katharine Clifton—she controls Subplot One in *The English Patient*—enters the novel in Chapter Four, named "South Cairo: 1930–1938." Katharine has no name when she enters. She is masked by this image: "a woman in Cairo curves the white length of her body up from the bed." She enters late in the novel; early in the film. Katharine's core story is King Replacement. Once she chooses Almásy, there is no going back for Katharine, her lover, or her doomed boy-husband. Once Katharine enters, the camera stays on her.

Checklist for Subplot One

☐ Does Subplot One follow the path of your antagonist? (If not, rethink.)

☐ Name the scene where Subplot One starts.

☐ When Subplot One starts, which character has the point of view? Protagonist? Antagonist? Helper? Walk-on?

☐ How is the Subplot One character connected to the other characters? Blood? Money? Love? Friend from the past? Enemy? Power situation: teacher-student, master-slave, officer-private, jailer-prisoner?

☐ What is the secret held by your Subplot One character?

☐ Is your Subplot One character a Monster or a Death Crone?

☐ What is the core story for your Subplot One character?

☐ Do you need more back story on your Subplot One character?

☐ How many scenes are in Subplot One? Do you need more scenes?

☐ What object have you attached to the Subplot One character? Does this object belong to another character? Who else wants this object?

☐ Where does Subplot One peak? (Name the scene.)

☐ Where do you cap off Subplot Two? (Name the scene, give the page number.)

Exercises for Rewriting Subplot One

1. CONNECTIONS

How is your Subplot One character connected to other characters? Child? Parent? Sibling? Cousin? Teacher? Student? Master? Slave? Stepchild? Prisoner? Jailer? Boss? Worker? Private? Officer? Cop? Killer? Victim? When you rewrite your own Subplot One, make sure you tighten the character connections.

Startline: My Subplot One character connects to . . .

Writing time: ten minutes

2. LIST OF SCENES FOR SUBPLOT ONE

If you can make a scene list from memory, you're in good shape. This is a bare-bones scene list—character, action, object—that leads to the Index Cards and CUT TO's. You might narrow your focus to ritual action—kissing, drinking, eating, crossing thresholds—and unearth an insight.

Writing time: Take seven minutes for the bare-bones list

3. STRUCTURAL DIAGRAM

Use a diagram to position your subplot in the structure. This is a snap-shot. Take notes on scenes where subplots collide with each other, where they collide with the plot.

Time for the diagram: twenty minutes

4. INDEX CARDS

Index cards expand the information for each scene in the subplot. A chance to change the sequence, make it more dramatic. A chance to add a new scene if you need one.

Writing time: two hours

5. CUT TO'S

Working from memory, write CUT TO's for Subplot One. Have fun here as the momentum of your story speeds up.

Startline: We fade in with . . .

Writing time: ten minutes

6. QUICK SCENE FIX

If the scene is short—two to three pages—you can rewrite using the Quick Scene Fix. Follow the steps:

Step One: Use sense perception to lock down the point of view.

Step Two: Use action to express emotion.

Step Three: Put a second character into the scene. If you're writing a crime novel, the other character could be a witness, a suspect, a fellow sleuth, a supervisor.

Step Four: Write some dialogue.

Step Five: Now lock down the object in the scene: a book, a chair, a computer for research, drawing materials, a cell phone, a fountain pen, a weapon.

Step Six: Bring on the intruder. Witness, boss, suspect, etc.

Step Seven: Describe the setting. Is the place a bedroom? A prison cell? A library? A local pub? A cave?

Step Eight: Ratchet up the suspense by adding a time limit. What if the mission has to be completed by midnight?

7. THE THIRTY-ONE-MINUTE SCENE TEMPLATE

Use the Scene Template for rewriting master scenes.

- I am writing a story about . . . (one minute)
- This is a scene about . . . (five minutes)
- **Setting:** The time was/the place smelled of . . . (five minutes)
- **Character A on Character B:** His/her hairdo looked like . . . (five minutes)
- **Action and Dialogue:** What are you looking at? (5 minutes)
- **Intruder/Complication:** What are you guys up to? (5 minutes)
- **Climax/Resolution:** Using the long sentence release (see "Weekend 8," p. 129), extend the action to a dramatic climax. (5 minutes)

The Rewrite: Writer X Rewrites Subplot One

Paging through his battered Marvin manuscript, Writer X discovers character traits for Kate's husband, the antagonist named Charles D'Amboise. His name in the Marvin manuscript was Charley F. He drove a gold Mercedes and lived in a big fake castle in a canyon outside Santa Barbara. For his rewrite, X moves the castle to a hill in Provence, overlooking vineyards and Mont Ventoux in the distance. The castle becomes Kate's home, owned by her husband (cheating Charles) and her mother-in-law, renamed Madeleine.

LEARNING CURVE

With Rhoda's guidance, X builds a new character grid. The grid isolates the plot from the subplots; it isolates Subplot One from the other subplots. There are more antagonists to block Kate's access to the house.

Rhoda applauds. "Mr. X," she says, "you have defined Kate's resource base, her object of desire. What if Madeleine Ventoux owns the house—it was inherited from her father—and 60 percent of Ventoux Vineyards? What if Charles wants to sell the vineyards to a sleazy developer? What if Kate's biker works for the same developer? What if the developer's name is April? What if she has a daughter named . . . Julie Jean? What if their last name is Jardine?"

GRID: *A HOUSE IN PROVENCE* SUBPLOT ONE

Name	Role	Core Story	Object	Entry	Exit
Kate	Protagonist	Rags to Riches	Camera	Act 1	Act 3
Charles	Antagonist 1	Queen Replacement	Mercedes	Act 1	Act 3
Biker	Helper	Grail Quest	Bike	Act 1	Act 3
Raoul	Antagonist 2	Coming of Age	Racquet	Act 1	Act 3
Madeleine	Antagonist 3	Scapegoat Sacrifice	Key	Act 1	Act 3
April	Antagonist 4	Scapegoat Sacrifice	Blueprints	Act 1	Act 3
Julie Jean	Antagonist 5	Queen Replacement	Bikini	Act 1	Act 3

The grid helps X focus on a specific task: Subplot One in *A House in Provence* belongs to Charles D'Amboise. Charles is a Monster with a Queen Replacement core story; he's had several mistresses while married to Kate. Charles is a cool dresser. He drives a fancy Mercedes. He hates dirt, hates managing Ventoux Vineyards. When he meets April Jardine—she's on a real estate tour in France—Charles sees a way out of his cage. To rewrite Subplot One, Writer X uses index cards followed by CUT TO'S.

Index Card #1

Subplot One opens with Charles in a hotel bed watching April Jardine drop a business card on his bare belly.

Index Card #2

Sitting in his big leather chair, Charles makes check marks on Kate's expense list with his gold ballpoint. A deep frown as he writes a check, a spring in his step as he exits without a word.

Index Card #3

A fancy high-priced restaurant on the French Riviera where April Jardine introduces her daughter, Julie Jean, to Charles. His face beams with admiration for Julie Jean's beauty.

Index Card #4

The setting is the player's box at Stade Roland Garros in Paris. Sitting between Julie Jean and his mother, Madeleine, Charles applauds a winning shot by his son, Raoul.

LEARNING CURVE

Index cards start the process, then X switches to the CUT TO exercise. After the CUT TO's, he rewrites the weaker scenes. Fixing Subplot One takes only four and a half hours. The rewrite is on solid ground with the house as the object of desire. What will happen when the Biker discovers that Madeleine owns the house? What if April uses Julie Jean to enslave Charles? What if Kate's son, Raoul, has an auto accident that pulls Kate and Madeleine to Los Angeles? What will Madeleine do when she discovers that Charles wants to sell her family home to developers?

CUT TO:

Charles miffed as Kate intrudes looking crude and old and low class in her rough peasant sandals.

CUT TO:

A sidewalk café where Julie Jean laughs at a story told by Charles and they are interrupted by Raoul arriving.

CUT TO:

April's conference room at her tennis resort in California showing Charles the scale model of the hotel-resort complex that will eat up the family vineyards and replace the ancestral family home, five centuries old, on the hill in Provence.

CUT TO:

Poolside at April's resort where Charles clicks glasses with three chubby moneymen, backers of April's hotel-resort complex. They want Charles on their board.

CUT TO:

Charles wearing a hard hat staring at Julie Jean in skimpy clothes while a bulldozer rips through the last orange grove in California.

Weekend 5: Rewriting
Subplot Two

Tom Buchanan, husband of Daisy, moves with a heavy-booted tread through Subplot Two of F. Scott Fitzgerald's *The Great Gatsby*. Tom's archetype is Monster. His core story—he shares this with another man of property, Mr. Rochester of *Jane Eyre*—is Queen Replacement. His role in the book and in the film adaptations is Antagonist Two. Tom guards the treasures of East Egg. After Daisy cheats on him, Tom ejects the intruder; a day later, he engineers the intruder's execution.

Tom is the first character Nick meets in the book.

The setting for the meeting is Tom's estate at East Egg, a big Georgian house, a monster lawn sweeping from the mansion down to the beach. The mansion has French windows that glow gold in the sunset, a metaphorical backdrop for Tom in riding boots on the front porch. He stands wide-legged, a studied power posture. His leg muscles strain the high-polish leather boots. A great pack of shoulder muscle verifies his strength, depicted with a key Fitzgerald descriptor: *a cruel body*.

What you need to remember as you rewrite your book, sorting characters for your subplots, is that, during the rewrite of *The Great Gatsby*, Tom Buchanan came close to being promoted to protagonist.

The confused writer almost replaced Gatsby with Tom.

How did this happen?

A Lesson in Rewriting

Fashionable East Egg, home of Daisy and Tom, two world-class antagonists, is Fitzgerald's fictional, symbol-rich name for Manhasset Neck, a peninsula nestled between Hempstead Harbor and Manhasset Bay, on Long Island, east of New York City. The protagonist of the novel, Mr. Jay Gatsby, lives in West Egg, across the Bay from East Egg. West Egg is Fitzgerald's fictional name for Great Neck, a smaller, shorter peninsula.

When Fitzgerald got the idea for writing *The Great Gatsby*, he and wife Zelda were renting a house in Great Neck, aka East Egg. His 1925 Jazz Age novel about booze and fast cars and a love story between a bootlegger and a deadly Southern belle made Fitzgerald famous. This novel still sells today. Warning sign for your rewrite: During the rewrite, the author came close to tossing his protagonist, replacing Gatsby with Tom Buchanan.

Here's what happened. Revising the *Gatsby* manuscript in the mid-1920s for editor Maxwell Perkins, Fitzgerald lost his grip on Gatsby's character. The author still held tight to his basket of power symbols—green light, yellow car, hearse, City of Sin, valley of ashes, Dr. Eckleburg's Bespectacled Eyes—but his writing grew stale on that road from New York City with Daisy the Death Crone steering the yellow car toward murder in the valley of ashes. Gatsby was indistinct, Fitzgerald complained to his editor, a shadowy figure out of reach, and he was ready to turn the lead role in the book over to rich man Tom Buchanan, Daisy's womanizer husband.

> **TIP FOR YOUR REWRITE**
>
> Follow Fitzgerald's lead with Tom-Daisy-Gatsby. Use a sexual triad to connect the plot to Subplots One and Two.

Fitzgerald, confused about his rewrite, was ready to replace the protagonist with his Subplot Two character.

Perkins, a great editor, ordered Fitzgerald back to work. More detail, he urged, more word pictures. Carrying drawings of Gatsby's face made by his wife Zelda, Fitzgerald poked around in the back story (what happens to your characters before Page One) and unearthed the sexual triad that would make him famous. The triadic connections start in the back story, when Gatsby meets Daisy in Louisville:

- boy meets girl
- boy loses girl
- girl marries Monster
- boy gets girl at last
- boy dies in swimming pool

Rewriting Subplot Two

When you rewrite Subplot Two, you can rewrite the scenes early, using the scene profile and the Thirty-One-Minute Template. Or you can warm up to your task by taking the same five steps you took to rewrite Subplot One. Let's list those here:

1. *Character Arc*—entrance and exit—marks the subplot in the structure.
2. *List of Scenes* fills in the parts of the character arc.
3. *Structural Diagram* shows the subplot colliding with the plot to make key scenes.
4. *Index Cards,* on loan from screenwriters, is a way to expand scene content while getting a feel for structural changes.
5. *CUT TO,* another device from the world of screenwriting, lets you speed through the subplot. Speed gets your brain cooking, a handy jump start for the rewrite process.

STEP 1. CHARACTER ARC

Tom Buchanan has a long character arc. It starts early in Act One, a scene called Enter the Monster; it ends late in Act Three, when Nick runs into Tom on Fifth Avenue. The month is October and Tom justifies his action—sending Wilson to Gatsby's house—by saying he was in fear of his life because Wilson had a pistol.

STEP 2. BARE-BONES SCENE LIST FOR SUBPLOT TWO

- **Enter the Monster.** Tom enters flexing.
- **Crimson Room.** Tom exits to speak to Myrtle on the phone. Daisy follows him. Jordan tells Nick about Tom's mistress.
- **Wilson's Garage 1.** Tom introduces Nick to Myrtle.
- **Bloody Nose.** Tom breaks Myrtle's nose for saying bad things about Daisy.
- **Rivals Meet.** Nick introduces Tom to Gatsby in the lunch dive in New York City.
- **Intruders.** Tom and two East Eggers penetrate Gatsby's West Egg mansion.
- **Last West Egg Party.** Tom sizes Gatsby up.
- **Hot Lunch.** Daisy's Look of Love tells Tom she's having an affair with Gatsby.
- **Car Swap.** Tom takes possession of Gatsby's yellow car.
- **Wilson's Garage 2.** Myrtle thinks the yellow car belongs to Tom.
- **Verbal Combat.** Tom calls Gatsby a bootlegger. Daisy cries.
- **Wilson's Garage 3.** Tom hears about the yellow car, assumes Gatsby was driving.
- **Fifth Avenue.** Explaining to Nick, Tom justifies guiding Wilson to Gatsby's house.

STEP 3. ARCHITECTURAL DIAGRAM FOR SUBPLOT TWO

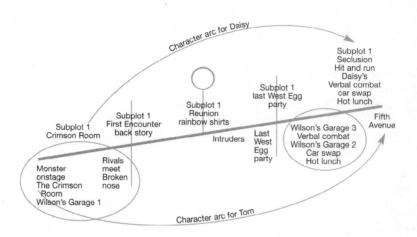

The diagram shows scenes for Tom's Subplot Two running under the straight line. Daisy's subplot runs above the line. The diagram shows Tom absent for most of Act Two. Intruders is a short scene where Tom penetrates Gatsby's closed circle, where he ridicules Gatsby's manners. The Last West Egg Party has Daisy defending Gatsby and Tom deciding to have him investigated. After that party Act Two is almost over.

A grouping of five scenes—Hot Lunch, Car Swap, Wilson's Garage 2, Verbal Combat, and Wilson's Garage 3—show Tom's power. He grabs Gatsby's car; he calls him a crook; he blames the hit-and-run on Gatsby. Tom's exit in Fifth Avenue gives Nick the opportunity of condemning Tom and Daisy—"they smashed up things and then retreated back into their money"—for being Upper World rich and Upper World careless.

There is a class struggle buried in *The Great Gatsby*. Jordan Baker cheats at golf while George Wilson sweats over machinery in his garage. Jordan Baker is Upper World. George is Lower World. The valley of ashes is Hell. Use this kind of conflict in your rewrite: Lower World character (bad resources, good genes) vs. Upper World character (good resources, bad behavior).

All the dead characters are blue collar, working class. The result: automatic drama between the haves and the have-nots.

STEP 4. INDEX CARDS FOR SUBPLOT TWO

Index Card #1—Enter the Monster

The Monster mansion in East Egg verifies good resources. The lawn is huge. The rose bed is half an acre. Tom's muscles—his legs straining the leather boots—verify good genes. In college, Tom played football. Tom's bad behavior shows itself in the next scene. (Tip: Bring your strong characters on early.)

Index Card #2—The Crimson Room

Daisy tells Nick that Tom vanished when their daughter was born. When Tom vanishes to answer the telephone, Jordan leaks the mistress secret, then drops Gatsby's name. Daisy gasps: "You know Gatsby?" and King Replacement throbs in the subtext. Tom grabs Nick's arm, hauls him to the dinner table.

Index Card #3—Wilson's Garage I

On the way into the city, Tom teases George Wilson about cars. Then Tom orders Myrtle Wilson to hop the next train for the city. Symbolism: The valley of ashes is a wasteland Hell. Polar opposite of East Egg, a lush garden.

Index Card #4—Broken Nose

Action: Myrtle cries Daisy; Tom breaks her nose. Bloody towel symbolism. More bad behavior from Tom.

STEP 5. WRITING CUT TO'S FOR SUBPLOT TWO

We open with Tom Buchanan on the porch of his East Egg mansion, his muscles shouting "good genes."
CUT TO:
Tom crushing Nick's hand.
CUT TO:
Tom on the phone with Myrtle watching Nick chat with Daisy and Jordan.
CUT TO:
Tom on the train in the valley of ashes talking to Nick about money.

CUT TO:

Wilson's garage in the valley of ashes where Tom runs an Upper World power trip on George Wilson before telling Myrtle to meet him in the city.

CUT TO:

A party in a hotel room in the city where Myrtle screams Daisy's name, where Tom breaks Myrtle's nose and there's blood everywhere.

The Power of Perspective in the Rewrite

When subplots meet, you have a scene. In the Crimson Room, for example, there are four subplot characters: Nick, Jordan, Daisy, and Tom. The reader sees the scene from Nick's point of view. If you use the power of analogy, putting yourself in Fitzgerald's shoes, you could see the scene from Daisy's point of view when you rebuilt Subplot One. You would see the scene from Tom's point of view when you rebuilt Subplot Two.

When you shift perspective on a scene, you enhance your control over the material. The setting is the same. You start with the same objects. But changing one action or one dialogue line can make the difference between okay and very good. Let's say you have a scene where Subplots One and Two collide with the plot. Let's say you rewrote the scene from the protagonist's point of view; now you rewrite it from the point of view of the antagonist, the character in Subplot One. Lightning flashes and thunder roars as your insight illuminates the bones of story. You never know unless you take the leap.

Reviewing the Function of Subplot

Subplots have three main functions: to isolate the protagonist and make a place for dramatic irony; to contain secrets; and to build texture.

SUBPLOTS ISOLATE THE PROTAGONIST

Tom sends George Wilson to kill Gatsby; Wilson kills Gatsby, then shoots himself. Tom's role is safe. Gatsby is locked in the plot. He does not know George Wilson; he cannot see what's cooking in the subplots. The reader sees Tom and George in the first Wilson's Garage scene. If you could warn Gatsby about George, would you take the shot? The writer creates dramatic irony.

SUBPLOTS CONTAIN SECRETS

In the Crimson Room, Jordan leaks Tom's affair with Myrtle to Nick. The secret whirls through the subplots—from Daisy to Jordan to Nick—but never penetrates the plot.

- Secret One. Tom does not know that his wife (Daisy) is cheating on him.
- Secret Two. Gatsby does not know that Tom's cheating on Daisy. So when Daisy kills Myrtle, Tom's mistress, with Gatsby's yellow car, he has no idea that he will die, shot dead by Myrtle's husband, who was sent by Tom.
- Secret Three. Daisy does not know that Gatsby bootlegs illegal booze from storefronts called "drugstores."

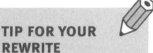

TIP FOR YOUR REWRITE

Choose your moment, a location in the structure, to let the secret out.

SUBPLOTS BUILD TEXTURE

In the grid below, Gatsby has the top slot, the slot for plot and protagonist. Daisy's subplot runs under the plot. Tom's subplot runs under Daisy's subplot. Myrtle, Tom's mistress, runs under Tom. George, her husband, runs under Myrtle. These five characters do stuff to each other. Nick the Narrator observes; he gets the lovers together; he never gets hurt. Other characters die, but not Nick. He's alive at the end. Jordan Baker is the writer's Greek Chorus: her role is leaking secrets. Nick and Jordan have the lower-level subplots.

GRID: PLOTS AND SUBPLOTS IN *THE GREAT GATSBY*

Name	Role	Plot/Subplot	Entry	Exit	Fate	Core Story
Gatsby	Protagonist	Plot	Act 1	Act 3	Dies	Rags to Riches
Daisy	Antagonist 1	Subplot 1	Act 1	Act 3	Lives	King Replacement
Tom	Antagonist 2	Subplot 2	Act 1	Act 3	Lives	Queen Replacement
Myrtle	Antagonist 3	Subplot 3	Act 1	Act 3	Dies	Rags to Riches
George	Antagonist 4	Subplot 4	Act 1	Act 3	Dies	Scapegoat Sacrifice
Jordan	Chorus	Subplot 5	Act 1	Act 3	Lives	Grail Quest
Nick	Helper	Subplot 6	Act 1	Act 3	Lives	Coming of Age

Raiders from Subplot Two

In each novel you write, watch out for those Subplot Two characters. They start out small; they promise to help with the story. Suddenly, they are begging for more ink. Ink is a character's lifeblood. You give them more ink and they grow. They preen, they swagger, they break stuff, they throw things, they inject energy into your rewrite. Earlier, we saw what almost happened in *The Great Gatsby*. The same thing almost happened in *The Accidental Tourist*, the model novel for the first *Weekend Novelist* book.

The Subplot Two character in *The Accidental Tourist* (by Anne Tyler) is a dog-trainer named Muriel Pritchett. Macon Leary, the protagonist, hires Muriel to train his dog, Edward. By Midpoint, Muriel has Macon in her bed, where they share secrets and compare wounds. Muriel's core story is Rags to Riches. Like the waitress in *As Good as It Gets*, Muriel has a sick child. The child fills the void left in Macon's life when his son was killed in a shoot-out in a hamburger joint. As you can see from the drawing below, Muriel takes over most of Act Two.

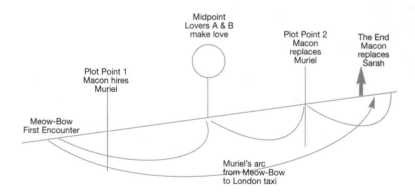

The sketch shows Muriel entering the story in the middle of Act One.

Macon's wife, Sarah, has gone, leaving Macon to care for the house, one cat, and one dog. Macon meets Muriel when he takes Edward the Dog to Meow-Bow, a pet clinic. At the end of Act One, Macon hires Muriel to train Edward. Their love affair starts at Midpoint in Act Two, when they discover that they are both wounded. They make love. Macon accepts Muriel's son. At Plot Point Two, Sarah reenters the story, replacing Muriel. Her lease has run out; she wants to come home. Macon dumps Sarah at the climax, bringing Muriel back for the ending, sunlight on raindrops in London.

SUBTEXT: MURIEL AND MACON
AND THE THREE GOODS

Macon has the house (a resource) and a good job writing travel books (a resource). His brothers and sisters are very bright (good genes) and a little eccentric (bad behavior possible). Macon is lost without Sarah; he needs a female to guide him through life. Muriel is poor (bad resources), but filled with motherly love for her son (good behavior). When Muriel appears in Act One, her wardrobe shouts bad taste: a V-neck black dress *splashed* with big pink flowers, padded shoulders, skimpy skirt, outrageous high-heeled sandals. Muriel is Character C, the third leg of the sexual triad (Sarah-Macon-Muriel) at the heart of *The Accidental Tourist*.

TIP FOR YOUR REWRITE

Subplot Two characters need watching. They are sneaky folk, plotting takeover.

When Hollywood turned Tyler's novel into a feature film, the director filled the Muriel Pritchett role with Geena Davis. Davis dominated the film and won an Oscar that year for Best Supporting Actress. Muriel has Subplot Two. And she's here in this example because what happened in *The Accidental Tourist* can happen in your novel.

Checklist for Rewriting Subplot Two

☐ Name the scene where Subplot Two starts.

☐ Are you introducing the Subplot Two character with a monologue? A First Encounter? A burst of action?

☐ What core story does Subplot Two follow?

☐ How many scenes are in Subplot Two? Do you need more scenes? Do you need to cut some scenes?

☐ In which key scenes does Subplot Two surface?

☐ What object have you attached to the Subplot Two character? Does this object belong to another character? Who else wants this object?

☐ Where does Subplot Two peak? (Name the scene.)

☐ Where do you cap off Subplot Two? (Name the scene, give the page number.)

☐ Have you done a Subplot Profile for Subplot Two?

Exercises for Rewriting Your Subplot Two

1. CONNECTIONS

How is your Subplot Two character connected to other characters? Child? Parent? Sibling? Cousin? Teacher? Student? Master? Slave? Stepchild? Prisoner? Jailer? Boss? Worker? Private? Officer? Cop? Killer? Victim? When you rewrite your own Subplot Two, make sure you tighten the character connections.

Startline: My Subplot Two character connects to . . .

Writing time: ten minutes

2. BACK STORY

If your Subplot Two character feels thin, write some back story. Use the character connections from Exercise 1, above. Suggestion: Start in school if you can.

Startline: My name is. . . I have Subplot Two. I met Character E in high school when . . .

Alternate Startline: What if Character C met Character D back in . . . when they . . .

Writing time: twenty minutes

3. BARE-BONES SCENE LIST FOR SUBPLOT TWO

If you can make a scene list from memory, you're in good shape. This is a bare-bones scene list—character, action, object—that leads to the index cards and CUT TO'S. You might narrow your focus to ritual action—kissing, drinking, eating, crossing thresholds—and unearth an insight.

Writing time: Take seven minutes for the bare-bones list

4. DIAGRAM

Use a diagram to position your subplot in the structure. This is a snapshot. Take notes on scenes where subplots collide with each other, where they collide with the plot.

Time for the diagram: twenty minutes

5. INDEX CARDS

Index cards expand the information for each scene in the subplot. A chance to change the sequence, make it more dramatic. A chance to add a new scene if you need one.

Writing time: Two hours

6. CUT TO'S

Working from memory, write CUT TO'S that integrate Subplot Two with the plot and at least one other subplot. Have fun here as the momentum of your story speeds up. Pay attention to the rhythm.

Startline: We open Subplot Two with Character C tossing . . .

Writing time: twenty minutes

7. QUICK SCENE FIX

If the scene is short—two to three pages—you can rewrite using the Quick Scene Fix. Follow the steps.

Step One: Use sense perception to lock down the point of view.

Step Two: Use action to express emotion.

Step Three: Put a second character into the scene. If you're writing a crime novel, the other character could be a witness, a suspect, a fellow sleuth, a supervisor.

Step Four: Write some dialogue.

Step Five: Now lock down the object in the scene: a book, a chair, a computer for research, drawing materials, a cell phone, a fountain pen, a weapon.

Step Six: Bring on the intruder: witness, boss, suspect, etc.

Step Seven: Describe the setting. Is the place a bedroom? A prison cell? A library? A local pub? A cave?

Step Eight: Ratchet up the suspense by adding a time limit. What if the mission has to be completed by midnight?

TIP FOR YOUR REWRITE

To rewrite a scene twice, try changing the point of view. For example, if you had rewritten a hot scene from Character B's point of view when you worked through Subplot One, then you would rewrite the same scene from Character C's point of view when you worked through Subplot Two.

8. THE THIRTY-ONE-MINUTE SCENE TEMPLATE

Use the scene template for rewriting master scenes.

- I am writing a story about . . . (one minute)
- This is a scene about . . . (five minutes)
- **Setting:** The time was/the place smelled of . . . (five minutes)
- **Character A on Character B:** His/her hairdo looked like . . . (five minutes)
- **Action and Dialogue:** What are you looking at? (5 minutes)
- **Intruder/Complication:** What are you guys up to? (5 minutes)
- **Climax/Resolution:** Using the long sentence release (see "Weekend 8," p. 129), extend the action to a dramatic climax. (five minutes)

The Rewrite: Writer X Rewrites Subplot Two

For his Subplot Two character, Writer X demotes Marvin the Biker from protagonist to helper. Rhoda advises a name change. An intense discussion with Rhoda births a name: Harry Thornburg. X adds details. Harry is a high school athlete; he served time in the U.S. military; he works for April Jardine, teaching tennis at her tennis club in Santa Barbara.

"Excellent," Rhoda says. "How do you separate Harry Thornburg from Marvin Krypton?"

"Core story first," X says. "Old Marvin was on a Grail Quest. That's why the plot wandered. Harry will replace Kate's husband, Charles, so his core story is King Replacement. Marvin was a computer geek with no visible income source. Harry's an ex-jock, ex-soldier. How about he's in debt to April? How about he owes her and he's working off his debt teaching tennis to restless housewives?"

"Good start," Rhoda says. "To stabilize this character, you need some back story. Start in high school and move forward to his job at the tennis club."

X Writes Back Story for Harry Thornburg

Using a series of what-ifs, X probes the back story of Harry Thornburg: What if Harry knew April in high school in Pasadena? What if Harry was two years older, a senior with jock super-status? What if April had a crush on Harry? What if Harry was hooked up with a rich girl? What if April, rejected by Harry, takes up with a bad guy and gets pregnant at sixteen? What if the pregnancy produced Julie Jean?

X reads the what-ifs to Rhoda.

"Good," Rhoda says. "Don't stop. Keep going."

X keeps writing: Harry joined the Army. He had a knack for languages, so they sent him to the Defense Language Institute in Monterey, California. He studied Vietnamese and French, spent time in Southeast Asia doing military intelligence. Came back to the DLI to study German and Italian, got stationed in Paris, and then Berlin. Married a German girl named Ilse, brought her to San Diego, where she left Harry for a fat banker. Losing his wife drove Harry to drink. He went into debt, taught pick-up lessons at public courts, played in a tournament at April Jardine's tennis club. Went to work for April at the tennis club and found he was a good teacher.

April took Harry into her bed, bought up his debts, and signed him to a five-year contract. If he split before the debt was paid off, she would send the law after him. When April meets Charles D'Amboise, she sends

Harry to France. He speaks French; he's had experience poking around in people's lives. Harry's mission: to purchase properties bordering Ventoux Vineyards.

In Paris, Harry rents a BMW bike from an old Army buddy. He borrows a leather biker suit and sets out for Provence with his pockets full of euros. In the square at Avignon, Harry spots Kate before he knows she is married to Charles D'Amboise. She grabs his heart, this lonely lady shooting photos of nothing in the slowly falling rain. When Kate drops a lens cap, Harry picks it up. Wheeling through the Ventoux Valley, Harry recognizes Kate's house from April's photos. He likes the house. Feels sad knowing that April plans to tear down most of the house, leaving a few old walls standing as a nod to history, and erect a hotel complex with an expensive view of the valley.

LEARNING CURVE

Writing back story helps Writer X transform a character from the Marvin manuscript into a character for the Kate manuscript. Writing back story also gives Harry a secret—he's working for April Jardine, the nasty lady who wants Kate's house—which builds suspense in the subtext. What will happen when Kate discovers Harry's secret?

Rhoda guides Writer X to the next step: pulling scenes out of the back story. Then fitting those scenes into the Kate manuscript. "The tool to use," Rhoda says, "is the index card followed by some CUT TO'S for Subplot Two."

The index cards track Harry's subplot from his first sighting of Kate in the square at Avignon to the phone call at the end of Act Two. The call comes from a hospital in Los Angeles. Kate's son, Raoul, has been hurt in a car accident. Kate leaves Harry in Provence and flies to Los Angeles to be with Raoul. Back in Provence, Harry discovers that Madeleine Ventoux—and not her son, Charles—owns the lion's share of the properties coveted by April Jardine. Kate's house and Ventoux Vineyards are controlled by Kate's mother-in-law. The same mean woman who stole away Kate's son, Raoul.

Down there in Subplot Two, Harry burns with secrets:

- First, he's in love with Kate.
- Second, he works for the enemy, April.
- Third, Charles D'Amboise cannot sell either the house or the vineyards without Madeleine's consent.

The secrets drive Harry to the hospital in Los Angeles, where Kate waits for Raoul to recuperate from his wounds. Writer X has ten index cards for Harry's subplot. "Secrets have power," Rhoda says. "Use your next index cards to show how your Harry character deals with the inner strife. Confession, followed by redemption."

Index Card #11. Subplot Two.

Los Angeles Hospital where Kate visits her son, Raoul, in a white bed in a white room. Harry waits for Kate. When she appears, he confesses: He's working for April, a real estate developer who wants Kate's house.

Index Card #12. Kate's Plot.

Kate turns away. Tears in her eyes. Watches Harry exit, shoulders slumped.

Index Card #13. Subplot Two.

The Teaching Court at April's tennis club. Harry exits the court, leaving a group of pretty housewives practicing their strokes.

Index Card #14. Subplot Two.

The Private Conference Room at April's tennis club. Harry shoots photos of the scale model for April's project, now called Club D'Amboise. The scale model shows Kate's house buried under a fancy resort complex. The Ventoux Vineyards are gone, replaced by a golf course.

Revved by his progress on the rewrite, X follows the index cards with some CUT TO's, fitting Harry's subplot into Kate's plot, then integrating scenes from the husband's subplot. X starts his CUT TO's in the hospital corridor in California, where Harry confesses to Kate; the CUT TO's wind up in Paris with Harry handing Kate the photos that she will carry to the climax.

"Very good, Mr. X. Your biker has become a mythic helper. Where did that come from?"

"Redemption was your idea," X says.

"And you made good use of the photos."

Writer X nods. He's feeling super.

Rhoda jots some notes on X's pages, then hands them back to X. He sees a short list of words, written in Rhoda's careful hand. The words are: *sacred object, scale model, envelope,* and *photos.*

"This is quite good," Rhoda says, "because it's quite cinematic. The scale model is a sacred object. It embodies the hopes and dreams of our secondary antagonist, April Jardine. To Charles D'Amboise, the scale model represents escape. His idea is a barter ritual. He can trade the family land for wealth and status. With the money from this deal, he can escape Provence and Kate. He can also end his dependence on his mother, Madeleine. When you rewrite the scenes between Charles and his mother, you might consider amplifying his debt. He's a grown man still asking Mommy for money."

Back to Harry's subplot.

"By confessing to Kate," Rhoda says, "Harry jump-starts his redemption. His first act of redemption is taking those photos, stealing the image of the scale model from April. His second act is delivering the photos to Kate. The best part is structural: you have used the sacred object to connect three subplot characters (Charles, April, and Harry) to Kate's plot. When Kate delivers the photos to Madeleine, you use the same object to connect to her subplot. The book gets tighter. How do you feel?"

"I need a beer," X says.

"Before the beer, Mr. X. You must make a grid."

"What for?" X says.

"A grid," Rhoda says, "for the lower subplots."

"Work, work," X says. "Always work."

Weekend 6: Rewriting Subplots Three, Four, and Five

Subplot Three runs under Subplot Two, which runs under Subplot One, which runs under the plot.

Subplot Four runs under Subplot Three.

Subplot Five runs under Subplot Four.

These three subplots—Three, Four, and Five—mark pathways for your minor characters. Most of the time, these subplots have shorter character arcs and fewer scenes. Characters in shorter subplots have specific functions. For example, Richard Mason, the Subplot Three character in *Jane Eyre*, is a whistle-blower. His main function in the novel is to help expose Rochester as a married man, thereby spoiling Jane's wedding.

Character Arc and Scenes

Mason enters the novel in Act Two, shivering in his overcoat. He exits in Act Two after a visit to sister Bertha's cage in the tower at Thornfield. He attends a party, gets stabbed by Bertha, and shows up in the Wedding Chapel scene near the end of Act Two, just in time to blow the whistle on Rochester.

For a contrast to Richard Mason, let's look at Myrtle Wilson, the Subplot Three character in *The Great Gatsby*. Myrtle enters in Act One, vanishes in Act Two, and surfaces in Act Three just in time to get killed. Myrtle's function in the novel is victim. She dies so that Gatsby may die—shot by Myrtle's husband.

Whereas Richard Mason appears and disappears—we have no idea where he lives or what he eats—we see Myrtle Wilson at home in Fitzgerald's Hades, a wasteland called the valley of ashes. Her domicile is a shabby apartment above her husband's garage on the highway between suburban East Egg and the metropolis of New York City.

We get to know Myrtle better than we do Richard Mason because she has five solid scenes.

1. **Wilson's Garage:** After toying with Myrtle's husband, George, Tom Buchanan makes a date with Myrtle. Tells her to hop the train for the city.
2. **Dog of New York:** Tom buys Myrtle a pet dog.
3. **Bloody Nose:** At Myrtle's impromptu midafternoon New York City cocktail party, Tom slugs Myrtle, breaking her nose. The reason: Myrtle won't stop screaming "Daisy! Daisy! Daisy!"
4. **Yellow Car:** Looking down from her bedroom window above the garage, Myrtle spots Tom behind the wheel of Gatsby's yellow car. Spotting Jordan Baker in the back seat, Myrtle makes the assumption that will get her killed: She assumes that the yellow car belongs to Tom.
5. **Hit and Run:** Spotting the yellow car coming back from New York City, Myrtle tries to flag it down and gets killed by Daisy.

Myrtle has no scenes alone. She has four scenes with Tom and Nick; one scene with Daisy and Gatsby. We learn about Myrtle through her sister, Catherine, a walk-on character who functions as a Greek chorus. In the Bloody Nose scene, Catherine analyzes Myrtle's affair. Since Myrtle can't stand George, and since Tom can't stand Daisy, they should both get divorces and marry each other.

Four pages later, Tom breaks Myrtle's nose.

Lower subplot characters are offstage more than they are onstage. They are hidden from the reader. They get less ink, but they still require careful handling. Myrtle Wilson gets real when her nose bleeds. Richard Mason gets real when he bleeds from Bertha's knife. When you're working your minor characters, give them a function and a motive and make them bleed.

Four Steps for Rewriting the Lower Subplots

1. FIND THE MOTIVATION

What drives Myrtle Wilson's affair with Tom? Answer: money. Tom is rich. Myrtle's husband, George, is poor. Tom is clean; George Wilson has

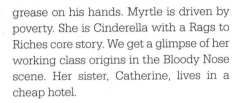

TIP FOR YOUR REWRITE

If you can't figure out the motivation for a character in one of your lower subplots, spend ten minutes writing some back story.

grease on his hands. Myrtle is driven by poverty. She is Cinderella with a Rags to Riches core story. We get a glimpse of her working class origins in the Bloody Nose scene. Her sister, Catherine, lives in a cheap hotel.

2. FIX THE CHARACTER ARC

Lock down each subplot with a core story. Mark the entrances and exits of any character with a subplot. Richard Mason enters and exits in Act Two, Myrtle Wilson vanishes for all of Act Two.

3. BUILD A SCENE LIST

Before you start rewriting, make a scene list and add action for each scene.

4. PROBE ROLE AND FUNCTION

Make sure you know what these lower subplot characters are up to. Why are they in the book? What is their function? Keep it simple. Myrtle Wilson is a victim. Richard Mason is a whistle-blower. Jordan Baker (she has Subplot Five) is a Greek chorus. She comments on the action. George Wilson's function is executioner. If you're writing a mystery, you could have a red herring character, or a witness who turns into a suspect, or a suspect who turns into a friend.

Character Transformation: From Suspect to Friend

Let's say your rewrite unearths a really strong character in Subplot Three. A character who starts as an antagonist, but who changes roles along the way. A character with brains and a lot of force. A character outside the sexual triad formed by the protagonist and the folks from Subplots One and Two. A character who becomes a helper for the protagonist. If that happens in your rewrite, you need a model. The model must include the magic of character transformation based on role change.

Fairy tales have magic. Realistic fiction has character transformation.

Our example of character transformation comes from *Gorky Park*, where the sleuth, Arkady Renko, bonds with an American detective named William Kirwill. Kirwill is New York City tough. He's a big guy with a cynical sense of humor. He enters the story in Act One as an antagonistic suspect. He fights with the sleuth. He performs the choral role of a lower subplot character, mocking Russian policework as amateur and corrupt. Near the end of Act One, however, Renko loses a detective, Pasha Pavlovich, from his homicide team.

The death of the Russian homicide detective opens a slot for a much-needed helper-replacer-friend, and here comes Kirwill, a cop from America, who changes roles, from antagonistic suspect to helper-sidekick. *Gorky Park* has a long cast roster with five subplots. Here they are in a grid.

GRID: GORKY PARK

Name	Role	Plot/ Subplot	Entry	Exit	Core Story
Renko	Protagonist	Plot	Act 1	Act 3	King Replacement
Osborne	Antagonist 1	Subplot 1	Act 1	Act 3	Revenge Quest
Irina	Antagonist 2	Subplot 2	Act 1	Act 3	Rags to Riches
Kirwill	Antagonist-Helper	Subplot 3	Act 1	Act 3	Revenge Quest
Iamskoy	Antagonist 3	Subplot 4	Act 1	Act 2	Grail Quest
Pribluda	Antagonist 4	Subplot 5	Act 1	Act 3	Revenge Quest

Running the Four Steps

1. MOTIVATION

Kirwill is in Moscow to avenge the death of his little brother, Jimmy, who is one of the three corpses found in Gorky Park to create the crime scene that opens the book. Back story: Both Kirwill brothers learned Russian from their parents, Russian émigrés who lived in New York City. Jimmy dies when he threatens to blow the whistle on the killer's smuggling of sables from Russia to America.

2. CHARACTER ARC

Kirwill's subplot starts in Act One and ends in Act Three.

3. SCENE LIST

Kirwill's subplot has eleven scenes:

- **First Fight.** The sleuth takes some body blows from Kirwill at the crime scene. Mystery: He's big and tough; no ID yet.
- **Suspect Interrogation.** A Moscow snitch fingers Kirwill as a suspect. Mystery: Kirwill speaks Russian, does not seem Russian.
- **Suspect's Lair.** In Kirwill's hotel room, the sleuth finds objects: a zip gun, a sketch of the crime scene, and a cop's badge from New York City. Sleuth's intuition: This guy Kirwill could help.
- **Male Bonding.** In the worker's dive in Moscow, Kirwill raises a glass to Pasha, the dead detective. "Hey," Kirwill says, "here's to your dead detective, huh?" Heart of the scene: Kirwill's back story, how he was raised by Russians escaping the Stalin regime. Role transformation from antagonist to helper. Now Renko has a buddy.
- **Victim's Lair.** Renko and Kirwill discover sable hairs.
- **Record Store.** Renko shares a tape of Osborne's voice. This voice, Renko says, killed your little brother.
- **Dacha Outside Moscow.** Kirwill saves Renko's life when he kills a pockmarked KGB agent. Now Renko owes Kirwill.
- **Moscow Bus Station.** Renko says goodbye to Kirwill.
- **New York's Barcelona Hotel.** Renko is under FBI guard when he gets a warning from Kirwill: Watch out for the FBI.
- **Snitch's Lair.** In rural New Jersey, Kirwill's snitch displays a sable pelt, a trophy from Osborne's sable farm. Kirwill's parting words: He will take care of Osborne.
- **Entrance to Osborne's Sable Farm.** Renko, flanked by three FBI agents and two agents of the KGB, finds the bodies of Kirwill and his snitch standing like statues. Kirwill's death adds motivation to the sleuth's revenge.

TIP FOR YOUR REWRITE

If you create a complex character for Subplot Three, make sure you explore the complexities of action vs. exposition and subtext (what's hidden) vs. symbolism (what's on the surface).

4. ROLE AND FUNCTION

Kirwill dies to start the climax. His function in the story is victim. He has a dual role: antagonist and helper. His core story (Revenge Quest) comes from his personality (he believes in an eye for an eye, a tooth for a tooth) and from his reason for being in Russia: He wants to avenge the death of his little brother Jimmy.

Action Vs. Exposition

- **Action.** Kirwill enters the story as a superactive intruder-antagonist. At Midpoint, even though he's still talking tough ("I'm going to get you first"), Kirwill shifts to a helper role. Because he's a cop like Renko, Kirwill can bring professional police experience to the investigation. Kirwill takes action. He drinks, he fights, he curses, he rescues the sleuth twice—once outside Moscow, again in New York—but his monologues are packed with cynical exposition.
- **Exposition.** The writer uses Kirwill to define modern Russia for the reader. When Renko reaches New York, Kirwill acts as guide, an echo of Virgil the poet leading Dante into the twisting labyrinth of the Inferno. His monologues about corruption in Russia and America ride on his explosive, cynical personality.

Subtext Vs. Symbolism

- **Subtext.** The Three Goods. Kirwill is large, tough, sentimental, fearless, and smart (good genes). He drinks too much (bad behavior), but he saves the sleuth's life (good behavior). He has a cynical sense of humor, showing wit, more evidence of good genes. He has enough money to travel to Russia, he has a house in New York (good resources).
- **Symbolism.** At the end of the book, the writer stations Kirwill's dead body at the entrance to the sable farm. The symbolism of the corpse is clear: If tough guy Kirwill could not kill the killer, then what are the survival odds for a pale, introverted sleuth from Moscow?

Checklist on Rewriting Subplots Three, Four, and Five

- ☐ How many lower subplots do you have?
- ☐ How many sexual triads?
- ☐ Have you taken the time to list the subplots in a grid?
- ☐ Have you tagged each subplot with a core story?
- ☐ Can you collapse one subplot into another?
- ☐ How is each subplot connected to the plot? To the other subplots?

☐ Are you using the blood connection? The money connection? The cultural connection (master-slave, teacher-student, etc.)?

☐ How many scenes in each of your lower subplots?

☐ Do you need more scenes?

☐ Have you sketched the subplots on a diagram?

☐ Have you defined the resource base for each lower subplot character?

☐ What secrets lurk in your lower subplots?

☐ Where does each lower subplot heat up?

☐ Where does each lower subplot end?

Exercises for Rewriting Subplots Three, Four and Five

1. MOTIVATION

If the motivation for your lower subplot characters feels thin, write some back story. Where do they come from? What don't they have? Is their behavior driven by genes or circumstance? What do they want?

Startline: Character D wants . . . because she . . .

Writing time: five minutes

2. CHARACTER ARC

> **TIP FOR YOUR REWRITE**
>
> Like Kirwill, lower subplot characters often die.

Make sure you mark entrances and exits for all your minor characters. In *Jane Eyre*, for example, Aunt Reed enters early in Act One, vanishes when she sends Jane off to school, and reappears near the Midpoint, just in time to lie gasping on her deathbed. If you get multiple arcs, return to clarity by drawing a structural diagram.

Writing time: ten minutes

3. LIST OF SCENES

List the scenes where your minor characters appear, and then make notes on the action in the scene. Who else is in the scene? What objects are present? Remember that your readers respond to character transformation.

Time for the list: thirty minutes

4. ROLE AND FUNCTION

Check the last couple of scenes for each minor character. What is their final act? Their final dialogue line? A minor character who dies is a victim. A minor character who helps the protagonist is a facilitator. Keep the role assignments simple. You already have a protagonist. Your minor characters can be helpers or junior antagonists.

Writing time: five minutes

5. CONNECTIONS

How do your lower subplot characters connect to other characters? Blood? Money? Child? Parent? Sibling? Cousin? Teacher? Student? Master? Slave? Stepchild? Prisoner? Jailer? Boss? Worker? Private? Officer? Cop? Killer? Victim? Sexual triad? When you rewrite your lower subplots, make sure you tighten the character connections.

Startline: My Subplot Three character connects to . . .

Writing time: ten minutes

6. SCENE PROFILE

Profile scenes that need rewriting. Scene profile is a warm-up. Use these categories:

Scene Name:
Position:
Ritual:
Setting:
Characters:
Objects Onstage:
Dialogue-Monologue:
Action and Climax:
Closed Circle + Intruder:
Secret:
Symbol/Archetype:
Writing time: ten minutes

7. QUICK SCENE FIX

Follow the steps below to a quick rewrite:

> Step One: Use sense perception to lock down the point of view.
>
> Step Two: Use action to express emotion.
>
> Step Three: Put a second character into the scene. If you're writing a crime novel, the other character could be a witness, a suspect, a fellow sleuth, a supervisor.
>
> Step Four: Write some dialogue.
>
> Step Five: Now lock down the object in the scene: a book, a chair, a computer for research, drawing materials, a cell phone, a fountain pen, a weapon.
>
> Step Six: Bring on the intruder. Witness, boss, suspect, etc.
>
> Step Seven: Describe the setting. Is the place a bedroom? A prison cell? A library? A local pub? A cave?
>
> Step Eight: Ratchet up the suspense by adding a time limit. What if the mission has to be completed by midnight?

The Rewrite: Writer X Rewrites His Lower Subplots

As the rewrite deepens, Writer X learns more about rewriting from Rhoda. On Weekend 6, bright and early, she arrives at X's condo with coffee and bakery goods. X loves blueberry muffins. Over coffee, they discuss the rewrite. X is stuck today, so Rhoda suggests a strategy.

"Look," she says. "It's only the sixth weekend and you have made solid progress. Your back story on Weekend Three, for example, transformed Kate: From a surprise walk-on in the Marvin manuscript, she became a worthy Rags to Riches protagonist who can carry an entire novel. You did the same thing with Charley D. and Harry Thornburg. Both of them came to fruition when you transformed characters from the old manuscript. So who's left?"

X checks his grid. He locates four characters: Madeleine (Kate's mother-in-law), April and Julie Jean Jardine (blondes who want Kate's house), and Raoul D'Amboise (Kate's only son). Madeleine gets Subplot Three. April gets Subplot Four. Julie Jean gets Five. Raoul gets Six. Working with Rhoda, X builds a new character grid:

GRID: *A HOUSE IN PROVENCE*, REVISITED

Name	Role	Plot/Subplot	Core Story	Object	Entry	Exit
Kate	Protagonist	Plot	Rags to Riches	Camera	Act 1	Act 3
Charles	Antagonist 1	Subplot 1	Queen Replacement	Mercedes	Act 1	Act 3
Biker	Helper	Subplot 2	Grail Quest	Bike	Act 1	Act 3
Madeleine	Antagonist 2	Subplot 3	Scapegoat Sacrifice	Racquet	Act 1	Act 3
April	Antagonist 3	Subplot 4	Scapegoat Sacrifice	Blueprints	Act 1	Act 3
Julie Jean	Antagonist 4	Subplot 5	Queen Replacement	Bikini	Act 1	Act 3
Raoul	Antagonist 5	Subplot 6	Coming of Age	Racquet	Act 1	Act 3

Using the four steps—motivation, arc, scene list, role and function—Writer X tracks Madeleine Ventoux, the character in Subplot Three.

1. **MOTIVATION.** Madeleine wants to save her grandson, Raoul. He represents genetic success. In the back story, Madeleine watched Kate lose two children in childbirth. When Raoul was born, Madeleine stole him away, seducing him with tennis. Had little Raoul on the court at three, stroking the ball with his chopped down racquet. Now Raoul is a top player, ranked number three in France and moving up, his face on billboards, television, magazine covers.

2. **CHARACTER ARC.** Madeleine enters the story at Plot Point One, at Stade Roland Garros in Paris, where she meets Julie Jean Jardine. She exits the story at the end, a woman transformed.

3. LIST OF SCENES FOR SUBPLOT THREE.

- **Meeting the Girlfriend.** Madeleine shakes hands with Julie Jean, Raoul's latest girlfriend, and feels danger. The girl is pretty; she speaks a bit of French; but she is too old for Raoul.
- **Sidewalk Café.** Madeleine ignores Kate; she promises to lend Charles some money; she bristles when Raoul kisses Julie Jean.
- **Airplane to America.** On the flight from Paris to Los Angeles, Madeleine lectures Kate on better budgeting. (Madeline does not know that Charles makes Kate beg for money to run the house.)
- **Hospital.** Madeleine sees that Julie Jean does not love Raoul.
- **Meeting April.** Madeleine finds April's tennis club garish. She sees Charles trying to hide his attraction to Julie Jean.
- **Goodbye at LAX.** As Madeleine departs for France, Charles asks for money.
- **Climax.** Seeing Kate's photos of the scale model (and of Charles and Julie Jean), Madeleine transforms from Kate's enemy to her friend.
- **Ending.** Madeleine approves of Harry Thornburg, a handsome man who can repair the house in Provence.

4. ROLE AND FUNCTION. Madeleine's function is protector, guardian of the gene pool. Raoul is the treasure, the gene carrier. Madeleine enters the story as an antagonist; she exits the story as a friend and helper to Kate.

Rhoda smiles as she reads X's work on Madeleine Ventoux and Subplot Three.

"Madeleine is the anchor character," Rhoda says. "How does she connect to the other subplot characters?"

"Okay," X says. "She connects to April through Charles. She connects to Julie Jean through Raoul."

"What is the resource base?"

"Two resource bases," X says. "One is Kate's house; the other is the land where the grapes grow. April Jardine wants Kate's house because she was born poor and now she has money and Kate's house represents stability. Maybe April saw a photograph of the house in an old magazine or online. With that Jardine name, maybe she has French roots.

"Like April DuJardin?" Rhoda asks. "Very good, Mr. X."

Rhoda likes the Rags to Riches core story for April Jardine. "Make her hungry," Rhoda says. "A hungry Death Crone with poor taste and a lust for the style and elegance of France. April is sexy; she uses men to get what she wants. When April gets older, she uses Julie Jean."

To thicken the subtext, X decides to keep April in the dark about who really owns Kate's house. A secret to be revealed later in the book.

Rhoda also likes making Julie Jean older than Raoul, which moves the girl away from the son and closer to the father. When Julie Jean sets her sights on Charles, she puts Kate in danger. Kate has already lost two children in childbirth; she has lost Raoul to Madeleine. If Kate does not act, Kate could lose her house. No base, no darkroom, no roof over her head.

CONNECTING WITH THE SEXUAL TRIAD

Writer X discovers four sexual triads and a fifth triad, a Mommy Triangle, composed of Kate, Raoul, and Madeleine. He connects the triangles with a diagram:

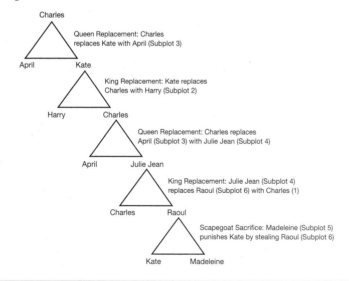

The first four triangles describe characters climbing into bed, changing partners while they scheme. The fifth triangle shows Kate competing with Madeleine for possession of Raoul. As the story opens, Madeleine is a replacement mom; Kate is out in the cold, shooting photos of emptiness, her inner state.

Working from the diagram, X spends the next two hours rewriting scenes from Subplots Three, Four, and Five. On the master scenes, he uses the Thirty-One-Minute Scene Template; on the shorter scenes, he uses the Quick Scene Fix. He starts by using a sense perception to lock down the point of view. He shoves an object into the dialogue. He jolts the action by bringing on an intruder. And he increases suspense by adding a time limit.

Rhoda is impressed by X's use of the tools.

The book feels tighter, but not finished.

Writer X is ready to rewrite his key scenes.

Rewriting:
Key Scenes

A *scene* is a single action or a series of connected actions that take place in a single setting in a finite period of time. A scene has a dramatic structure—action rising to a climax—that mirrors on a small scale the larger dramatic structure of Aristotle's three acts. A scene has standard component parts like setting, character, description, dialogue, action, and high point (miniclimax). A scene can be action-heavy or dialogue-heavy, but it still has a running time that works like an internal clock. When the scene is over, a little bell rings, a red light flashes. Time to pull the trigger, to shift to the next scene. The dramatic scene is the building block for your novel. You need forty to sixty dramatic scenes for your novel. A dramatic scene in a film script is too long at three pages; in a film, that's about three minutes on the screen. A scene in a novel gets long between pages seven and ten.

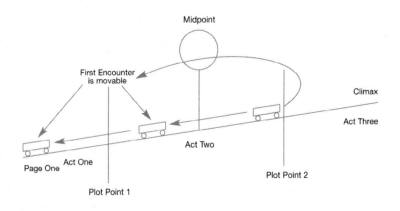

Key Scenes

There are seven key scenes: *First Encounter, Opening, Plot Points One* and *Two, Midpoint, Climax, and Ending.* Six of the key scenes are fixed in the structure (beginning, middle, end), but the First Encounter is movable. In a love story, the First Encounter works best in Act One or early in Act Two. The love story can't start until you write the First Encounter, a scene that crackles with energy and the Three Goods. Planted early, your First Encounter gives the lovers time to fall in love, back off, fight, doubt themselves, explore, doubt each other, cheat, feint, heat up, grow cool, split up, come back together—all those Firsts that do amazing structural work in good storytelling. Your first job before you rewrite a scene is placing that First Encounter scene in the structure.

FIRST ENCOUNTER

This is the scene where the protagonist meets the antagonist. In a mystery, the sleuth meets the killer and suspicion explodes in the subtext. In a love story, Lover A meets Lover B, and the subtext ripples with the ritual of sexual selection. Core stories collide as the two main characters compete. Example: When Jane meets Rochester on the icy causeway, the reader can feel the clash of rich vs. poor, male vs. female, possession vs. slavery, Upper World vs. Lower World, and age vs. youth (Rochester is thirtysomething; Jane is eighteen). Jane's core story is Rags to Riches. Rochester's core story is Queen Replacement. As these core stories collide, the characters slam into each other and drama builds on the page. Jane has her virtue. Rochester counters virtue with his selfish desires, his monstrous nastiness. Use this kind of power display for your First Encounter and your rewrite will zoom to the finish line.

The First Encounter scene is important because it starts the love story. When two lovers meet for the first time, they bring along a handy structural device called a String of Firsts: First Sighting, First Words, First Touch, First Fight, First Separation, etc. If you locate the First Encounter deep in your structure—Act Two or even Act Three—then you have lots of good stuff (action, drama, objects, motives) fighting for space.

If you're like most novelists, you write the First Encounter late, once you have completed your character work and written lots of heated prose. If you wrote the First Encounter late in your rush to finish the rough draft, now is your chance to move it forward. First Encounter is the mother of key scenes. Don't let it get stuck in Act Two or even Act Three. It needs to move forward. It floats until you lock it down.

Example from the world of films: When he transformed *Leaving Las Vegas* (John O'Brien's exposition-heavy novel) into an Oscar-winning

> **TIP FOR YOUR REWRITE**
>
> Plant a sacred object on Page One that recurs in Acts Two and Three.

> **TIP FOR YOUR REWRITE**
>
> Repeat that sacred object.

film, director Mike Figgis moved the first encounter twice. Once from Act Three to Act Two. Then again from Act Two to Act One. In a novel with two strong protagonists (a drunk and a hooker in Las Vegas), your rewrite will go smoother if you have them collide early in Act One.

PAGE ONE AND AFTER

Page One is shorthand for the opening of your novel.

Page One must contain setting. Time, place, weather, temperature, indoors or out, mood, nuance, shadow or sun, atmosphere.

It must contain character, wardrobe, object, situation, problem.

If you don't have dialogue on Page One, make sure there's some on page two.

The reader reads Page One—maybe in a bookstore, maybe online—and makes a decision.

To keep reading or to stop reading.

To buy or nor to buy.

When you rewrite Page One, you need to know archetype and core story. You need to consider an intruder penetrating a closed circle. (See Page One of *The Big Sleep*, in which sleuth Philip Marlowe crosses the threshold of Sternwood Manor in Los Angeles. A classic tale with a classic opening scene, where one sweet line reveals the resource base: "I was calling on five million dollars.") You need to know *your* resource base, what the characters want (money, land, shelter, sanctuary, access to the precious waterhole) and who's got possession as the book opens. Experienced writers might open with snappy dialogue. I prefer a classic description that uses detail (objects, wardrobe items, vehicles, jewelry, weapons, crockery, etc.) and sense perception to lock down the point of view of a single character. When you rewrite, discipline is all.

PLOT POINT ONE

Your protagonist turns a corner, clears a major hurdle, takes a breather while preparing for the forest, labyrinth, steep mountain or emotional minefield in Act Two. Plot Point One ends Act One and opens Act Two.

MIDPOINT

This is the point of no return for your protagonist. A turnstile at the center of Act Two, the Midpoint needs to be strong, lots of action, lots of subplots intertwining with the plot. You can write one scene for the Midpoint, but a three-scene sequence is smarter. At the Midpoint, the antagonist is still stronger than the protagonist.

PLOT POINT TWO

Plot Point Two ends Act Two, opens Act Three. Plot Point Two is a miniclimax that makes everything worse for the protagonist. It's a great place for a wound that sends the protagonist offstage to the hospital or aid station, to a place of sanctuary. As you reach Plot Point Two, you start strategizing the approach to the climax.

CLIMAX

The action peaks here, after a breathless climb through a series of quick cuts, where things look bleak for your protagonist. The winner wins, the loser loses. In most commercial fiction, the protagonist lives. In thrillers with a bad guy protagonist, you have some decisions to make. (Lives or dies?) In literature *(Hamlet, Madame Bovary, Moby-Dick)*, the protagonist often dies.

THE END

This is the point where your protagonist gets the reward, taking possession of the resource base, where you have a chance to write a memorable final image: marriage, death, exile, ceremony.

TIP FOR YOUR REWRITE

By the Midpoint, that sacred object could be growing into a symbol. Symbols can make you famous.

TIP FOR YOUR REWRITE

That sacred object, grown into a symbol, should make you proud. A happy writer.

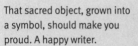

TIP FOR YOUR REWRITE

You need lots of strong verbs to write the action that explodes into the climax that leads to the end.

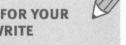

TIP FOR YOUR REWRITE

The repeated object, transformed into a symbol, closes your story.

You rewrite the key scenes to cinch up the plot. You rewrite the key scenes because the First Encounter launches the love story and also because each fixed scene locks down a chunk of the book's structure.

Plot Point One, for example, gives you a no-nonsense target for the action in Act One. If your goal is a three-hundred-page novel (a nice size for a first novel), Plot Point One needs to happen around page seventy-five. If your rewrite reaches page one hundred and Plot Point One has not appeared, then you need to check your scene list. Where is it? If you don't establish Plot Point One, then Act One gets longer. Because Act Two is twice as long as Act One, a hundred-page Act One means you're suddenly rewriting a four-hundred-page book. Longer books are tougher to rewrite; a long book is a hard sell for any first-time novelist. It pays to lock down those key scenes.

In a three-hundred-page book, your Midpoint should surface around page 150, Plot Point Two around page 225, leaving you seventy-five pages for the approach to the climax, which takes up most of a well-written Act Three.

When you rewrite one key scene, you'll get insights on rewriting two more scenes: the scene before and the scene after. That's good because, in a solid novel, the Midpoint and Plot Point Two are built with scene sequences. As you rewrite your key scenes, you'll be working the language (nouns, verbs, modifiers, metaphors) as part of the structure of the scene.

You rewrite the key scenes so you can push through the structure of the book from beginning to end in seven weekends. The heat of rewriting builds as you work. Act Three is hotter than Act One. Act Three is a template for rewriting Act One. When you reach Act Three, you know what the book is about.

When you rewrite, knowledge is power.

Seven Weekends, Seven Model Novels

For the next seven weekends you rewrite key scenes. If you get inspired, you should rewrite the scenes before and after each key scene. Work fast, use the tools. For working subplots, the model novel was *The Great Gatsby*. When you work key scenes, you'll see *Gatsby* and six other model novels. Here's a list of weekends and a model novel that demonstrates how a professional writer handles one key scene. We learn from the pros.

- **Weekend 7, First Encounter.** *Leaving Las Vegas* (John O'Brien). Ben the drunk meets Sera the hooker on the Las Vegas Strip. The First Encounter scene moved twice: once in the script, again in the film. Big lesson here.
- **Weekend 8, Page One.** *Amsterdam* (Ian McEwan). Vernon and Clive reminisce at the funeral of Molly, their ex-lover, now deceased. Two ex-lovers collide with a husband and a rival ex-lover. Lots of irony.

- **Weekend 9, Plot Point One.** *The Namesake* (Jhumpa Lahiri). Gogol, the Bengali protagonist, lies to a college girl about his name, then goes to court to change his name legally. College girl as mythic helper.

- **Weekend 10, Midpoint.** *Gorky Park* (Martin Cruz Smith). Homicide cop Arkady Renko rescues the femme fatale, then probes the killer's past for motive.

TIP FOR YOUR REWRITE

When you read a plot synopsis written by another writer, remember to probe for key scenes, core stories, mate selection, intruder and closed circle, and the resource base. Sniff out the subtext.

- **Weekend 11, Plot Point Two.** *The Great Gatsby* (F. Scott Fitzgerald). Gatsby crosses the threshold into East Egg and gets tagged for execution. A classic example of an intruder penetrating a closed circle.

- **Weekend 12, Climax.** *Eye of the Needle* (Ken Follett). A deadly spy runs afoul of a beautiful temporary Death Crone. Bad timing for that bad boy.

- **Weekend 13, Ending.** *Pride and Prejudice* (Jane Austen). Elizabeth Bennet, now married, coaches her younger sister: how a young woman with limited resources can penetrate the closed circle of polite society. A lovely example of Darwin's "survival of the fittest" several decades before Darwin.

Note: If you have not studied some of these novels, you can read short synopses in the following pages. For longer synopses on some novels, type *jane eyre plot,* etc., into your computer search engine. Hit the Enter key. Take the plunge into cyberspace.

SITE MAP FOR LOCATING YOUR PLACE IN THE REWRITE PROCESS

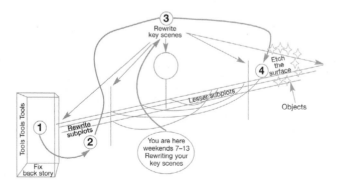

Weekend  : Rewriting the First Encounter

The First Encounter is the first meeting of protagonist and antagonist. There's lots of energy here, and you want to make sure this scene is not lost back there in Act Three.

In the First Encounter, the characters talk, they fence, they dodge, their agendas clash. Their motives are buried in the subtext. If your First Encounter is stuck way back in Act Two, try moving it to Act One before starting your scene rewrite.

The First Encounter scene is a ritual that readers recognize from real life. Let's say you're single and you meet this person in a supermarket parking lot. It's raining and windy. Your grocery bag breaks, spilling goodies into the wet. Your hair gets wet and messy. Your car won't start. You hate yourself. You hate your car. Along comes help, a handsome man in a Mercedes. He hauls out an expensive canvas toolkit. Extracts a pair of jumper cables. Hooks your battery to his battery. A hum starts inside your throat as your car coughs back to life. He buys you a cup of coffee. The coffee shop is warm. The women customers keep looking at this guy. He's handsome, well-mannered, he listens. Could be a keeper. The First Encounter has generated a scene in the coffee shop. If the coffee shop scene generates another scene, and another, you keep writing. Don't stop now. You're on a roll.

As in real life, so in fiction. When you wrote your rough draft, you might have penned this First Encounter scene late in the writing. You were writing hot. You could smell the finish line. The characters met, mate selection kicked in, the words flew fast and thick. Now when you rewrite, you move the scene closer to the beginning. You see the core stories. You deepen the secrets. You feel power in your style.

Example: The First Encounter in *The English Patient* occurs late in the novel as the desert explorer Count Ladislau Almásy watches Katharine Clifton step down from her husband's yellow airplane. The Cliftons are a young British couple, just married, and the boy-husband brings his bride to the Libyan desert. Almásy sees her from a distance before they meet up close. Standing transfixed, he registers khaki shorts (a wardrobe item) and bony knees (a body part). Already seducing him, Katharine the bride stands still for his First Sighting: "She stood there while the sand collected in her mane of hair."

TIP FOR YOUR REWRITE

It is time to change hats. Trade your novelist's golden helmet for the black baseball cap (a French beret, a pith helmet) of a film director. Be bold. Take control of your structure with both hands. Get a good grip. Use your legs for leverage. And shove that First Encounter way forward. Toward the beginning.

- In the novel, Katharine steps down from the plane to open Act Three.
- In the film adaptation, she steps down from the plane in Act One, around minute ten. When Lover B steps down from the yellow airplane into the story, the love story starts.

That forward shove helped director Mike Figgis turn a dark literary novel into an Oscar-winning film. The novel was *Leaving Las Vegas,* written by John O'Brien, published in 1990. Figgis wrote the script, started filming in 1995. He was two weeks into shooting when O'Brien committed suicide. Figgis dedicated the finished film to O'Brien's memory.

Remember this for your rewrite: When he wrote the novel, novelist John O'Brien hid the First Encounter in Act Three. To make the film, rewriter Mike Figgis unpacked Act Three.

Make this your mantra for your rewrite: A film adaptation is a major rewrite. There is compression in adaptation, squeezing two to three hundred pages (or more) down to a 120-page script. There is cutting: taking out what doesn't work. There is cast reduction: firing certain characters, some of them your favorites. With the characters that remain, there are promotions and demotions as one character gets more ink and another character gets less.

Synopsis—*Leaving Las Vegas*

Lover A is a Quester named Ben. Lover B is a Death Crone named Sera. They don't meet until Act Three. Until the lovers meet in Las Vegas, the love story cannot start. Before they meet, Ben buys booze in Los Angeles. He gets drunk, he wakes up with his face in a urinal. Trying to erase his past, he burns up his personal memorabilia: photos, etc. He can't buy booze in Los Angeles after two A.M., so he escapes to Las Vegas, where the liquor stores never close.

Before Sera meets Ben, she turns tricks in Las Vegas. She gets beaten up, bruised, cheated. Her pimp, a Middle Eastern guy named Al (short for Gamal), takes money and gives nothing back.

In the last quarter of the book, in the section called "plums" (fruit symbol on a slot machine), the doomed lovers meet in front of a casino on the Strip in Las Vegas. The time is night. Ben asks a question and Sera asks him what he means. Their first meeting starts with an edgy clash. On their first date, Ben is impotent. He wants to talk. He invites Sera to dinner. Sera dumps her pimp, goes to dinner, invites Ben to stay at her place to save money. She wants him to eat. He refuses food. She buys him a gift, a pink-and-green jungle shirt; he buys her earrings. On a date with Sera, Ben tears up a casino. Hunting for breakfast, he gets into a fight in a biker bar, and blood from his wounds ruins the new shirt. They escape to the desert, where the motel owner ejects them, saying, Go back to the city, you creeps. Back in Las Vegas, Sera goes to work hooking, and Ben gets revenge by bringing a rival hooker into Sera's bed. Finding Ben in bed with the hooker, Sera ejects him.

He calls her on the phone. She rushes to his bedside for one last orgasm. Ben dies. His Grail Quest is over. Sera the Death Crone presides over his deathbed.

Analysis—*Leaving Las Vegas*

If you study the structure of the novel, you can feel the writing heat up in Act Three. The heat starts to build at the First Encounter on the fabled Las Vegas Strip. It keeps on building until the First Phone Call, when Ben calls Sera to tell her he's dying. The novel is divided into four sections, each one with a label, printed in lowercase type. With each section, the point of view shifts:

1. **cherries:** Sera starts her plot in Las Vegas. We meet her pimp, Al/Gamal.
2. **bars:** Ben follows his plot in Los Angeles. He buys booze, wakes up in a public urinal, burns stuff from his past, and heads for Las Vegas. "bars," the title of this section, is a metaphor for the life of a drunk.
3. **lemons:** Sera picks up her plot again in Las Vegas. She's waiting for something, waiting for Ben.
4. **plums:** Ben checks into the Whole Year Inn, then heads for the Strip, where he meets Sera. Now that they are together, the story moves through a series of Firsts:

- **First Encounter.** Ben spots Sera on the Las Vegas Strip.
- **First Words.** Are you working?
- **First Fight.** What do you mean, working?
- **First Invitation.** Ben invites Sera to his room for sex.
- **First Barter.** Ben gives money to Sera in exchange for sex.
- **First Touch.** Sera helps Ben undress.
- **First Insight.** Sera realizes Ben wants to talk because he's lonely.
- **First Real Date.** Ben invites Sera to dinner.
- **First Separation.** Sera leaves Ben to check with her pimp.
- **First Threshold Crossing.** Sera takes Ben home.
- **First Gift.** Sera gives Ben a shirt; Ben gives Sera earrings.
- **First Bloodshed.** Wearing the shirt, Ben gets into a fight in the biker bar.
- **First Escape.** Ben and Sera escape to the desert.
- **First Emotion.** Sera goes to work; Ben is jealous.
- **First Queen Replacement.** Ben brings a hooker into Sera's bed.
- **First Phone Call.** Ben calls Sera; he's dying.

Act Three of O'Brien's novel is packed with drama. The writing got hot and the good stuff surfaced near the end. The film director comes along, studies the structure, and spreads the good stuff out across the structure of the film. In the diagram below, you can see the fullness of Act Three:

TIP FOR YOUR REWRITE

If you take the time to develop your own series of Firsts, you will plot at least a third of your rewrite in a flash.

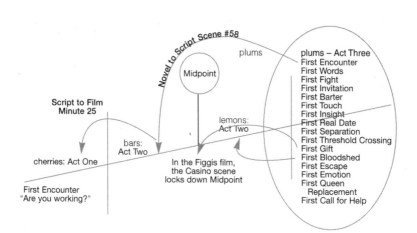

Novel to Script Scene #58

plums

Midpoint

plums – Act Three
First Encounter
First Words
First Fight
First Invitation
First Barter
First Touch
First Insight
First Real Date
First Separation
First Threshold Crossing
First Gift
First Bloodshed
First Escape
First Emotion
First Queen
  Replacement
First Call for Help

Script to Film
Minute 25

lemons:
Act Two

bars:
Act Two

cherries: Act One

In the Figgis film,
the Casino scene
locks down Midpoint

First Encounter
"Are you working?"

TAKE ACTION NOW

A diagram gives you a snapshot of your key scenes. Use a diagram to explore your structure. Where is the weight? Where does your structure tilt off-balance? If you need a moving van to transport your Firsts, hire a moving van now. Don't wait for the film director to save your book.

TIP FOR YOUR REWRITE

Unless your First Encounter scene appears in Act One, pull it up and plant it earlier. Don't brood about it. You cannot brood your way to moving the scene; you have to do the work of moving it. Time for some heavy lifting. Use the cut and paste function in your word processor. Cut the scene from its hiding place way back there near the end and trundle it forward on your hand truck to a spot closer to the beginning. Don't start rewriting the scene until you move it.

The preceding diagram shows the four sections of the novel—"cherries," "bars," "lemons," and "plums"—relabeled as acts. "Cherries" is Act One; "bars" and "lemons" are Act Two; "plums" is Act Three. Study the Firsts that occur after the First Encounter.

If you study the Figgis film script— it's in book form, with black-and-white stills from the movie—you'll find the First Encounter in Act Two, just before Midpoint. If you study the film, you can find the First Encounter at minute twenty-five. When he shot the movie, Figgis saw a way to move the First Encounter closer to the beginning.

Good scenes don't change much: That opening dialogue where Ben asks Sera if she's working does not change from novel to script to film. It moves like a building block from Act Three to Act Two to Act One. When the First Encounter moves, stuff happens. For example, the shirt in the novel (First Gift) is an ugly jungle-green splotched with pink. When the shirt appears in the film, it has transformed into an orange sunshine shirt that Ben wears to the casino on their First Date. The orange shirt brings temporary light to a dark tale of death, betrayal, and impossible love. Ben wears the orange shirt again when he gets beat up in the biker bar. That scene, First Bloodshed on the diagram, has moved from Act Three in the novel to Act Two in the film.

When you move a scene, you rattle the structure of your novel. It's like tearing a hole in fabric stretched tight. A gap appears. An opening gapes at you. The opening is your chance to improve the book when you rewrite.

Checklist for Rewriting the First Encounter

☐ Have you made a structural diagram showing the location of the First Encounter?

☐ Does the First Encounter need moving?

☐ Who meets whom in the First Encounter?

☐ Is there a third character in this scene?

☐ What is the closed circle? Who is the intruder?

☐ What is the setting? What time is it? What's the weather like? Hot? Rainy? Cold? Is the wind blowing? Is the meeting outdoors or indoors?

☐ How are your characters dressed?

☐ What are the rituals? Barter? Threshold crossing? Mate selection?

☐ If you move the First Encounter, what happens to the structure?

☐ Can you move other Firsts along with this key scene?

☐ Who speaks first?

☐ Do the characters touch?

Exercises—Rewriting the First Encounter

1. WARM-UP

Does the First Encounter need moving? If it needs moving, do it now, before you start rewriting. The best move is from the back of your manuscript (Act Three) to the front (Act Two or Act One), where the List of Firsts can do more work in your novel.

Startline: My first encounter needs moving because . . .

Writing time: twenty minutes

2. DIALOGUE

Dialogue is big in First Encounter. Ben asks a question: "Are you working?" Sera replies, her voice defensive: "Working? What do you mean, working?" And the conflict starts.

Choose a startline:

- **Your dialogue can start with a greeting:** "Hello."
- **Or a question about direction:** "Can you show me the way to . . .?"
- **You can go regional:** "Howdy, ma'am."
- **Your character can have one foot in Upper World:** "Excuse me, Madame, but . . ."
- **Or two feet trapped in Lower World:** "Got a light, sailor?"
- **Writing time:** fifteen minutes.

3. INTRUDER AND CLOSED CIRCLE

The big closed circle is Las Vegas, city of night, where you need money to enter the casinos, to enter the life of Las Vegas. The smaller closed circles are the circumscribed lives of Lovers A (the drunk) and B (the hooker).

The drunk's closed circle is alcohol. The hooker's closed circle is her body, selling sex for money. When the drunk gives money to the hooker, she lets him inside her closed circle. This is a barter ritual. The drunk's smaller closed circles—the car and the motel room—provide threshold crossings for the hooker.

To juice up the drama in your First Encounter, bring on a third character. A character with an agenda. For example, what if Lover A is a guy with a buddy? He meets Lover B. What does he do with the buddy? What if Lover B is a girl with a girlfriend? She meets Lover A, feels the pull of mate selection. What does she do with the girlfriend?

Startline: "Hi, I'm Kip and this is Mike. And you are . . .?"

Startline: From across the room, Kip nudges Mike. "Would you look at that?"

Writing time: ten minutes

TIP FOR YOUR REWRITE

After you write your dialogue, probe it for these five rules:
1) short lines for rhythm;
2) echo words for glue;
3) objects for stability;
4) links to what came before;
5) hooks to what comes after.

4. SETTING

Where is the meeting? Indoors? Outdoors? A public place? What is the time? What is the weather? How are your characters dressed? Example: Ben the drunk meets Sera the hooker on the street in the shadow of a casino. The time is night. Sera is working; Ben's hunting for a working girl. The air is balmy. The wardrobes are casual. Contrast the setting for Jane Eyre's meeting with Mr. Rochester on the icy causeway. Jane's on foot and Rochester is on his horse. He's wearing his rich man outfit, heavy overcoat and leather riding boots. Contrast the setting

TIP FOR YOUR REWRITE

Make use of wardrobe as an element in the Three Goods of mate selection.

for Almásy's meeting with Katharine Clifton at base camp in the African desert. She steps down from the yellow airplane and Almásy's heart stops. In the movie version, Katharine wears a leather flight jacket.

Startline: The time was . . . and the room/street smelled of . . .

Writing time: ten minutes

5. THE THREE GOODS

If you are rewriting a love story, the main ritual is mate selection, where you deploy the Three Goods. In *Leaving Las Vegas*, where there is no hope of genetic success, mate selection still controls behavior. Ben selects Sera because she's attractive: good hair, good skin, good body. Sera uses her body to barter with Ben for money, the visible resource base. Ben's a drunk with bad behavior that gets worse as the book stumbles toward the climax, but Sera shares her resources (food, apartment, love) with Ben while she tries to alter his bad behavior.

Startline: She looks at him and sees a handsome man with . . .

Startline: He exits the Mercedes wearing . . .

Writing time: fifteen minutes

6. FIRSTS

What Firsts travel with First Encounter in your novel?

Lots of choices here—First Encounter, First Sighting, First Words, First Touch, First Date, First Kiss, First Foreplay, First Sex, First Fight, First Making Up, First Proposal, First Engagement, First Wedding—and each one can trigger a scene.

Startline: My list of Firsts starts with . . . in Act . . . and ends with

First . . . in Act . . .

Writing time: fifteen minutes

7. THIRTY-ONE-MINUTE SCENE TEMPLATE

If you need a fresh look at your First Encounter, use the startlines from the template that follows. Writing time: one minute for the warm-up and five minutes for each for the six sections:

- I am writing a story about . . . (one minute)
- This is a scene about . . . (five minutes)
- **Setting:** The time was/the place smelled of . . . (five minutes)
- **Character A on Character B:** His/her hairdo looked like . . . (five minutes)
- **Action and Dialogue:** What are you looking at? (5 minutes)
- **Intruder/Complication:** What are you guys up to? (5 minutes)
- **Climax/Resolution:** Using the long sentence release (see "Weekend 8," p. 129), extend the action to a dramatic climax. (5 minutes)

The Rewrite: Writer X Rewrites His First Encounter

When he moves his First Encounter scene from a deserted beach in California to a deserted square in Avignon, in the south of France, Writer X triggers memories. He remembers a trip to Provence, meeting a French girl in Avignon. He was just out of college. The girl's name was Nicole and X fell in love and now when he rewrites his First Encounter scene there is a rosy glow around those small towns like Carpentras and Rousillon and Isle-sur-la-Sorgue and Menerbes.

For the rewriting of Kate's first encounter, Rhoda suggests that X work through the scene template: setting, character description, action and dialogue, intruder and closed circle, and a high point or hook to the next scene.

X says okay. He types in the word *setting* and starts rewriting.

SETTING: A cold morning, the dark before the dawn, as Kate threads her vehicle through the streets of Avignon. The city sleeps. When she arrives at the Place du Palais (the Palace Square), the square is empty, with soft rain just starting.

Action: Kate stands under a café awning, photographing the emptiness. She shoots empty benches, empty chairs, empty tables. She shoots trash cans overflowing with tourist trash from the day before. She shoots the massive stone hump of the Palace of the Popes. Kate's camera is a Hasselblad with a manual crank rewind. The whole world has gone digital, and Kate's best camera is twenty years old.

INTRUDER AND CLOSED CIRCLE: The roar of an engine makes Kate frown. It is too early for the tourists. The delivery trucks unload at the open market on the other side of town. Lights flicker on stone, and then a motorcycle enters the square.

CHARACTER A DESCRIBES CHARACTER B: The rider wears black.

Action: Kate shoots the motorcycle rider, using the last frame before turning to head back to her vehicle. It is raining harder and time to go. She tucks her camera under her jacket. The rain feels cold on her face.

HIGH POINT: She reaches her car, an ancient Renault station wagon, opens the door, and climbs behind the wheel. The starter sounds like a wornout sewing machine. The engine coughs, then sputters. Kate presses hard on the accelerator and the engine catches. A knocking on the driver's side window forces her to turn her head. A black figure stands there. The man from the motorcycle, holding something out. An object. Kate can hear his voice on the other side of the glass. He is not speaking French.

HOOK TO THE NEXT SCENE: Kate drives away. Before she makes her turn onto Rue de Mons, she sees a single headlight in her rearview mirror. Her hands are shaking. She turns a corner, then heads east, toward her house.

Rhoda analyzes the parts of X's scene.

"Very good work," she says. "You have two closed circles. First, the square penetrated by the motorcycle; second, the car, an enclosure, which keeps the Biker outside. The third closed circle is Kate's house. The Biker will use the lens cap—the Object Left Behind—to gain entrance. The Hasselblad is a good choice for a classic camera. It shows that Kate cares about old things that still have value. The battered car reinforces Kate's lack of money. Her husband keeps her poor, makes her beg for money. Shooting emptiness is the perfect metaphor to express the vacuum in Kate. So you have a woman feeling empty. What happens next?"

"Well," says Writer X. "Harry returns the lens cap. That's a threshold crossing. Kate's house is the closed circle; she lets the intruder in. I need a scene with Harry buying properties. I need Kate shooting the same property, not knowing it's empty because of Harry."

"What key scene is next?" Rhoda asks.

X checks his diagram.

"Page One and After," he says.

Rhoda beams.

"I love it, Mr. X, when you talk structure."

Weekend 8: Rewriting Page One and After

How many concrete nouns can you load into your Page One?
How many objects?
How many body parts?
How many landmarks?

Page One of *Leaving Las Vegas*, for example, opens with Sera the hooker drinking coffee. *Coffee* is a concrete noun. Her Styrofoam *cup* has a plastic *lid*. The lid has a *hole*. She's in front of a *7-Eleven* store, feeling out of it. She sits on the *curb*. Body parts tighten the focus on Sera as she hugs her *knees*, bends her *head*. Her *arms* create a *cave* for her head. Like an intruder, a *stream of light* runs between her *thighs*. The light ends in black *lace* and a short leather *skirt*. A *bus* passes, someone in the *window*. Her *head* is thrown back, her dark brown *hair* fanning around her *shoulders*. Concrete nouns give us a verbal picture of setting, character, a wardrobe that suggests Sera's profession, and point of view.

Page One of *The English Patient* opens with the Nurse in a garden. *Garden* is a concrete noun. To get back to the *house*, a ruined villa on a hillside, she climbs over a low *wall*, feels *raindrops* on bare *arms*. To get to her patient, she climbs *stairs*, walks along the *hall*, toward an open *door*. There's a man on the *bed*. The room has a *painting* on the *wall*. The body parts come fast now: *black body*, *destroyed feet*, *ankles*, *shins*, *bone*, *penis*, *hips*, *hip bones* of Christ. The concrete nouns give us setting, character, point of view, weather (raindrops), and the plight of the man on the bed.

To rewrite your Page One, you inject concrete nouns. There are three classes of concrete nouns: objects (bus, candle, pistol, etui, brooch, tiara); body parts (arm, leg, eye, hair, fingernail); and landmarks (town, city, village, mountain, valley, cave, castle, tower).

Concrete nouns are visible. You can touch them, taste them, feel them hard at work. Concrete nouns keep your story on the page. Abstract nouns, on the other hand, are mostly polysyllabic—*administration*, *coordination, indication, insubordination, speculation, verification*—heavy and hard to read. Abstract nouns that are not polysyllabic (*time, world, love, year*, etc.) are still mental constructs inside the head. You can't see an abstract noun. Can't touch one or taste one. If you are writing well, you can use abstract nouns in dialogue to define character. Puffy characters use puffy nouns: "In *essence*, it is assumed by the *administration* that *verification* would actually be advisable unless *insubordination* becomes less a *speculation*." If you use abstract nouns in your description or your narration, your story will rise from the page like a phantom and float past the reader, into the ozone.

Page One opens your novel. When you rewrite, you should pack Page One with concrete nouns. Why take a chance that your reader will read past a weak and fuzzy Page One? You can't risk that. You need to open your book with substance: a sharp word-picture that introduces character. My example for a solid Page One that leads to a strong opening scene comes from *Amsterdam*, by Ian McEwan. Page One of *Amsterdam* mixes crisp dialogue with concrete nouns—*arm, Dorchester Grill, cab, propeller, bed, cream, mirror, acanthus, bresaiola,* and *sickroom*—that tell the story of the demise of Molly Lane. *Bresaiola*, also spelled *bresaola* (without the *i*), is an Italian word; it means a kind of dried salted beef. When Molly lost her sense of taste for bresaiola, she saw a doctor. By the time she saw the doctor, it was too late for a medical solution. Page One introduces two of Molly's former lovers, burned-out men recalling their memories of Molly. Here's a bare-bones synopsis.

Synopsis—*Amsterdam*

Two friends, a contemporary composer named Clive (Lover A) and the editor of a tabloid magazine named Vernon (Lover B), brave the February London cold to attend Molly Lane's memorial service. In the back story, both Clive and Vernon were among Molly's lovers. Clive shakes hands with Molly's husband, who introduces Lover D, an American who was intimate with Molly in the back story, when she was sixteen. The husband passes Clive on to Lover C, a high-ranking cabinet minister, who insults Clive's manhood.

Stung by this insult, Clive gets drunk, does destructive work on his symphony, then signs a mutual suicide pact with Vernon. They agree to poison each other and die in Amsterdam, in a friendly, no-pressure environment of assisted euthanasia.

With the death pact throbbing in the subtext, Molly's husband peddles naughty photos to Vernon. The photos show Molly in underwear and Lover C, the cabinet minister, in a dress. When the photos are published, Lover C's wife, a prominent physician, attacks Vernon in a televised interview.

Vernon loses his job. He decides not to die from poison after all, then flies to Amsterdam, where he encounters Clive, who is depressed about his mangled symphony—his last hope for fame fading in a cacophonous discord.

Following the death pact, Clive does poison Vernon and Vernon does poison Clive. Molly's ghost presides over both their deaths. Feeling smug about eliminating competition, the husband and Lover C shepherd the bodies of the two dead lovers to England.

Back in London, the husband rings the doorbell of Vernon's widow. The husband is smiling; he has his revenge; the widow, a handsome woman, is his reward.

Analysis—*Amsterdam:* Page One and After

Let's pretend that you're rewriting a book like *Amsterdam*. It's a book with no overt violence, no murder scenes, no car chases, no major characters under forty. An all-adult cast, educated people with solid footholds in society. The dialogue is crisp, the characters subtle and snide. *Amsterdam* is a satire—a good model if you have a yen to write irony—and it's also a good model for you to follow if your novel manuscript has two protagonists. This is a short novel—less than two hundred pages—something to think about when you rewrite.

Page One introduces the two protagonists. Lover A is Clive the composer. Lover B is Vernon the editor. In the scene that follows Page One, the writer brings on three more characters: the husband and two more lovers. The writing is compressed. The subtext is thick. There are echoes of *Death in Venice*, Thomas Mann's story about a protagonist who stays in Venice to die for beauty. Let's do a scene profile:

NAME OF THE SCENE. Molly's Ashes

LOCATION. Page One and After

SETTING. Crematorium, Grounds, Garden of Remembrance, London

TIME. February afternoon

WEATHER. Cold, frozen, bleak

RITUAL. Burial of the Dead

CHARACTERS. Lover A is Clive; Lover B is Vernon; Lover C is Julian Garmony; Lover D is Hart the American; Molly's husband is George Lane; Molly (evoked through memory) is the centerpiece.

Action. Walking, talking, shaking hands, shivering; Vernon answers his cell phone.

DIALOGUE. Digging up the past; barbs; insults; snide remarks.

CLOSED CIRCLES AND INTRUDERS. 1) Molly is inside the crematorium, inside her closed circle of fire and ashes. 2) Vernon and Clive, both jilted by Molly, form their own closed circle of sad jilted lovers. George, the husband, uses the American ex-lover to penetrate their circle of bitter remembrance. 3) Julian, the British Foreign Secretary, pulls Clive into his closed circle of fawning admirers. Trapped inside Julian's little power circle, Clive insults his stance on hanging; Julian responds by evoking Molly's words to question Clive's manhood: "She told me you were impotent and always had been."

CLIMAX. Julian's insult climaxes the opening scene.

CONCRETE NOUNS. Objects are *cab, propeller, bed, cream, mirror, acanthus, bresaiola*, and *sickroom*; body parts are *backs* and *arm*; landmarks are *chapel, crematorium*, and *Dorchester Grill*.

SECRETS IN THE SUBTEXT. The American Hart is the Secret Lover from Molly's past. The husband thrusts Hart at Clive and Vernon like a spear. They are shocked by this unwelcome information. A new guy splits the memory of Molly into more pieces. The husband's action reveals his vengeful agenda: The revenge that dooms the protagonists starts here in this opening scene.

ARCHETYPE AND CORE STORY. Clive the composer is a Quester; fame is his Holy Grail. Vernon the editor is a Sick Man who will use photos of Molly and Julian to boost tabloid circulation; his core story is Scapegoat Sacrifice. Husband George wants revenge on all Molly's ex-lovers; his core story is Revenge Quest. Julian the British Foreign Secretary is a Wonder Boy; his core story is Coming of Age. Molly Lane, the female at the center of these empty men, is a Death Crone; her core story is King Replacement. The Page One and After scene from *Amsterdam* contains the seeds of the book—not only the two protagonists (Clive and Vernon) and their plots, but also the major characters (Molly, husband George, and Lover C) and their subplots. In a novel with two protagonists and three major characters, you would be smart to take control with a grid, followed by a structural diagram. Here's a sample grid for *Amsterdam*.

GRID: *AMSTERDAM*

Name	Role	Plot/Subplot	Archetype	Core Story	Entry	Exit
Clive	Protagonist 1	Plot	Quester	Grail Quest	Act 1	Act 3
Vernon	Protagonist 2	Plot	Sick Man	Scapegoat Sacrifice	Act 1	Act 3
Molly	Antagonist 1	Subplot 1	Death Crone	King Replacement	Act 1	Act 3
George	Antagonist 2	Subplot 2	King	Revenge Quest	Act 1	Act 3
Garmony	Antagonist 3	Subplot 3	Wonder Boy	Coming of Age	Act 1	Act 3

Lessons from *Amsterdam*

Lesson One is Molly and the Three Goods. The grid shows Molly Lane, a powerful female, alone with four adult males. As we learn later in the novel, Molly is a free spirit. She practices sexual liberation and careful mate selection.

- Vernon the foreign correspondent is bright (good genes); his life is filled with adventure (exciting behavior).
- Clive the composer is talented (good genes); he has a shot at fame (good behavior).
- George the husband is a rich man (good resources); he tolerates Molly's affairs (good behavior); a meaner man would beat Molly up.
- Julian the cabinet minister is powerful (good behavior); his children verify his good genes.

Males compete for females. Molly is a walking resource base that draws men to her company. As she moves from one lover to another, Molly forces her lovers to share. She has control. They have no choice. Irony lurks in Molly's mate selection: Sex for recreation is not sex for procreation. But biology has power. Molly's genes want genetic success. Her genes keep trying, no matter what.

TIP FOR YOUR REWRITE

You must explore biology (genetic success and the Three Goods) before you rewrite Page One and After.

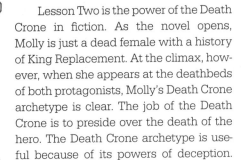

TIP FOR YOUR REWRITE

If you don't yet have a Death Crone in your character list, there is still time. The smart writer taps into myth and ritual.

Lesson Two is the power of the Death Crone in fiction. As the novel opens, Molly is just a dead female with a history of King Replacement. At the climax, however, when she appears at the deathbeds of both protagonists, Molly's Death Crone archetype is clear. The job of the Death Crone is to preside over the death of the hero. The Death Crone archetype is useful because of its powers of deception. On the surface, Molly is beautiful. Beauty is the perfect mask for a Death Crone.

Lesson Three is the importance of early planting. *Amsterdam* has five major characters: two protagonists (Clive and Vernon) and three antagonists (Molly, George, Julian). All five are planted onstage in the scene that starts on Page One. The two other antagonists, Julian's wife, Rose, and a sly junior editor named Frank, enter the story later. With so many characters crowding your stage, you need a diagram like the one below to chart entrances and exits.

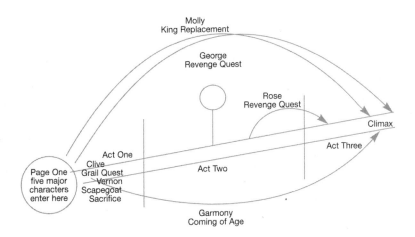

The two parallel lines rising to the climax represent the paths of the two protagonists, Vernon and Clive. They open the book on Page One outside the London crematorium at Molly's memorial service;

both protagonists die in *Amsterdam*, in separate hotels, the result of a mutual suicide pact. The longest arc belongs to George Lane, Molly's widowed husband, who closes the book with a visit to Vernon's widow, Mandy. The second longest arc belongs to Julian Garmony, who encounters Clive at Molly's memorial service, and who helps George return the dead protagonists to England. The shortest arc belongs to Rose Garmony, who enters the story in Act Two, with one purpose: to attack Vernon for attacking her husband. Rose is a fierce mother archetype defending her boy-husband.

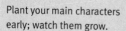

TIP FOR YOUR REWRITE

Plant your main characters early; watch them grow.

TIP FOR YOUR REWRITE

The best way to manage subtext when you rewrite is core story and archetype.

Lesson Four from this opening scene is how to contain the power of drama in the subtext. If you're rewriting a Cinderella tale, you have lots of action taking place on the surface. The power of a Rags to Riches story comes from the sweaty climb and the presence of the Triple Goddess (Virgin-Mother-Crone, three aspects of the major female archetype). If you're rewriting a novel like *Amsterdam*—subtle, ironic, understated, referential—you must know your subtext.

Checklist for Rewriting Page One and After

☐ How many objects on Page One? How many body parts? What are the landmarks?

☐ Which character opens the story? Protagonist? Antagonist? Helper? Narrator?

☐ What's the location for Page One? What's the time? The temperature? The season?

☐ What are the characters wearing?

☐ What action takes place?

☐ Is there dialogue?

☐ What's the closed circle on Page One? Who is the intruder?

☐ What core stories are you setting up on Page One?

☐ What secrets lurk in the subtext?

Exercises—Rewriting Page One and After

1. ANALYSIS

Read over your Page One. Circle all the nouns and then make two columns. One column for concrete nouns (arm, leg, bike, dagger, cave); and one column for fat, often polysyllabic, always abstract nouns (reassurance, politics, religion, organization, transportation). The two columns give you a ratio. The ratio is objective proof of grabbing power. An okay ratio is 8:1, eight concrete nouns for every abstract noun. If you want to grab the reader, use concrete nouns on Page One.

2. SYNTACTIC FLEX

Rewrite Page One using three rhetorical devices: short sentences, chaining, and long sentence release.

SHORT SENTENCES. Short sentences compress your prose, squeezing it down. As you write short sentences, you feel restricted, caged. You want to break out, write longer. That way you can breathe. When you read aloud, you listen for a staccato voice, the rhythm of your forced restriction. In Greek rhetoric, this technique is called *asyndeton*, the conscious removal of conjunctions like *and, but, so*.

Rewrite example

It was nine A.M. The month was July. The car lurched up the drive. Character A drove. The horn tooted. A burst of melody. The horn sang its trilling song. The door opened. Character A climbed out.

Writing time for short sentences: five minutes.

CHAINING. Rewrite Page One using a *chaining* exercise in which you start the next sentence with the word that ends the sentence that came *before. Before* you have time to *think. Thinking* returns you to robot *prose. Prose* to fill magazines and newspapers and bad TV shows with words like elegant and unique and *wonderful. Wonderful* to take a break with chaining.

When you chain, three things happen:

- First, you feel trapped in a lockstep sequence that warps information transfer;
- Second, your ambitious brain leaps to the end of the sentence and that sets you free;

- Third, when you're set free, you start to have fun; your prose edges closer to poetry.

When you chain, your writing develops rhythm. Rhythm jangles information—what you wanted to say when you started writing. Writing your way through the chain, you'll look ahead to the end of your sentence, writing on automatic now, as you plan the beginning word of the next sentence. In Greek rhetoric, this technique is called *anadiplosis*.

Rewrite example

The time was nine in the morning. Morning of a summer in West Egg. Egg that stares at your face like one single eye. Eye of Dr. T.J. Eckleburg. Eckleburg the optometrist whose spectacled face broods over the valley of ashes. Ashes in the valley to represent a wasteland. Land of Fitzgerald implanted into the American brain. Brain where . . .

Writing time for chaining: ten minutes.

LONG SENTENCE RELEASE. The long sentence opens the writer up to sudden release. As you write longer long sentences—going for fifteen minutes or more—you unearth sharp insights that help you see where the rewrite wants to go. Best of all, when you get jazzed, you keep the language alive for the rest of us. In Greek rhetoric, this long sentence technique is called *polysyndeton*. The conscious addition of conjunctions like *and, but, so*. The same conjunctions that you removed when you wrote short sentences.

Rewrite example

July of a long hot blistering summer and the yellow car lurching up the drive bumping the rocks of West Egg the clock reading nine o'clock and my stomach churning with hunger and the horn toots a burst of melody and the door swings open and Character A climbs out wearing . . .

Writing time for the long long sentence: fifteen minutes.

3. INTRUDER AND CLOSED CIRCLE

The big closed circle in *Amsterdam* is London. The circle inside London is men who knew Molly Lane. Clive and Vernon have their own tight little circle. They want to eject Julian Garmony, the cabinet minister. Then George Lane, Molly's widowed husband, shoves the American in their faces. What are the closed circles in your novel? Which closed circles appear on Page One?

Startline: On Page One of my novel an intruder named X penetrates
the closed circle of . . .
Writing time: ten minutes

4. THE THREE GOODS

Which of the Three Goods lured Lovers A and B to Molly Lane? She
was beautiful (good genes); she kept leaving men behind (bad
behavior if you were the one left). After leaving all those men, Molly
married George Lane for his money (good resources), but still kept up
her wild behavior with men of power like Secretary Garmony. Power
is a resource. Which of the Three Goods appear on Page One of your
rewrite?

Startline: She looks at him and sees . . .
Startline: He looks at her and sees . . .
Writing time: fifteen minutes

5. SCENE LIST FOR ACT ONE

Using the First Encounter as a launch pad, combine Firsts (First Words,
First Touch, First Date, First Rejection, First Fight, First Separation, First
Reunion, First Kiss, First Sex) with rituals like rebirth, barter, threshold
crossing (birthday, wedding, funeral), and incorporation (eating, chewing,
digesting, defecating). Make a list down the page and start jotting down
actions and possible locations for each scene. You need at least ten scenes
for Act One.

Writing time: twenty minutes

6. THIRTY-ONE-MINUTE SCENE TEMPLATE

Use this exercise to extend the scene past Page One. Writing time:
Take one minute for the warm-up and then five minutes each for the
six sections:

- **Warm-up:** I am rewriting Page One because . . . (one minute)
- This is a scene about . . . (five minutes)
- **Setting:** The time was/the place smelled of . . . (five minutes)
- **Character A on Character B:** His/her hairdo looked like . . . (five minutes)
- **Action and Dialogue:** What are you looking at? (five minutes)
- **Intruder/Complication:** What are you guys up to? (five minutes)
- **Climax/Resolution:** Using the long sentence release (see p. 129), extend the action to a dramatic climax. (five minutes)

The Rewrite: Writer X Rewrites Page One and After

"The scene in the square in Avignon," Rhoda says, "is a classic First Encounter where two characters collide for the very first time. There is no dialogue, but there is drama: the half-dark, an intrusion by the Biker in leather, the knocking on the window, the single cyclopean headlight in her rearview mirror." Over coffee, they discuss Writer X's next move. He's eager to press on down the road, leap from Page One to Plot Point One. Rhoda wants him to rebuild his scene list for Act One.

"I've already got a scene list," he says.

"When you made the first scene list," Rhoda says, "you did not have a firm grasp on your subplots."

> **LEARNING CURVE**
>
> The scene list tightens the structure between Page One and Plot Point One.

"Is that a compliment?"

Rhoda smiles.

"You're writing awfully hot, Mr. X."

"Thanks to you."

"Where is that list of Firsts?"

Writer X sighs. Work, work, work. He grabs his spiral notebook, sits on the floor, knees up, his back braced against the wall, and combines his list of Firsts with scenes from Subplot One, pushing through Act One.

- **First Encounter.** We open in Kate's point of view in the square at Avignon shooting photos of emptiness when the Biker interrupts. We know the Biker is Harry, but to Kate he is an intruder in black leather. She shoots the Biker, drops the lens cap on her way to the Renault station wagon. When Harry knocks on her window, Kate shakes her head and drives off.
- **First Touch.** Crossing the threshold into Kate's house, Harry returns the lens cap to Kate and their fingers brush.
- **First Date.** Kate and Harry have lunch in the sun in the courtyard of a small Provençal hotel. Kate's eyes are shining. In Harry's eyes, she looks like an earth goddess, tanned arms and a wide smile when she laughs.
- **April's Hand Off.** A fancy restaurant on the Promenade des Anglais in Nice where April Jardine introduces Charles to her film starlet daughter, Julie Jean. April has a plane to catch. She leaves Charles and Julie Jean in Nice.
- **First Betrayal.** In the courtyard of a farmhouse that borders Ventoux Vineyards, Harry hands over a check to the homeowner.

- **First Separation.** Kate begs for money from her husband, Charles. She owes the merchants, the maid, the gardener. Charles laughs, a sharp contrast to Harry.
- **Hall of Records, Avignon.** In a dusty office, Harry discovers that the owner of Ventoux Vineyards is not Charles D'Amboise, but instead his mother, Madeleine Ventoux.
- **Closed Circle.** Madeleine sits beside Julie Jean in the Player's Box at Stade Roland Garros in Paris. Charles frowns at Kate, who arrives looking like a Provençal peasant in her rough sandals and floppy sun hat. Kate is the intruder.
- **Sidewalk Café.** Charles sits next to Julie Jean. Madeleine chats with Raoul. Two chummy couples leave Kate outside, clutching her camera.
- **First Reunion.** The train station at Avignon where Kate runs into Harry's arms.
- **First Sex.** A small hotel in that same village overlooking the hotel courtyard where they had lunch. Kate falls in love with Harry.

"Good work, Mr. X. What is the resource base?"

"The vineyards and the house," X says.

"Why is the resource base important?"

"These are bad people," X says, "trying to steal Kate's house. Gives her something to fight for."

"My, my," Rhoda says. "Aren't we perky today?"

Weekend 9: Rewriting Plot Point One

Plot Point One ends Act One and opens Act Two. In a three-hundred-page novel, Plot Point One should appear around page seventy-five. Lots of my workshop writers are write-and-see novelists. They go for it from Page One, writing hard, waiting to see what happens, and when, and why. Write-and-see novelists do not plot; they feel restricted, their creativity held back by the three-act structure. It's too formal, they say. Too tight. Not enough room to be really creative. Write-and-see novelists can write 150 pages or more and not find the end of Act One. Write-and-see is a good strategy for the rough draft, but not for the rewrite.

In the rewrite, you have to study structure.

If you're this far into the process and still hoping to wrestle it through with write-and-see, stop rewriting and study a couple of good films. If the film is on DVD, you can fast-forward to the thirty-minute marker. Somewhere between twenty-eight and thirty-two minutes, you'll find Plot Point One. Act One is over; Act Two has begun. Using the power of analogy, you can transfer your new skill to:

- find Plot Point One in films
- find Plot Point One in model novels
- find Plot Point One in your novel

In *Leaving Las Vegas*, the novel, Plot Point One appears at the end of section one, called "cherries" in lowercase. Sera the hooker is in a taxi. She's just had bad sex with an abusive john. Her body aches, her face is bruised. Seeing her bruised face in his rearview mirror, the driver asks what happened. Nothing, Sera answers.

And the curtain falls on Act One.

And opens in a bar, where Ben the drunk is sucking up the booze. Act Two has started.

Did you catch what happened?

- Act One ends in *Las Vegas*.
- Act Two opens in *Los Angeles*.
- A shift in location marks Plot Point One.

In most dramatic structures, Act Two is longer than Act One. Act One is about the same length as Act Three. In *Leaving Las Vegas*, the novelist locates Plot Point One at the end of "cherries," a quarter of the way through the book. In the film adaptation, because the director moved the First Encounter forward, Plot Point One takes place in Ben's room at the Whole Year Inn. The scene is First Date, part of the string of Firsts started by the First Encounter. Ben has just arrived from Los Angeles. He sees Sera on the street. Plot Point One starts with a dialogue line when Ben asks the question, "Are you working?"

Whether you're rewriting a literary novel, a mainstream novel, or a genre novel (mystery, romance, horror, sci-fi), finding plot points will speed up your rewrite. If you're rewriting a mystery, for example, you can use Plot Point One as the First Encounter between killer and sleuth. That's what happens in *Gorky Park*. The sleuth has been tracking the killer through some choppy voice tapes and now he appears, naked except for a gold watch, in a dressing room of a Moscow bathhouse that caters to bigwigs in the Communist regime. The killer is dark, with white hair and black eyes. The dark skin comes from the sun. The implied sun power is picked up by a gold ring and a heavy gold watch and a cigarette lighter made of gold and lapis lazuli. The description presents Osborne, the killer, as a sun god, handsome and wealthy, bristling with confidence. The killer toys with the sleuth and the subtext hums with secrets:

- The killer is sleeping with Irina Asanova, Lover B.
- The killer is stealing furs from Russia and trading them for gold.
- The killer steals the sables with the help of the sleuth's boss, who is also in the dressing room.

To summarize, Plot Point One in *Leaving Las Vegas* comes with shifts in location (Las Vegas to Los Angeles) and point of view (Sera to Ben). Plot Point One in *Gorky Park* comes with a First Encounter between killer (John Osborne) and sleuth (Arkady Renko). The killer is a rich American (good resources); the sleuth is a low-paid Russian cop (bad resources). The killer is tanned and fit (good genes); the sleuth is pale and underfed (weak genes). The killer is a murderer (bad behavior); the sleuth is dogged and honest (good behavior). The antagonist outclasses the protagonist, which guarantees conflict. A good strong antagonist forces the protagonist to grow, maybe even change. Let's see what happens in our model novel for Plot Point One, *The Namesake*, by Jhumpa Lahiri.

Bare-bones Synopsis—*The Namesake*

A baby is born to Bengali parents living in America. The father names the baby Gogol, after Nikolai Gogol, a Russian writer. Gogol the Bengali hates his Russian name. He is a high school senior when he meets Kim, a college girl. She asks his name; his name is Nikhil, he says, lying. She smokes, they kiss. One magic kiss from Kim gives Gogol courage: He goes to court and changes his name to Nikhil. Changing his name starts Gogol's transformation. Kim is Lover One.

Gogol meets Lover Two on a train. She is a college girl named Ruth. Gogol falls in love. He's in college now. The love affair is going great until Ruth flies to England to study at Oxford. When she does not return, Gogol is heartbroken. He mopes around. He survives. Gets his degree in architecture. Goes to work in New York City, a good place to meet women.

He meets Lover Three at a party in a loft. Her name is Maxine. She is tall, slender, smart, educated, arty (good genes, good resources). She has blonde hair and long legs and modern parents who accept Gogol like a future son-in-law. After a night together, the lovers share breakfast with the parents. The parents trust their daughter's judgment, a display of good behavior.

There is a problem: Gogol's parents—both full-blood Bengalis—are not so modern. They do not accept Maxine. Gogol is hurt by their bad behavior. And surprised that he still needs their approval. While Gogol and Maxine are building their relationship, his father dies in a city far from home. Gogol fetches the body. His father's death kills his connection to Maxine. She is hurt by his bad behavior. She stops calling.

Gogol meets Lover Four at work. Her name is Bridget (good genes) and she has a husband in a small town outside the city. During the week, she has sex with Gogol. Bridget does not last.

Gogol meets Lover Five at a party. Her name is Moushumi. Like Gogol, she is 100 percent Bengali. She remembers him from childhood. He does not remember her, but Moushumi has ripened into a sexy female with a hot body (good genes) and an expert knowledge of love-making gleaned from multiple affairs. The lovers get engaged. They get married in a traditional Bengali ceremony, surrounded by family and friends. (Good behavior, good resources.)

Moushumi takes him to Paris. She speaks fluent French. She adapts to France like a native. Men swarm around her like bees. A warning bell sounds, but Gogol ignores it. Moushumi is his wife. She is a Bengali. His mother approves.

Back in New York, Moushumi exhibits bad behavior by starting an affair with a Frenchman named Dimitri. She remembers Dimitri from her past. He barely remembers her.

The name Dimitri is new to Gogol.

When he asks the question, Who is this Dimitri guy, his wife gasps, revealing her secret affair.

One evening, Gogol returns to the apartment to find Moushumi has moved out.

At Christmas, Gogol goes home to his mother's house. He sits in his father's study, reading "The Overcoat," a short story by Nikolai Gogol, the Russian writer he was named after. This scene, Gogol the Bengali reading the words of Gogol the Russian writer, loops back to his father's near-death moments before Gogol was born: a train wreck, his father trapped, dropping a page from "The Overcoat." The page caught the meager light, the light was seen by rescuers, and the father's life was saved. To pay homage to the writer whose single page had saved his life, the father named his son Gogol. Sitting there, holding the book of short stories, Gogol the Bengali forgives his father.

Analysis of Plot Point One in *The Namesake*

Plot Point One starts with a kiss (ritual) and ends with a name change. Gogol is reborn as Nikhil. Kim is a mythic helper who helps Gogol cross the threshold from boyhood to manhood. Gogol meets Kim in 1986. She's a college girl, older than Gogol, who smokes, and who accepts him as a fellow college student. She asks his name; he seizes the opportunity to escape his old Gogol Ganguli tradition-bound Bengali self. He suppresses the name Gogol and offers the name Nikhil. Authorial irony smolders in the subtext. Nikhil is close to "nihil," which is short for *nihilum*, the Latin word for "nothing." A boy who feels like nothing chooses a name that means "nothing." Kissing Kim the college girl gives Gogol courage. Courage to act, courage to confront his parents, courage to cross a threshold into a court room, to sign his new name on checks and application forms. Kissing Kim helps Gogol with his rebirth.

Diagram—*The Namesake*

To locate your Plot Point One, to fix it in your mind, draw a diagram with three acts and a little bubble for a Midpoint. A diagram helps you focus on the key scenes, their location, the way they connect to each other.

In the diagram below, Plot Point One is marked by the big bubble about a quarter of the way through the book. The year is 1986 when Gogol kisses Kim. After Kim he meets Ruth and Maxine and Bridget and Moushumi. He meets Moushumi, the last of his five women, in 1999. Their marriage makes a good Plot Point Two, a transition from bachelorhood to husband. Plot Points One and Two mark the boundaries of Act Two. Gogol's relationship with Maxine marks the Midpoint. A diagram gives you a snapshot of the novel. Here's the diagram for *The Namesake*:

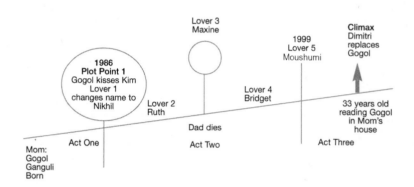

Subtext in Plot Point One

Remember that rewriting means working the subtext. Subtext is the stuff lurking under the surface of your prose. Subtext under the surface comes from emotions boiling inside your characters, the greed under the smile, the hatred in the heart. Subtext allows for harmless deception—Character B pretends to listen to Character A while all the time thinking about last night in the kayak with Character C, a handsome boy (good genes) wearing a ragged shirt (bad resources)—or it could get stronger. What if Character B is afraid, guilty, filled with desire, hatred, lust, and greed? What if Character B is plotting to betray Character A any minute? What if Character B is ready to steal, maim, or commit murder (killing Character B), and all the while making heated love with Character A?

Action and object work together to reveal what's cooking in the subtext.

- What if your Character B lights a cigarette, blows smoke at the ceiling, says something like "That's cool," and kisses Character A?
- What if Character B lights a cigarette, blows smoke in the face of Character A, and says, "Take off your clothes"?

- What if Character B lights a cigarette, blows smoke at the window, puts her lighter back into her purse, says, "Take off your clothes," pulls a 9mm pistol from her purse, and blows a hole in Character A? What if Character B knew about the pistol in the subtext (her little secret), while Character A did not know?

When you rewrite your novel, you deepen the subtext by using fictional devices like mythic helper, threshold crossing, closed circle and intruder, sexual triad—devices that the reader senses but does not see. As trained writers, we can see these devices working in Plot Point One of *The Namesake*. Let's have a closer look:

TIP FOR YOUR REWRITE

Find the mythic helper in your novel.

MYTHIC HELPER

To escape his Bengali identity, Gogol needs help and Kim appears just like Cinderella's Fairy Godmother. One taste of Kim's magic lips in that kiss and Gogol wants more. More kisses mean more women. The ritual kissing with Kim at Plot Point One launches the Journey of Love with Four Females: Ruth, Maxine, Bridget, and Moushumi.

TIP FOR YOUR REWRITE

Find a threshold crossing near page seventy-five in your novel.

THRESHOLD CROSSING

When a character crosses a threshold, s/he changes states. Gogol's threshold is the doorway to the courtroom where he changes his name. He changes states from boyhood to manhood.

CLOSED CIRCLE AND INTRUDER

When an intruder penetrates a closed circle, the action creates drama. There are two thresholds at *The Namesake*'s Plot Point One. The first closed circle is the dorm room at the college where Gogol meets Kim. She is the gatekeeper; he is the intruder. When she asks him his name, she's inviting him inside the circle. His reward for penetrating that closed circle is a kiss. The second closed circle is the courtroom where Gogol changes his name. After an interrogation by the judge, Gogol exits with his second reward, his new name, Nikhil.

REBIRTH

In Act One, Gogol feels suffocated, isolated, caged. Like Cinderella buried in ashes, Gogol exists in a state of near death. He starts his rebirth by lying to Kim and tossing out the name Nikhil. When his name change becomes official, Gogol feels new life surging through him. By changing his name, he takes control of his destiny. He has been reborn.

SEXUAL TRIAD

The sexual triad is a plot device that generates drama. Two characters form a closed circle called a couple. A third character penetrates the closed circle, causing drama. Two characters have balance; a third character means two against one, an imbalance. When Gogol meets Kim, she forms the first sexual triad with Gogol and his mother. The sexual triad connects Gogol's plot to his mother's subplot and to Kim's brief appearance as a walk-on character. The first sexual triad buried at Plot Point One sets up sexual triads through the rest of the book.

TIP FOR YOUR REWRITE

If you aren't using the closed circle–intruder device at Plot Point Two, now is your chance.

TIP FOR YOUR REWRITE

Put your character into a cage that represents near death. Then write in a ritual like threshold crossing to indicate rebirth, a breath of life at Plot Point One, so the character can keep going through Act Two and Act Three.

> Mother+Gogol+Kim
> Ruth+Gogol+Maxine
> Maxine+Gogol+Bridget
> Bridget+Gogol+Mousuhmi
> Gogol+Moushumi+Dimitri
> Moushumi+Gogol+Mother

Stacking Subplots

When you're rewriting and you come to Plot Point One, you need to stop and stack up your subplots. To identify a subplot, you attach a core story to each main character. If you don't know your subplots by now—you're at the curtain that separates Act One from Act Two—then you need to recheck your cast roster and then check your structure for entrances and exits.

If you don't have a subplot at Plot Point One, then you need to locate your subplot characters in the structure. Have they entered the story yet?

TIP FOR YOUR REWRITE

When in doubt, deploy the sexual triad.

Do they enter soon after Plot Point One? Stacking subplots helps you get organized.

In *The Namesake*, for example, Gogol Ganguli (aka Nikhil) is the protagonist. He has the plot and most of the point of view. The sexual triads on the preceding page show him wandering from one female to the next, replacing one woman with another until he gets replaced by Dimitri in Act Three. Because of the lengthy time span of this novel (two decades stretching from Gogol's boyhood to his divorce at age thirty-three), Plot Point One takes place without any help from the three major subplot characters: Moushumi the Death Crone; Maxine the would-be Mother; and Ashoke Ganguli, the sad Bengali father who saddled his Bengali son with the name of a dead Russian writer.

Gogol's core story is Queen Replacement. His archetype—Wounded Knight-Errant—comes clear when Moushumi wounds him with her betrayal. In order to reach Moushumi, Gogol must pass through Plot Point One and four other female characters. With the plot identified, let's check out the first three subplots:

- **Subplot One** belongs to Moushumi, the Death Crone antagonist, who does not enter the story until Act Two. Her core story, King Replacement, comes from her sexual history: Before she met Gogol, Moushumi had lots of affairs. This pattern of replacing one man with another does not change when she marries Gogol. Moushumi, like most Death Crones, is a very strong character. She's sexy, attractive, aggressive. Her deception when she betrays Gogol with Dimitri gives Gogol a chance to grow. Instead, he retreats. This novel is all about waiting for the Death Crone. Her character contains the fire of fiction.
- **Subplot Two** belongs to Maxine, the tall blonde goddess who embodies, with her family, the cultural freedom of America. Maxine has super-good genes. Her family has good resources. Sex is easy with Maxine. Maxine is fun to be with. Her parents like Gogol. Her Loving Mother archetype opposes the self-centered betrayal of Moushumi. Maxine's Holy Grail is marriage to Gogol; she wants to replace Gogol's mother; her core story is Queen Replacement. Ejected from Gogol and his family, Maxine exits the story. The exit of the American girl leaves a gap to be filled by a Bengali girl: Moushumi. Excellent story technique here.
- **Subplot Three** belongs to Gogol's father, Ashoke, the guy who named his son Gogol after the Russian writer. Ashoke represents

the Bengali culture. He came to America; what does he want for his son? The son is confused by his Russian name. This confusion swirls below the surface of the novel. The father is not amused when his son changes his name. He does not take a Bengali name; he does not take an American name. He takes a name that means nothing. Trapped in his subplot, the father loses control of his son. Plot Point One in *The Namesake* takes place with no parents around. The only other characters are two walk-ons: the college girl in the dorm and the judge in the courtroom.

TIP FOR YOUR REWRITE

If you don't have a Death Crone when you reach Plot Point One, create one now. The Death Crone is deadly; she brings the threat of fear to your story. Without fear, you have no drama. Without drama, you lose readers.

Checklist for Rewriting Plot Point One

- ☐ What page are you on when Plot Point One starts?
- ☐ How many pages does it run?
- ☐ How many scenes?
- ☐ What happens at Plot Point One?
- ☐ Does the action drive a location change?
- ☐ Is there a switch in the point of view?
- ☐ Is your character getting help from a mythic helper?
- ☐ What discovery does your protagonist make?
- ☐ Does a new character enter the story?
- ☐ If your First Encounter is not in Act One, can you place it here at Plot Point Two?
- ☐ Any sexual triads at Plot Point One?
- ☐ Any money changing hands?
- ☐ What is the closed circle?
- ☐ Who is the intruder?
- ☐ What symbols float in the prose?

Exercises for Rewriting Plot Point One

1. DIAGRAM

Draw a diagram of your structure—three acts, key scenes, character entry and exit, objects that might grow into symbols—and locate the action at Plot Point One. What happens? Who's there?

2. LOCATION CHANGE

Find page seventy-five in your manuscript and check what's happening. Is there a location change between pages seventy and eighty-five? Where to where?

Startline: Act One of my novel ends when . . .

Startline: Act Two of my novel opens when the protagonist rams . . .

Writing time: ten minutes for each writing

3. POINT OF VIEW SHIFT

Working those same pages (seventy to eighty-five), shift the point of view from your protagonist to another character. This is good practice. Shifting the perspective gives you a better look at what's cooking in your scene.

Startline: Standing in the center of the room, s/he stared hard at the face of . . .

Writing time: fifteen minutes

4. MYTHIC HELPER

Turn one of your characters into a mythic helper who guides the protagonist from Act One to Act Two. Check *The Accidental Tourist*, in which Act One ends when Macon hires Muriel Pritchett to be his dog trainer. Macon has Act One and Muriel dominates most of Act Two.

Startline: The mythic helper in my novel enters the story wearing . . .

Writing time: twenty minutes

5. ACTION

Two actions in *The Namesake*—the kiss and the threshold crossing—should trigger ideas for action at your Plot Point One.

Startline: At Plot Point One of my novel, the protagonist slams into . . .

Writing time: fifteen minutes

The Rewrite: Writer X Nails Plot Point One

For rewriting his Plot Point One, Writer X starts with a sequence of four scenes.

- Scene One is the Sidewalk Café in Paris where Kate feels shut out of the family circle. Being shut out drives Kate back to Harry.
- Scene Two is Kate's Reunion with Harry at the train station in Avignon. The technique is a location change.
- Scene Three is lunch at their favorite outdoor courtyard café in Isle-sur-la-Sorgue. Kate gets tipsy, tells Harry about meeting Charles. Harry does not tell Kate his secret.
- First Sex. Kate and Harry make love.

Rhoda does a quick sketch, shows it to Writer X. The sketch shows index cards framing a short string of CUT TO's. Rhoda calls it a framing template.

```
FRAMING TEMPLATE
     Index Card

       CUT TO
       CUT TO
       CUT TO
       CUT TO

     Index Card
```

"The transition between acts is difficult," Rhoda says. "The tension builds and builds to a release—in your book, that's First Sex—and then you have to start building again for the next act. The Sidewalk Café scene is grooved in your brain. Use that scene for your first index card. Scoot through the other scenes, and use the second card for the intruder scene. It's your doorway into Act Two."

"What intruder scene?" X asks.

"Let's say Raoul the Wonder Boy has been eliminated from the tournament. Let's say further that he brings the girl home to Kate's house. What does Kate feel?"

"Invaded," X says.

"Get to work," Rhoda says.

Index Card #1: Starting Plot Point One

Setting: *Paris. A sidewalk café.*

Characters: *Charles and Julie Jean; Madeleine and Raoul; Kate.*

POV: *Kate has the point of view.*

Objects: *drinks, cigarettes, Julie Jean's low-cut blouse, Kate's camera.*

Dialogue: *Madeleine whispers to Raoul; Julie Jean giggles.*

Action: *Parisian pedestrians jostle Kate. She spills her drink.*

Intruder and Closed Circle: Kate is the intruder; she is outside the closed circle of couples.

Subtext: *Kate has lost her only son to Madeleine. She could lose her husband to Julie Jean. If she loses her husband, she loses the house.*

LEARNING CURVE

Once again, Writer X discovers that if he uses the tools, the rewrite zooms along. After he admits to being a slow learner, he moves on to the Midpoint.

CUT TO:

Avignon, the train station. Kate runs into Harry's arms, gives him a hug. Tears on her cheeks from being home, from being shut out in Paris.

CUT TO:

The road. Wearing a crash helmet, Kate sits close behind Harry on the BMW, arms holding him tight, her face pressed against his broad back. The wind dries her tears.

CUT TO:

Isle-sur-la-Sorgue. A hotel courtyard beside a clear running stream. Harry orders another bottle of wine. Kate is tipsy. She's drowning her sorrow in drink. Harry looks good. He's tanned and fit.

CUT TO:

Hotel room, Isle-sur-la-Sorgue. Kate exits the bed, walks to the window and calls down to a waiter for coffee. The waiter salutes Kate. Feeling reborn, Kate smiles back.

Index Card #2: Doorway to Act Two

Setting: *Kate's house in Menerbes.*

Characters: *Kate, Raoul, Julie Jean.*

POV: *Kate has the point of view.*

Objects: tennis gear, racquets, balls, Julie Jean's cute outfit, Raoul's tight shorts.

Action: Finding Raoul and Julie Jean on the orange clay court, Kate hugs Raoul and shakes hands with Julie Jean.

Dialogue: Raoul compliments Julie Jean on her tennis game.

Subtext: Raoul is shirtless and brown. Julie Jean is golden and ravishing. It's a mating dance. Kate feels old. She feels invaded.

Weekend 10: Rewriting the Midpoint

The Midpoint is a massive turnstile in the middle of Act Two, in the structural center of the book. When your characters click through this turnstile at the Midpoint, you have reached the heart of your novel. From here, there is no going back.

Act Two thickens after the Midpoint.

Core stories collide when subplots meet the plot. Character agendas clash, secrets throb in the subtext, and your protagonist digs up the past and makes a discovery. You'll need three to four scenes for your Midpoint. With that many scenes, your Midpoint becomes thicker and more substantial. A solid Midpoint stabilizes your book. Let's look at a couple of examples.

Midpoint for *Jane Eyre*

The Midpoint in *Jane Eyre* has five scenes; Deathbed, First Reunion, Trickster, First Kiss, and First Proposal. Let's look at them in sequence:

- **Deathbed.** Aunt Reed dies at Gateshead. "I covered her cold and clammy hand with mine."
- **First Reunion.** Jane returns to Thornfield; Rochester mocks her shadowy reappearance: "She came from the other world, from the abode of people who are dead."
- **Trickster.** Rochester toys with Jane about his upcoming nuptials: "You, Miss Eyre, must get a new situation." (Jane thinks he's going to marry Blanche Ingram.)
- **First Kiss.** Rochester kisses Jane and she responds: "Do you think, because I am poor, obscure, plain and little, that I am soulless and heartless?" (Like he is.)
- **First Proposal.** Rochester proposes to Jane in his usual nasty style: "But Jane, I summon you as my wife."

The Midpoint climaxes with Rochester's proposal. The fact that he's already married doesn't bother this guy. The fact that his crazy wife is locked in the tower doesn't matter. Rochester is a rich man in love, an older man who wants Jane. She is young and fertile and full of fire and ethics. She needs Rochester's resources. First Kiss and First Proposal and First Reunion continue the string of firsts that starts with their first encounter on the icy causeway.

This is a very strong Midpoint.

Technique is important here. *Jane Eyre* is written in first person. First person isolates the protagonist, who cannot know secrets until they are released like snakes from the subplots. Rochester conceals the secret of his wife in his Queen Replacement subplot, while Jane feels herself rising several steps in her ascent from Rags to Riches.

Midpoint for *Leaving Las Vegas*

At the Midpoint of the novel *Leaving Las Vegas*, Ben the drunk wakes up on the floor of a urinal just south of Malibu. Surprised to be alive, Ben goes to a restaurant where he orders dry toast and two double Bombay tonics. He pays with his credit card. He cleans up in the restroom. He smells the coffee machine. He's leaving Los Angeles. He misses the screaming seagulls already.

As the turnstile clicks, the story shifts to Las Vegas, where Sera wakes up in bed with Al/Gamal, her pimp. Ben had the point of view in Los Angeles; Sera has the point of view in Las Vegas. Al worries about the bruises on Sera's face. Al has lost his jewelry. He's losing his grip on his hooker.

The Midpoint has three scenes—Urinal, Dry Toast, and Bruises. It has a location change from Los Angeles to Las Vegas. It has a switch in the point of view, from Ben to Sera. The scene with Al/Gamal triggers Sera to follow her King Replacement core story, the first encounter scene that opens Act Three of the novel.

Midpoint for *Gorky Park*

Our model Midpoint is a thick four-scene sequence from *Gorky Park*. Published in the early 1980s, *Gorky Park* did for Martin Cruz Smith what *Eye of the Needle* did for Ken Follett: It made the writer world-famous. After moderate successes with books like *Canto for a Gypsy* and *Gypsy in Amber*, Smith switched to a Moscow location and a homicide cop named Arkady Renko. Renko is depressed, underfed, moody, romantic, intuitive, and dogged.

To give Renko a solid opponent, the writer created killer John Osborne, a rich American fur trader who's stealing sables from Mother Russia. To create a sexual triad for the heart of his novel, Smith developed a female character named Irina Asanova, a Siberian Cinderella. Irina is thin, depressed, brilliant, ambitious, ironic, and deadly. The book is written in the third person, but Smith never switches the point of view away from Renko. Like Jane the Governess and Jay the Bootlegger, Renko is locked inside his plot. We see what he sees, feel what he feels. When he gets stabbed at the end of Act Two, we feel the thrust of the blade. When he rescues Irina at Midpoint, we feel relief mixed with dread.

I'm using *Gorky Park* as an example because I want you to have a strong Midpoint for your novel. If you're like most first-time novelists, your Midpoint is weak. The Midpoint is the heart of your novel. If the heart is weak, the book is weak. Now is your chance to build up the heart muscle. As you read, try to locate the Midpoint of Gorky Park.

Bare-bones Synopsis—*Gorky Park*

- Lover A, Arkady Renko, is a sleuth. He works in Moscow for the People's Militia.
- Lover B, Irina Asanova, is a prop girl in B movies.
- They meet at a film shoot in Moscow. The season is winter. The day is gray and cold. Renko tracks Irina using an object: ice skates borrowed by her dead friend.
- Irina's dead friend with the borrowed skates is one of three corpses killed in the back story.
- Renko enters the story because he is a homicide detective hunting a killer. He falls in love with Irina when she puts her cigarette out on the white trunk of a birch tree. She burns the tree. He feels the burn in his flesh.
- Irina has a secret. She is sleeping with the killer who murdered three people, one of whom wore Irina's borrowed ice skates.
- Renko meets the killer in a fancy bigwig bathhouse, when the killer enters the dressing room, naked.
- The killer is a rich American working with a corrupt Russian—Renko's boss—who sends KGB agents to kill Renko's best detective.
- With the detective dead, Renko bonds with William Kirwill, a New York City homicide cop, whose brother was one of the three corpses found at the crime scene that opens the book.
- The sleuth's boss sends agents to kill Irina in the metro tunnel.

- Renko rescues Irina.
- He takes her to his doctor.
- He takes her to his apartment in a state of near death.
- When she wakes, Irina wraps herself in a sheet and goes to Renko.
- They make love.
- Renko uses his father, a retired general, to probe the killer's back story.
- Twenty-five years before, the killer executed three German prisoners in wartime. Motive unknown.
- The killer tries to bribe Renko.
- Refusing the bribe, Renko hurries to save Irina from a second murder attempt by Renko's corrupt boss in the shallow pool of the university fountain. Renko kills the henchman. He gets stabbed. Irina shoots his corrupt boss.
- In his own state of near death, Renko heals from his wounds.
- Meanwhile, the killer whisks Irina to New York.
- In the Fur Palace in Leningrad, five KGB officers send Renko to New York because they want their sables back.
- The killer confesses to Renko about killing the three prisoners of war twenty-five years ago because they laughed at his innocence, his American naïveté.
- Renko confronts the killer at his sable farm in rural New Jersey.
- Warming up for Renko, the killer kills seven more victims: one NYC homicide cop, one snitch, two agents of the KGB, and three agents of the FBI.
- The killer wounds Renko.
- While Irina watches, Renko kills the killer.
- Irina exits the killing scene with the car keys. She wants to experience America.
- As he releases the caged sables, Renko drips blood onto the snow.

Analysis—Midpoint in *Gorky Park*

The Midpoint of *Gorky Park* is a four-scene sequence—Male Bonding, Metro Rescue, Father and Son, and Bedsheet—where the novel thickens as the plot collides with three different subplots. The plot belongs to Arkady Renko, intrepid Moscow homicide cop. Subplot One belongs to Mr. John Osborne, a rich American fur trader. Subplot Two belongs to Irina Asanova, a beautiful Siberian Cinderella. These three characters form a powerful sexual triad. Subplot Three belongs to Detective William Kirwill, a New York City homicide cop.

MALE BONDING

Renko the sleuth drinks with William Kirwill, who wants revenge on the killer for killing his brother, Jimmy Kirwill. In a Moscow dive, the two weary policemen drink a toast to Renko's detective friend Pasha, murdered by Iamskoy's KGB goons. Renko is outnumbered and outgunned. He needs help. He joins forces with Kirwill.

CORE STORIES CROSSING
Renko's core story is King Replacement; he has the plot. Kirwill's core story is Revenge Quest; Kirwill has Subplot Three. The plot device that unites them is the dead detective, Pasha, killed by Iamskoy's KGB goons. Iamskoy's subplot lurks in the shadows of this scene.

METRO RESCUE

Renko (Lover A) rescues Irina Asanova (Lover B) from the same KGB goons who killed his detective, Pasha. The rescue takes place in a tunnel of the Moscow Metro, where Irina is dying from poison from a hypodermic needle. Renko rushes her to his doctor friend. Then takes her home to his apartment. Irina, a bitter Siberian Cinderella, caps off the rescue by mocking Renko, calling him an idiot, a fool, and a government toady.

CORE STORIES CROSSING
Renko (King Replacement) is falling in love with Irina (Rags to Riches), who is sleeping with the killer, Mr. John Osborne (Scapegoat Sacrifice). The killer is a rich American; Irina is a poor girl from Siberia. She barters her body for passage to America. Her body-barter unites the sleuth with the killer in a dangerous sexual triad. Irina's secret—she has slept with the killer—is buried in her subplot. The sexual triad connects the plot to Subplots One and Two.

FATHER AND SON

To crack the killer's motive, Renko pays a visit to his father, a retired Soviet Army general, sometimes called "The Butcher of the Ukraine." In an interview, Renko learns that Osborne executed three German officers who were prisoners during the Siege of Leningrad (1944). The killing twenty-five years ago occurred at a picnic in the woods, with champagne and chocolates. According to the general, Osborne killed the officers for fun. (The real motive, buried in Osborne's subplot, will surface in Act Three; for now, it is another secret churning in the subtext.) The killer's presence invades the room where the sleuth listens to his father, showing the power of the killer even in the retelling.

CORE STORIES CROSSING

The general is a walk-on. He makes a brief appearance and then retires into the wings. But his story of execution adds weight to the killer's subplot. The killer has killed before; once you have killed, it's easier to kill again. With this information, Renko acts on his King Replacement plot.

BEDSHEET

Renko returns to his apartment with groceries and shampoo. Irina grabs the shampoo and exits. She reappears wet from the shower, wrapped in a bedsheet tied at the waist with one of his belts. The dialogue changes their relationship. He calls her "Comrade"; she tells him to use her first name. He tells her the KGB will come first to his apartment; she should go away and stay with a friend. She replies, "I can drag a friend down or I can drag you. I've thought it over. I want to take you." Desire pulses in the subtext. A few pages later, they make love.

TIP FOR YOUR REWRITE

For your Midpoint, you need to intertwine core stories. The Midpoint in Gorky Park reveals the power of core story. The general's story about an execution buried in the back story shows that the killer is evil; he kills for no apparent reason; his core story is Scapegoat Sacrifice. Irina's core story is Rags to Riches. For her, the killer is another step on the economic ladder leading up from poverty. Before she gives herself to the sleuth, Irina buries him in hostile dialogue. The sleuth takes the punishment because he wants her. The Midpoint sets up the climax in Act Three, where the three lovers take the stage together, and where the sleuth fulfills his King Replacement plot by killing the killer.

Lessons from *Gorky Park*

Lesson One is thickness. Four scenes connect the plot with the three major subplots:

- Male Bonding entwines the plot with Kirwill's Revenge Quest (Subplot Four).
- Metro Rescue entwines the plot with Irina's desperate Rags to Riches climb (Subplot Two).

- Father and Son entwines the plot with Osborne's Subplot, Scapegoat Sacrifice (Subplot One).
- Bedsheet brings the sleuth back home, back to Irina and her bitter Rags to Riches scramble for survival (Rags to Riches).

Lesson Two is digging up the past: Renko uses his own father to unearth the killer's first killing. It happened twenty-five years ago in wartime Leningrad. The killer was young back then. He shot three German officers after treating them to champagne and chocolate. What was his real motive? The writer keeps that secret buried until Act Three, a couple of scenes before the climax. Renko digs up the past and now the body count is up to six dead corpses.

Lesson Three is the biology of the sexual triad: Irina is the classic shared female resource. She is smart, bitter, needy, and sexy. She has good genes and no resources. She makes up for sleeping with the killer (bad behavior) by sleeping with Renko (good behavior). Her balancing act creates the sexual triad: Renko-Irina-Killer. When Renko meets the killer, Irina swims in the subtext; when Renko meets Irina, the killer swims in the subtext. The sexual triad implies two powerful rituals: barter (Irina barters her body for a trip to America) and mate selection: She chooses Renko. Reread that bit of dialogue, where Irina says, "I've thought it over. I want to take you." The lovers are locked together; if she dies, he dies. That's Irina's idea of true Siberian love.

Lesson Four is the power of character transformation: When Renko loses a detective (Pasha is killed by KGB goons), he is replaced by William Kirwill, the homicide cop from New York City. Kirwill entered the book as an adversary, an antagonist. He did not trust Renko because he was a Russian. Russians, by definition, are corrupt. But Renko is a wounded knight with tarnished armor. Honest to the core. At the Midpoint, when he toasts the dead detective, Kirwill shifts roles: from Antagonist Four to Helper.

Checklist for the Midpoint Rewrite

☐ How many scenes in your Midpoint?

☐ How many subplots intersect the plot?

☐ How many core stories entwine?

☐ How many closed circles? How many intruders?

☐ What rituals—barter, threshold crossing, mate selection—are working at your Midpoint?

☐ How many sexual triads?

☐ If the protagonist is not in all the scenes, why not?

☐ What objects appear at your Midpoint? Do the objects tie the Midpoint to other key scenes?

☐ Who has possession of the resource base at the Midpoint? Who takes possession?

☐ How much time passes at the Midpoint? Minutes? Hours? Days?

☐ How can you compress the time?

☐ Dialogue: Who talks to whom? Who has the power? The edge?

Exercises for Rewriting the Midpoint

1. THICKNESS

The effect that readers call a "plot twist" comes from a collision of plot and subplot. The protagonist wheels along, singing and whistling, until she runs into an antagonist. To find your Midpoint, go to the middle of your manuscript and seek out those intersections. If your manuscript is three hundred pages long, search for the Midpoint ten pages before page 150 and ten pages after. Write a narrative summary overview using this startline.

Startline: The Midpoint for my novel starts when . . .

Writing time: ten minutes

2. INTRUDER AND CLOSED CIRCLE

At the Midpoint in *Gorky Park*, one closed circle is Renko's apartment. He brings Irina inside the circle, where she buries him in bitterness and scorn. She is poison, but he loves her anyway. A few pages after the Midpoint, the lovers make love. A second closed circle appears when Renko uses his father to reenter the back story for insights into the killer. The old man knows he's being used, but he invites his son back: "You'll come again? It's good to talk."

Startline: The closed circle at my Midpoint is . . . and the intruder penetrates because . . .

Writing time: ten minutes

3. OBJECTS AT THE MIDPOINT

Glasses and a bottle in Male Bonding. Knives and guns in Metro Rescue. Cigarette ashes and bulldozers in Father and Son. Soap and shampoo and a damp bedsheet in Bedsheet. Objects keep your writing close to the page. If you add arms and legs and eyes and hands, you write even closer.

Startline: The main object at the Midpoint is . . .

Writing time: ten minutes

4. RITUAL

When Renko visits his father in *Gorky Park*, the ritual is Digging Up the Past. When he drinks with Kirwill, the ritual is Male Bonding. When Irina tells him not to call her Comrade, the ritual is Language Lesson—she's teaching him how to address her, modifying his behavior. Language Lesson is part of mate selection and Irina, a Siberian Cinderella, has chosen Renko, a Muscovite Sleuth. Ritual gains in focus with archetypes: Irina is a femme fatale. Renko is a wraith, pale of face and lank of hair. His archetype is Wounded Hero.

Startline: The ritual that guides my Midpoint is . . .

Writing time: ten minutes

5. REWRITING SCENES USING THE THIRTY-ONE-MINUTE SCENE TEMPLATE

For a strong Midpoint, you need at least three scenes in a sequence. If you have two scenes and need a third, you can write a scene using the scene template. Exercises 1–4 should give you three to four scenes to rewrite. Three scenes will take ninety-three minutes. Use the startlines from the template below. Take one minute for the warm-up and then five minutes for each of the six sections:

- **Warm-up:** I am rewriting my Midpoint because . . . (one minute)
- This is a scene about . . . (five minutes)
- **Setting:** The time was/the place smelled of . . . (five minutes)
- **Character A on Character B:** His/her hairdo looked like . . . (five minutes)
- **Action and Dialogue:** What are you looking at? (five minutes)
- **Intruder/Complication:** What are you guys up to? (five minutes)
- **Climax/Resolution:** Using the long sentence release (see "Weekend 8," p. 129), extend the action to a dramatic climax. (five minutes)

The Rewrite: Writer X Rewrites the Midpoint

The Subtext at Midpoint

Rhoda helps X probe the subtext at the Midpoint. "Dramatic tension," Rhoda says, "comes from two sexual triads. The first triad is Harry+Charles+Kate. Kate's in love with Harry; Charles does not suspect. If he's not attracted to Kate, how could anyone else be? The second sexual triad is Charles+Julie Jean+Raoul. The father cuckolds the son. Kate knows there is another woman (Charles has a history of flagrant infidelity), but she does not yet suspect Julie Jean.

"The quick sale of the neighboring properties shows the raw power of money: Homeowners who never thought they would sell give up the family homestead for money. There is danger here for Kate. Without Charles, she has no income and no house."

To refine his Midpoint, Rhoda suggests that Writer X summarize the subplot characters. What does each character want? How do their drives affect the protagonist? Writer X starts with Julie Jean Jardine.

- Julie Jean wants to marry a rich guy. She's having sex with Raoul while she reels in Charles.
- Charles wants to replace his son, Raoul, in the arms of Julie Jean.
- April Jardine wants Harry to dig up divorce dirt on Kate. Subtext: April does not know that Harry's love for Kate will provide its own divorce dirt.
- Harry wants out from under his debt to April. He's trapped between what he owes April and his love for Kate. Every time he buys a house or a piece of Provençal real estate, Harry betrays his love for Kate.
- Raoul wants to keep on having sex with Julie Jean.
- Madeleine worries that Raoul is no match for Julie Jean.
- Kate, seeing her husband, Charles, drooling over Julie Jean, worries about losing her house if Charles replaces her with Julie Jean.

As the story approaches its Midpoint, Harry heads for Paris. Alone and brooding, Kate hikes through the Ventoux Valley, shooting photos of empty houses that once were full. Where have all the owners gone?

Index Card #1

The Empty House. The setting is Provence, the Ventoux Valley. Kate knows the people who lived here. They always gave her cool water and a shady place to rest. No one in the house. No dogs, no vehicles, no one to water the garden. Subtext: This was the first property acquired by Harry Thornburg for April's real estate corporation.

LEARNING CURVE

Charles wants nothing to get in the way of selling the house to April Jardine for her resort complex.

CUT TO:

Charles barging into Kate's darkroom to announce surprise dinner guests who are expecting a good steak, grilled American-style.

CUT TO:

Kate on the patio using cooking secrets learned from her Uncle Julian: six steaks *à l'Americain.*

CUT TO:

The guests (film people scouting locations). Kate okays a film shoot in her house. She can use the money. Charles says not so fast.

CUT TO:

Kate's passing out photos of the empty houses. There is a mystery here, she says. Two weeks ago, these houses were inhabited. Some of them have been in the same family for four hundred years. Where did the home-owners go? Enraged, Charles rips up the photos.

Index Card #6: Midpoint Climaxes.

Setting: Kate's kitchen.

Characters: Charles and Kate.

POV: Kate has the point of view.

Objects: dirty dishes, knives, dish towels, wine glasses, bloody white handkerchief.

Action: Charles slaps Kate. She slaps him back, pushes him off his feet. Charles orders her to behave, grabs her. She whacks him with a desk lamp, cutting his cheek.

Dialogue: Charles says he's bleeding. Apologizes for his behavior.

Action: Tears come to his eyes. He backs off, holds a white handkerchief to his cheek. Kate dresses his wound.

Subtext: Kate is afraid Charles will want to make love. But he goes to bed like a child, nursing his cheek.

Learning Curve Q&A:

Writer X: Why does the rewrite feel smoother and faster?

Rhoda: Because you have laid a foundation.

Writer X: What foundation?

Rhoda: First, back story. Second, subplots and their scenes. All those index cards, all those CUT TO's. Each time you run a CUT TO, your characters cross thresholds. They meet, they fight, they argue, they make love. And you have not stopped the structural work to retrofit your style.

Writer X: I'll drink to that. How about a beer?

Rhoda: One beer, then on to Plot Point Two.

Weekend **''** : Rewriting Plot Point Two

Plot Point Two ends Act Two and launches Act Three. Plot Point Two entwines the plot with one or more subplots. Character agendas collide. Objects get transferred. Secrets buried in the subtext force their way to the surface, where they explode. Explosions bring pain and loss. Pain unearths emotions like greed, envy, hate, love, hunger, longing, fear.

Plot Point Two is a miniclimax that sets up the major climax in Act Three.

A great Plot Point Two drips with dramatic tension.

Your rewrite this weekend will end the second act and launch you into Act Three. Last weekend, you were halfway through and working hard on the Midpoint. This weekend, you are three-quarters done. Plot Point Two is thick with dramatic tension because you've been digging up secrets in Act Two, unearthing dark stuff in the hearts of your characters.

As Act Two ends, you have a chance to cap off one or more subplots, clearing the stage for the final confrontation between antagonist and protagonist. Let's look at some examples.

Plot Point Two in *Jane Eyre*

Plot Point Two in *Jane Eyre* is a scene sequence that starts in the wedding chapel, where Richard Mason's solicitor accuses Rochester of being an incipient bigamist. Jane, in her wedding dress, learns for the first time that Rochester has a wife locked in the tower. The next scene takes us to the tower, where Jane has a face-off with Bertha Mason Rochester. Jane saw Bertha once before, in a fire dream, the night she rescued Rochester from his burning bed. Seeing Bertha in the flesh (not in the dream) sends Jane packing.

She must leave Thornfield, leave behind safety and sanctuary, but before she does, Rochester unearths his back story in a Confession Scene.

The placement of this scene is perfect. We know Jane's heading out. We know Rochester's a lying bastard. But the style of his confession is a testimony to his wit, his charm, his ability to spin the words out—a sharp talker shows evidence of good genes and a brain that calculates well. In this back story, Rochester admits to having three different women in Europe (far away in space; way back in time). He reasserts his nonfatherly connection to Adele. And, in a flourish of snappy dialogue, and without using the word "mistress," he asks Jane to stay on at Thornfield.

No way, Jane says.

The last scene in Brontë's Plot Point Two shows Jane leaving Thornfield. She has no money and will spend the first pages of Act Three starving on the heath.

TIP FOR YOUR REWRITE

As you rewrite one key scene, watch for insights into other key scenes. At this stage of the rewrite, a single insight into structure or character is pure gold to the writer. If you get an insight on the ending when you are rewriting Plot Point Two, you should follow the insight. Jump to the ending, work fast, and then leap back to finish up your work on Plot Point Two.

Plot Point Two in *Gorky Park*

If you're writing a mystery or a thriller, you can juice up Plot Point Two with weapons, ritual combat, and death. If you kill off a character, you also end a subplot. In *Gorky Park*, the writer uses Plot Point Two to reduce the cast of characters, thereby clearing the stage for the climax.

Plot Point Two in *Gorky Park* is ritual combat in a fountain pool at the University of Moscow. The time is night. Iamskoy, the boss of Lover A (Arkady Renko, the sleuth), has brought a German hitman to murder Irina Asanova, Lover B, the femme fatale who's been sleeping with both the killer and Renko, alternating them in her bed.

At the high point of the fountain scene, Renko kills the German hit man. Iamskoy aims a pistol at Renko but Irina rescues him by killing Iamskoy. The screen fades. Irina goes to America with the killer. Renko, wounded, descends into a state of near death, which sets up his rebirth in Act Three. After he heals from his wounds, Renko goes to New York to execute the killer. If you are writing a mystery or a thriller, the formula requires that you pile up the victims. A stack of victims justifies the execution of the killer at the climax.

For a powerful Plot Point Two, have the intruder penetrate a closed circle. For example, let's say you have this intruder. He's been outside the closed circle since Page One and now, at Plot Point Two, he gets invited inside. It's hot inside the closed circle; he's a Lower World guy and the insiders, the folks inside the closed circle, are very Upper World. Some weird stuff happens inside the hot circle. He gets kissed; a secret leaks out; he loses a sacred object. He gets into a fight where secrets explode in midair. He exits, makes one mistake, and dies the next day. His death is an execution caused by a threshold crossing: a single penetration of the closed circle.

This closed-circle situation comes from *The Great Gatsby*, by F. Scott Fitzgerald. Like *Jane Eyre*, another Rags to Riches story, *Gatsby* has enjoyed a long shelf life. It was published in 1925, and still sells over five hundred thousand copies a year. Year after year, *The Great Gatsby* keeps reappearing in new versions. It's been studied by scholars, taught in literature classes, mined for symbols, adapted into films (four of them so far) and a stage play. The name Gatsby stands for America in the Roaring Twenties. To study Plot Point Two in this model novel, we'll start with a synopsis followed by a recap of key scenes. There are some juicy secrets buried in the subtext. A recap gathers them up.

Bare-bones Synopsis—*The Great Gatsby*

Lover A (Gatsby) meets Lover B (Daisy) in the back story. He's a poor boy from out West; she's a rich girl dressed in virginal white. Her vehicle is a sleek white roadster. There's a war on "over there" in Europe and Gatsby sails away to do his duty as a soldier. While he's away, Daisy marries a rich man. They have a child. The rich man gets into trouble with a hotel maid.

The novel opens in Daisy's house, a mansion inside a closed circle of rich people like her husband. At a small dinner party, Daisy learns that her old flame, Gatsby, keeps throwing wild parties in a mansion across the lake. The narrator, a cousin to Daisy and a neighbor of Gatsby, engineers their Second Encounter, where the lovers rekindle their back story love.

Daisy has a secret: she uses her affair with Gatsby to get revenge on her husband, the rich man who keeps a mistress in a dead land called the valley of ashes.

The affair is underway when Daisy invites Gatsby to lunch—the first (and last) time he penetrates the closed circle of the moneyed rich. In the living room, Daisy kisses Gatsby. In the hot dining room, she reveals their affair with the Look of Love, seen by her husband.

To escape the heat, the party of five (Gatsby and Daisy, her husband, her old friend Jordan, and Nick the narrator) drive to the city.

The husband drives Gatsby's car, a yellow convertible. In the valley of ashes, the husband's mistress spots him behind the wheel and assumes that he owns the yellow car. In the city, Gatsby has a verbal duel with the husband, and Daisy, the object of desire, responds with tears.

The party is over. Gatsby takes possession of his car and drives away with Daisy. To calm her frayed nerves, Gatsby turns the wheel over to Daisy. In the valley of ashes, the mistress tries to flag down the yellow car and Daisy kills her dead.

Nice work.

- Gatsby hides the car and stands vigil outside Daisy's house, waiting for her to appear.
- Daisy's husband tells his mechanic (he's the husband of the murdered mistress) where to find the yellow car.
- Tracking the owner of the yellow car, the bereaved husband kills Gatsby, shooting him in the swimming pool of the rented mansion.
- The killer kills himself.

Gatsby is buried on a rainy autumn afternoon. Daisy does not show up for the burial. Instead, she takes a long vacation with her rich-man husband. The narrator, soured on the events, returns to his hometown in Middle America.

Analysis—The Road to Plot Point Two

Gatsby is the protagonist; he has the plot. Daisy is the antagonist; she has Subplot One. This is a Cinderella fairy tale with two changes in casting: Cinderella is transformed into a guy and the Death Crone is neither old nor ugly. She is young, beautiful, deceptive, and deadly. No happy ending here.

The dramatic tension in *The Great Gatsby* comes from the class struggle.

Gatsby is Lower World.

Daisy and Tom are Upper World.

Gatsby wants inside their closed circle.

He gets inside the circle at Plot Point Two.

As punishment for his intrusion, Gatsby is executed at the climax by a garage mechanic, another denizen of Lower World.

As you can see from the diagram that follows, Fitzgerald plots a course for his boy-Cinderella starting in the Crimson Room scene—where

Jordan Baker drops Gatsby's name, making Daisy gasp—and ending in the Swimming Pool scene where Gatsby dies. To reconnect his doomed lovers, the writer uses two messenger-facilitators. One is Jordan Baker, Daisy's pal from Louisville; the other is Fitzgerald's narrator, nosy neighbor Nick Carraway. Gatsby is hot to reconnect; he's in love with Daisy, her white dress, her access to Old Money. (There's a great line in the novel that made it into the film, where Gatsby says: "Her voice is full of money.") Following the money, Gatsby winds up dead. The diagram below highlights the road that leads Lover A (Gatsby) to Plot Point Two.

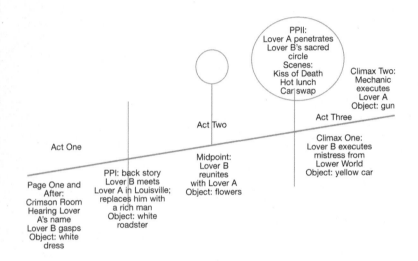

Expanding Information from the Diagram

Plot Point Two in *The Great Gatsby* is composed of three interlocking scenes—Kiss of Death, Hot Lunch, and Car Swap. Let's compress the action for each scene:

EXPANSION: KISS OF DEATH

The Kiss of Death is the first of a powerful three-scene sequence where emotions roil at Daisy's East Egg mansion. The season is late summer, and Daisy the antagonist invites three guests to lunch: Jordan, Nick, and Gatsby. Gatsby's threshold crossing is ominous. He's inside the closed circle just this once, and his lady is showing her fangs. It's a hot day, even in sumptuous East Egg. To keep herself in a ditzy play-mode, Daisy clogs on the fireplace in the Crimson Room. Then, in front of Nick and

Jordan, she kisses Gatsby on the mouth. The kiss marks him for death and it's time for lunch.

EXPANSION: HOT LUNCH

In the dining room at East Egg, Daisy zaps Gatsby with the Look of Love. At the head of the table, Tom sees Daisy's look, realizes he's being cuckolded, and orders everyone out to the patio. As the threshold guardian of East Egg, Tom will take action to protect his property. He owns Daisy. He has caught Gatsby stealing his possession.

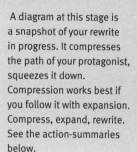

TIP FOR YOUR REWRITE

A diagram at this stage is a snapshot of your rewrite in progress. It compresses the path of your protagonist, squeezes it down. Compression works best if you follow it with expansion. Compress, expand, rewrite. See the action-summaries below.

EXPANSION: CAR SWAP

While the ladies change clothes for a quick run into the city, Tom seats himself behind the wheel of Gatsby's yellow car. The symbolism is very alpha male: because Gatsby has stolen Tom's wife, now Tom grabs Gatsby's yellow car, his prize possession. When Tom stops at Wilson's garage in the valley of ashes, Myrtle assumes that he owns the yellow car. When Myrtle spots Jordan Baker in the back seat, she mistakes Jordan for Daisy. This mistake will get Myrtle killed.

Build an Action Chain

Action chain is a great exercise. It lays out specific actions that connect two key scenes. Action chain teaches you to cut exposition. If the action chain is strong enough, there is no need for long passages of exposition because good action carries the story. Here's a model from *The Great Gatsby* that connects Plot Point Two to the double climax:

- **Action One.** Daisy kisses Gatsby, making their secret affair no longer secret. Tom is offstage, and does not see the kiss.
- **Action Two.** Back onstage, Tom sees his wife, Daisy, tag Gatsby with the Look of Love.
- **Action Three.** In the driveway at East Egg, Tom grabs Gatsby's yellow car. Sits behind the wheel, orders Gatsby to ride with Daisy. This is a barter deal with Tom calling the shots. The ritual is powerful: wife-swap leads to car-swap.

- **Action Four.** Gatsby does Verbal Combat with Tom in the hotel. When Gatsby claims Daisy's undying love, Tom calls him a crook. Daisy hides behind her tears.
- **Action Five.** Gatsby gives the wheel of the yellow car to Daisy. He sees Daisy's tears. Thinking it will steady her nerves, Gatsby lets Daisy drive.
- **Action Six.** Daisy kills Myrtle with Gatsby's yellow car.
- **Action Seven.** Tom sends Wilson to Gatsby's house at West Egg.
- **Action Eight.** Wilson kills Gatsby in the swimming pool.

Checklist for Rewriting Plot Point Two

☐   How many scenes form your Plot Point Two?

☐   What ties them together? Action? Recurring Object? Dialogue?

☐   On your structural diagram, have you located Plot Point Two and its relation to the other key scenes?

☐   What is the closed circle? Who is the intruder?

☐   Which characters are present? How are they dressed?

☐   What core stories converge?

☐   How many subplots end at Plot Point Two?

☐   What decisions have you made about cast reduction?

☐   What is the setting? What time is it? What's the weather like? Hot? Rainy? Cold? Wind blowing? Does the action take place outdoors or indoors? Both?

☐   How does your Plot Point Two connect to the climax? To the midpoint? To other key scenes?

☐   Dialogue. Who talks? Who has the power? Who gets slapped around?

Exercises for Rewriting Your Plot Point Two

1. INTRUDER AND CLOSED CIRCLE

Gatsby is the intruder. East Egg is the closed circle. Daisy invites him in, kisses him, tags him for execution with the Look of Love. She lives; he dies.

Startline: The closed circle at Plot Point Two is . . . and the intruder is . . .

Writing time: twenty minutes

2. REWRITE PLOT POINT TWO

Use the Thirty-One-Minute Scene Template. One minute for the warmup; five minutes for each section after that.

- **Warmup:** I am rewriting my Plot Point Two because . . . (one minute)
- This is a scene about . . . (five minutes)
- **Setting:** The time was/the place smelled of . . . (five minutes)
- **Character A on Character B:** His/her hairdo looked like . . . (five minutes)
- **Action and Dialogue:** What are you looking at? (five minutes)
- **Intruder/Complication:** What are you guys up to? (five minutes)
- **Climax/Resolution:** Using the long sentence release (see "Weekend 8," p. 129), extend the action to a dramatic climax. (five minutes)

3. CONNECTIONS

What connects your Plot Point Two to the Midpoint? What connects it to your climax? To the Ending?

Startline: Plot Point Two connects to the climax through . . .

Writing time: ten minutes

4. ACTION CHAIN

Study the action chain for Plot Point Two in *The Great Gatsby*, and then build an action chain that connects three or four scenes at the end of your Act Two.

Writing time: ten minutes

5. STORY

Write a bare-bones synopsis. If your first synopsis took twenty minutes, cut the time in half and write for ten minutes. Start with Lovers A and B. If there is no love story in your novel, take a moment to rethink. *Eye of the Needle*, a thriller, has a powerful love story.

Startline: Lover A meets Lover B when . . .

Writing time: ten to twenty minutes

6. CHECK YOUR VERBS

Find a Plot Point Two passage that needs work. Circle the verbs and make two lists. One list for strong verbs like *hit, smash, chop*, and *wheedle*. One list for weak verbs (interiors, infinitives, passive voice, and subjunctive-conditionals starting with *would, should, could*, etc.). At Plot Point Two, your strong verbs should outnumber the weak verbs. Find the ratio of weak verbs to strong verbs. A good ratio would be 2:1, two strong verbs for every weak verb.

If your weak verbs outnumber the strong verbs, you can rewrite using the long sentence release. Set your timer for fifteen minutes and write one long sentence using the connectors *and, so, then, when, and so, and when, and then.* You can use the occasional *but*, but avoid words that swerve the prose toward explanation, like *if, however, nevertheless, although.*

Time for the lists: twenty minutes

Time for the long sentence release: seven minutes

The Rewrite: Writer X Rewrites Plot Point Two

Location change worked so well for Plot Point One—Paris to Provence and First Reunion—that Rhoda suggests the same technique for Plot Point Two. "Three or four scenes," Rhoda says, "connected by an action chain. And be sure to make good use of Kate's camera."

ACTION CHAIN

- **Action One.** Kate takes her Hasselblad to Avignon for repairs and Harry loans her his digital Nikon. (Subtext: The new camera is easy to carry.)
- **Action Two.** Raoul's auto accident initiates the phone call from the hospital that forces Kate to borrow money from Madeleine for plane fare to Los Angeles. (Subtext: Rags to Riches Kate is Cinderella growing old.)
- **Action Three.** On the plane to Los Angeles, Madeleine lectures Kate. Don't be a spendthrift, she says. (Subtext: Madeleine does not know that Charles makes Kate beg for money.)
- **Action Four.** At the hospital, Kate witnesses her husband, Charles, kissing Julie Jean Jardine. (Subtext: Kate sees her house slipping away.)
- **Action Five.** After a few minutes with Raoul, Julie Jean leaves. Raoul blames Kate for not making Julie Jean feel more welcome. (Subtext: Kate does not tell Raoul about the furtive kiss.)
- **Action Six.** On a lonely walk, Kate stops at a pricey wine bar to use the bathroom, where she sees Charles at a table with Julie Jean and her mother, April. They are poring over blueprints. (Subtext: As she shoots pictures with Harry's camera, Kate does not know that the blueprints mean the end of her house in Provence.)
- **Action Seven.** In a lonely hospital corridor, Harry confesses to Kate. He works for April Jardine. He came to France to buy up properties bordering Ventoux Vineyards. He fell in love with Kate. He knows that Madeleine, not Charles, owns the house and the vineyards. (Subtext: Secrets explode at Plot Point Two.)
- **Action Eight.** Kate pushes Harry away. Her life is over. She will lose everything: her son, her husband, her home. (Subtext: Kate does not tell Harry she has missed her period. She could be pregnant with his child.)

LOOKING AHEAD TO THE CLIMAX

After praising X on his action chain, Rhoda suggests a structural diagram that highlights the key scenes in his rewrite. X needs to connect Plot Point Two to the climax.

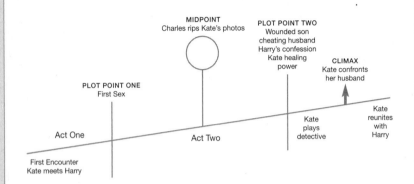

The diagram is a snapshot of X's rewrite to this point. First Encounter to open the book. First Sex to close off Act One and start Act Two. Rhoda emphasizes biology as a dramatic force: The pregnancy initiated at Plot Point One increases her need for a stable home at the same time that she feels her house slipping away. The baby is Kate's secret.

At the Midpoint, Charles rips up Kate's empty house photos because of another secret: He knows the houses were purchased with money from April. Kate is locked in her plot, isolated from Charles and April, so she does not know. While Harry tells Kate about working for April at Plot Point Two, Kate does not tell Harry about the baby in her womb.

"What happens to Harry?" Rhoda asks.

"He still owes April," X says. "He goes back to work."

"Why not have him vanish in Mexico?"

"Harry deserves a second chance," X says.

"Does Kate still love Harry?"

"You bet she does."

"Kate has all the secrets," Rhoda says. "But her time is running out. She knows about April's plan. She knows Charles has stolen Raoul's lady. Why doesn't she just tell everything to Madeleine?"

"Madeleine is tough," X says. "She sees Kate as weak and useless, a pushover."

"Madeleine would make a natural ally," Rhoda says.

"All right," X says. "How does that happen?"

"What about the scale model?" Rhoda asks.

"I got it," X says. "Harry delivers photos of the scale model to Kate."

"When?" Rhoda says.

"Right before the climax. She dumps the photos. Madeleine changes from nasty lady to good guy."

"Brilliant story work," Mr. X. "Now I would like one of your beers, please."

Rhoda smiles as she settles herself on the sofa. She's barefoot this afternoon. She runs a hand through her hair. X shakes his head. No matter how hard he works, Rhoda stays two steps ahead. He hands her the beer. She raises her glass in a toast.

"Photos at the climax, right?"

Rhoda nods. Her eyes are shining.

"Exactly," she says.

Weekend 12: Rewriting the Climax

Climax is the moment of maximum intensity in your novel. This is the moment of confrontation between protagonist and antagonist, the final struggle between the forces of Good and Evil. Let's look at a couple of examples. One is violent; the other is low-key.

The Day of the Jackal, a thriller by Frederick Forsyth, climaxes with the shooting execution of the bad guy protagonist.

The protagonist is an assassin hired to kill the president of France. His code name is Jackal. To reach the climax, the Jackal dyes his hair, repaints his vehicle, murders innocent people who block his way. As we approach the climax, the Jackal snakes his way through tight police security by disguising himself as a wounded war veteran. His bloody trail ends in Paris, a small room in a small hotel that overlooks a patriotic ceremony where the president is an easy target down below. The Jackal has the president lined up in the crosshairs when the door bursts open and he swivels around to see a rookie cop and a man in a business suit. Both men are armed.

The man in the business suit is the Head Cop, the guy who headed the manhunt that tracked the Jackal's journey from the French Riviera (he smuggled the weapon in from Italy) to the climax in Paris.

The object at this climax is a sniper's rifle, custom made to look like a chrome crutch. The weapon, a one-shot single loader, is designed for long-range shooting, not for close quarters. The weapon kills the rookie cop. While the Jackal sweats to reload, the Head Cop shoots him dead.

The Jackal's core story is Rags to Riches. He is a poor boy, a male Cinderella figure planning one last gig before his retirement from killing. His last gig is executing the head of a nation-state.

TIP FOR YOUR REWRITE

At the climax, does the object work for the protagonist? Or does it fail?

In a role reversal, the Head Cop is the antagonist. He and the police are the hunters; they have Subplot One. The Head Cop's core story is Revenge Quest: he's out to get payback for the murders committed along the road to Paris, as the assassin eliminates witnesses.

Contrast this bloody, shoot-out climax in *The Day of the Jackal* with the soft-pedal climax of *The Accidental Tourist*. The scene shifts from Paris to London, to another small hotel, where the protagonist, travel writer Macon Leary, lies in his bed suffering from back pain. Macon's wife, who left him alone in Chapter One, feeds him pain pills packed with narcotics that keep the protagonist in bed. The wife (Sarah Leary) is busy taking over Macon's life's work—writing travel books for the Accidental Tourist series.

The wife's core story is Scapegoat Sacrifice—she's punishing Macon for not showing the required emotions about the death of their son, murdered in the back story in a multi-victim shootout that took place in a hamburger joint. Macon's core story is Queen Replacement. At the Midpoint, he replaces his wife with Muriel the Dog Trainer. A temporary replacement, as the wife invades Macon's life at the end of Act Two. She wants her house back. Muriel reenters the novel at the end, when Macon plucks her from a London street corner.

Muriel's archetype is Cinderella. Macon's archetype is Wounded Knight. When his wife doses him with pain pills, she reveals her archetype: Sarah Leary is a Death Crone administering a deadly elixir. The climax occurs when Macon palms the pain pill, foiling Sarah's relentless takeover of his job and his life. Rejecting Sarah, Macon grabs a taxi, finds Muriel on a London street corner, and orders the cab to stop.

To see a variation on the Queen Replacement core story, check out the climax of *The Namesake* (by Jhumpa Lahiri), which takes place in a flashback while the protagonist, Gogol Ganguli, rides a train home to visit his mother, where he will spend Christmas. Riding the train triggers Gogol's memory of an earlier train ride, taken with his wife, Moushumi, a year before. On this same train, Gogol discovered that his wife was having an affair with a foreign student named Dimitri. As he thinks back, Gogol remembers that the secret affair popped up in a line of dialogue, where Moushumi was quoting her lover: "Dimitri says Siena is something out of a fairy tale." Hearing the strange name, Gogol feels shock. The name Dimitri is familiar to Moushumi, but unfamiliar to Gogol. He asks one question: Is Moushumi having an affair? She nods. Her nod shatters the marriage.

If we stand at the climax and look at the rituals in *The Namesake*, we can see Gogol replacing one woman with another. He replaced Kim with Ruth, Ruth with Maxine, Maxine with Bridget, Bridget with Moushumi. As the core stories collide—Gogol's Queen Replacement slams into Moushumi's King Replacement—the reader feels the irony.

What happens at the climax? What goes on at the point of maximum dramatic intensity in your novel? Answer: Emotions explode, actions get serious and sometimes deadly; someone wins and someone else loses. The winner gains control of the resource base—treasure, secret elixir, castle on the hill, kingdom, piece of land, or Holy Grail—and the loser either dies or gets exiled or tossed into a dungeon. Climax comes from *klimax*, the Greek word for "ladder." A footrace climaxes in seconds and the fastest runner wins. An election climaxes on election night, and the best politician wins. In a novel, the climax happens near the end of the book, in Act Three in a final struggle between Good and Evil, where the protagonist represents Good, and the antagonist represents Evil.

The climax is a competition for control or possession of a resource base. The loser dies; the winner lives; the winner gets the resource base. In popular fiction, the hero stays alive and the monster dies. In the western genre, the good guy in the white hat kills the bad guy who wears a black hat. In a good mystery, the sleuth executes the killer.

Resolution at the climax means a fitting end to the dramatic tension that has been building in your story since Page One. To rewrite your climax, you start with an archetypal synopsis of the novel. You probe the synopsis with an analysis that focuses on character motivation (survival, the Three Goods) and important structural stuff like subplots colliding with the plot. The analysis will cough up insights that trigger your rewrite. By now, you have at least three ways to rewrite a scene:

1. Use the startlines from the scene template ("The time was; the room smelled of . . . ").
2. *Use syntactic flex*: short lines, then chaining, then long sentence release; end with dialogue (see "Weekend 8," p. 129).
3. Start in the middle of the scene by rewriting old dialogue and then insert an object.

Model Climax: *Eye of the Needle*

Our model climax comes from *Eye of the Needle*, by Ken Follett. Let's start with a synopsis.

SYNOPSIS

The time is the mid-1940s. The Great Nations are at war and the Allies are preparing to invade German-held France. Lover A's job is to assess invasion strength, troops and tanks, and airplanes being collected in England.

Lover A is a German spy who carries a stiletto, a knife with a blade like a long needle. His code name is Needle. On his quest for evidence, Lover A kills his English landlady when she finds him with his secret communication device. He kills one of his own, a neophyte German spy, for clumsiness. He kills five British soldiers in the Home Guard because they discover his mission: taking photos of a D-Day deception plan—canvas planes and cardboard tanks—to verify a huge Allied invasion force. And then he heads across England to rendezvous with his U-boat and take the photos to Berlin.

The MI5 spy-hunters, led by a professor of medieval studies, are hot on Lover A's trail. Tracing Lover A's back story, the professor locates Billy P., a boy from the rooming house of the dead landlady, now a soldier in combat. He extracts Billy P. from combat and puts him on a train to finger Lover A. But Lover A, wily as ever, kills poor Billy. The amateur is no match for the professional. Lover A steals a bicycle, then steals a car. When the car breaks down, he hitches a ride to Aberdeen, on the east coast of Scotland, where a big storm has beached all boats. Lover A, daring the elements, steals a boat and heads for his rendezvous. The storm wrecks his stolen boat and tosses him onto the rocky beach at Storm Island. In a state of near death, Lover A climbs the cliff face and arrives at the cottage of Lover B.

Lover B is a beautiful young woman married to a man with no legs. A determined ex-Spitfire pilot, the husband hauls himself up the stairs with his powerful arms. He drives around the island in a refitted Jeep. Lover B has a small child and wants more children. She rescues Lover A. Finds him handsome, polite, mysterious. Admires his strength—who else could survive that storm and climb that sheer cliff face? Wooed by Lover A, Lover B climbs into his bed.

The husband suspects Lover A's cover story. Using his Jeep, retrofitted for a man with no legs, the husband tries to kill Lover A by driving off the cliff. Showing the daring of a Spitfire pilot, the husband is willing to give up his life to kill Lover A. But the husband is an amateur. Lover A kills the husband. He kills Old Tom, the airplane spotter, so he can use the short wave radio to signal the U-boat. Confused by this feeling of love, Lover A is unable to kill Lover B.

When she discovers evidence of her husband's death, Lover B fights for her life. She slams Lover A with the Jeep. She cuts off two of his fingers with an ax. When Lover A tries to contact the U-boat, Lover B blows the electrical circuits by sticking her fingers into a live light socket. The U-boat surfaces. With the precious photos strapped to his chest, Lover A climbs down the same cliff he climbed up to reach Lover B.

Lover B drops a rock on his head.

He loses his grip.

He dies on the rocks below.

ANALYSIS

Lover A's name is Heinrich (Henry) Faber. Henry's archetype is Monster. He is the protagonist and his core story—he kills innocent people to assure the success of his mission—is Scapegoat Sacrifice. Lover B's name is Lucy Rose. Lucy is the antagonist. She works her way through the three aspects of the Triple Goddess archetype. Before she urges her husband, David, to make love, Lucy is a Virgin; when she gives birth, she becomes a Mother; when her husband dies and her child is threatened, Lucy transforms into a deadly Death Crone.

TIP FOR YOUR REWRITE

To confront a Monster, create a magnificent Death Crone.

Lucy has Subplot One. Subplot Two is the professor of medieval studies (his name is Godliman). Subplot Three belongs to a spy-hunter named Bloggs, an MI5 agent who works with the professor. Subplot Four gives us the German point of view from generals and the U-boat commander. Subplot Five belongs to the boy-soldier, Billy Parkin, who gets killed when he spots Henry on a train.

The professor's archetype is Wise Old Man. He shares the Revenge Quest core story with the spy-hunter, Bloggs. Both of these spy-hunters want payback for the deaths of all the innocent victims. The professor, the police, and the MI5 agents act for society. The writer keeps the spy-hunters close behind, but not close enough to nab Henry.

By the time we reach the climax, we have seen Henry take eight lives and we want him dead.

The power of the climax in *Eye of the Needle* comes from role reversal: The bad guy has the plot; the good girl—Lucy—has Subplot One. The writer gets added power from biology and mate selection.

Henry likes Lucy's body. Lucy is impressed with Henry's strength, verified by his climb up the cliff face, pelted by wind and rain. Unlike David, Lucy's crippled husband, Henry has legs. He can stand, walk, run, make love. Lucy controls visible resources: a cottage, a warm bed, food, shelter. Before she discovers Henry's betrayal (he lied about killing David), Lucy even gives him her husband's clothes. The island is isolated. It has a radio, another resource that Henry needs to contact the U-boat that will take him back to Germany.

TIP FOR YOUR REWRITE

A stack of bodies justifies the killer's execution at the climax.

Lucy is torn between guilt and desire until she discovers that Henry has betrayed their love. He kills her husband, then lies to her about it. No way can you trust a lover who lies. Maybe if he hadn't lied to her. Maybe if he had suckered her into his mission. Confused by the power of biology (Lucy's lovely body), Henry hesitates, giving the advantage—and the point of view—to Lucy.

Remember this technique for your rewrite:

TIP FOR YOUR REWRITE

There is still time for you to move one of your female characters through the three aspects of the Triple Goddess.

- This shift in the point of view from the Monster protagonist to the Death Crone is the turning point in the climax. When the point of view passes to Lucy, we see Henry reduced in size. First, he shrinks in the eyes of Lucy. Second, she whacks off two fingers with the ax, reducing the number from the biologically perfect five to a gimpy three, making him an instant cripple, in the same league, biologically speaking, as her husband, David. Third, when she drops the rock on him, Henry has shrunk to an insect on a rock wall. Fourth, when he falls to his death, Henry makes a very small corpse on the rocks.
- The switch in the point of view highlights Lucy's transformation from Virgin to Mother to Death Crone. By dominating the story, the Triple Goddess archetype sets this thriller off from hundreds of other thrillers.

Checklist for Rewriting Your Climax

☐ At your climax, which characters are still in the story?

☐ What objects do they bring to the climax? Any money? Jewelry? Vehicles? Garments? Lethal weapons?

☐ Which objects work? Which objects fail? Example: The protagonist of *Eye of the Needle* brings photos and a lethal dagger. The antagonist has a shotgun and an ax and a Jeep that runs out of gas, an example of object failure.

☐ What core stories collide at your climax? The protagonist's core story, Scapegoat Sacrifice, marks him for execution. The antagonist's core story, King Replacement, is always a good choice.

☐ Who lives and who dies?

☐ Who betrays whom?

☐ Who takes possession of the resource base? You're working with biology here—survival of the fittest and the working out of the Three Goods of mate selection. In *Eye of the Needle*, Henry displays his genetic fitness as he survives being slammed by a motor vehicle, losing two fingers to Lucy's ax, and he still has enough strength to climb down the cliff.

☐ Have you made good use of the intruder and closed circle? There are four closed circles in *Eye of the Needle*: Great Britain, Storm Island, the cottage, and the body of Lucy. The spy is trapped in Great Britain, the largest circle. He escapes by stealing a boat, but the storm tosses him on the beach. Lucy lets him into the cottage and then into her body. Each time he crosses a threshold, the spy risks exposure. When Lucy discovers he has lied to her, she ejects him from the series of closed circles.

☐ Does your novel have one climax? Two? Three? Example: The *Eye of the Needle* has four climaxes. First, the spy kills the husband; second, the wife chops off the spy's fingers; third, the wife blows a fuse by sticking her fingers into the light socket; fourth, the wife drops a rock on the spy, hitting his shoulder.

Exercises for Rewriting Your Climax

1. DIAGRAM

Draw a diagram locating your climax. If it's not at the end of Act Three, rethink. Your diagram should look something like this:

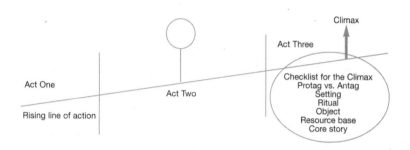

2. ACTION CHAIN

Build an action chain—half a dozen connected actions—that pulls the reader to the climax. Make sure to include one or more objects. The objects at the climax of *Eye of the Needle*, for example, are Jeep, shotgun, stiletto, light socket, and ax.

Writing time: ten minutes

3. THE THIRTY-ONE-MINUTE SCENE TEMPLATE

Rewrite the climactic scene using the Thirty-One-Minute Scene Template:

- **Warmup:** I am rewriting my climax because . . . (one minute)
- This is a scene about . . . (five minutes)
- **Setting:** The time was/the place smelled of . . . (five minutes)
- **Character A on Character B:** His/her hairdo looked like . . . (five minutes)
- **Action and Dialogue:** What are you looking at? (five minutes)
- **Intruder/Complication:** What are you guys up to? (five minutes)
- **Climax/Resolution:** Using the long sentence release (see "Weekend 8," p. 129), extend the action to a dramatic climax. (five minutes)

4. CHECK YOUR VERBS IN YOUR REWRITTEN SCENE

Circle the verbs on one page and make two lists. One list for strong verbs like *hit, smash, chop,* and *wheedle.* One list for weak verbs (interiors, infinitives, passive voice, and subjunctive-conditionals starting with *would, should, could,* etc.). In the climax, your strong verbs should out-number the weak verbs. A good ratio would be 2:1, two strong to one weak. Find the ratio of weak verbs to strong verbs.

If your weak verbs outnumber the strong verbs, you can rewrite using the long sentence release. Set your timer for fifteen minutes and write one long sentence using the connectors *and, so, then, when, and so, and when, and then.* You can use the occasional *but,* but avoid words that allow the prose to reach for abstractions, like *if, however, nevertheless, although.*

Startline: Lover B swings the skillet aiming at the fat face of . . . and then . . .

Writing time: fifteen minutes

The Rewrite: Writer X Rewrites the Climax

X dreams he's threading his way through a thick forest when he hears a knocking sound and a voice calling and he opens one eye to bright sunlight filling his bedroom and the bedside clock reads 11:25 and the knocking is louder now as he rolls out of bed grabs a robe and stumbles to the door.

Rhoda with her bike.

Rhoda in her biker outfit.

Blue helmet and bright yellow safety jacket and black shorts on slim legs and her hand holding out a sack from the Wireless Bakery and Café, her lips saying:

"Morning, Mr. X. Ready to work, are we? You take your shower while I brew your coffee. Time to rewrite that climax."

After the coffee pries his eyes open, X slumps on the sofa telling Rhoda how tired he is, how weary. He wants sympathy. Rhoda sits on the sofa next to X. Her shoes are off. Moving closer, she touches X's shoulder with her shoulder. X feels better when Rhoda is close. He wants to tell her about his dream in the forest when Rhoda says:

"Let's re-create Kate's journey."

"I know," X says. "Up the economic ladder like plain Jane Eyre. A tough climb, too."

"Let's focus on place," Rhoda says. "Starting with Kate's back story, when she moves from California to Paris."

"Okay. Places. California to Paris. That's in the back story."

"And after that?"

"Paris to Provence, when she married Charley."

"And after that?"

"Provence to Paris for Plot Point One."

"Excellent. And then?"

"I get it," X says. "Provence to California for Plot Point Two. California to Provence carrying all those ugly secrets. Provence to Paris for the climax."

"Very good. What secrets does Kate know?"

"She knows Charley's shagging Julie Jean. She knows Harry's working for April, buying up properties. She knows April wants the house. She knows Madeleine owns the house and the vineyards."

"What about her baby? Who else knows?"

"No one," X says. "Only Kate."

"Does April know that Madeleine, and not Charles, is the real owner?"

"Not yet."

"What objects surface at the climax?"

"Photos of the scale model," X says.

"And what happens when Madeleine sees the photos?"

"Character transformation," X says. "Madeleine shifts sides. She changes from enemy to friend."

"Feeling better, Mr. X?"

"I feel wired," X says. "Fired up and ready to roll."

With Rhoda's help, X builds an action chain that runs through a series of closed circles. The innermost circle is Madeleine's heart. Kate must reach that heart and transform Madeleine from enemy to ally. Madeleine is inside her Paris apartment, another closed circle. The apartment is on the third floor inside a building, another closed circle. If the elevator is broken, Kate must climb stairs. The outer circle is Paris, where Harry delivers the photos of the scale model. To build a ramp to his climax, X starts his action chain with Harry shooting photos of the scale model.

Action. In April's conference room, Harry shoots photos of the scale model.

Action. Gare du Nord, Paris. Harry delivers the photos to Kate.

Action. Kate crosses thresholds. Outer door. Stairs. Door to Madeleine's apartment.

Action. Kate brings photos to Madeleine. Before Kate can remove the photos from the envelope, Charles arrives with contracts and a check made out to Madeleine for fifteen million American dollars. Paris is pricey; this money from America will cushion Madeleine's golden years.

Madeleine is ready for some cash. Her rosewood desk is piled high with unpaid bills. Her landlord has just raised her rent. To purchase the Paris apartment would cost $2.5 million.

Action. Kate has lost. As she heads for the door. Charles makes a smart remark about her pregnant belly and Kate slaps him, a sharp crack in the Paris afternoon. Charles grabs Kate; she loses her grip on the envelope; photos from California spill onto Madeleine's white marble floor. Kate drops to her knees. Tears wet her face. Charles is frantic; growling, he snatches photos, cursing. He rips a photo. Madeleine studies the photos.

LEARNING CURVE

Throughout the novel, Madeleine has talked about selling a piece of land (vineyards take work to keep going); but never the house, with its orange clay tennis court built by her grandfather Antoine in the Twenties.

- a California orange grove turned into a strip mall—bulldozers, men with chain saws, hard hats
- April Jardine in a hard hat presiding over the destruction
- Charles studying a blueprint—a huge machine pouring concrete where once were orange groves
- a building complex going up
- a sweeping shot of the D'Amboise vineyards in Provence, April and Charles with a survey crew
- Harry's photo of the scale model of Club D'Amboise in Provence

LEARNING CURVE

The climax to *A House in Provence* uses the device of an intruder (Kate) penetrating a series of closed circles: Madeleine's building, Madeleine's apartment, and the sacred blood bond between Mother and Son. The intrusion works because Kate carries a sacred object— photos in an envelope—that prove Charles D'Amboise to be a louse.

Action. When Charles tries to snatch away the photo, Madeleine glares at him. Marching to the telephone, she calls her lawyer. Charles begs her to sign. This is a one-time offer. The buyers are impatient.

Action. Kate slips to the floor, passes out. Wakes to find herself in a small bedroom, hearing loud shouting, and then the bedroom door opens and Charles bursts in. He curses Kate. Calls her a whore, a slut, a common street *poule*. Accuses her of adultery. Madeleine sends Charles away. Sits on the bed, thanks Kate for saving the house in Provence. The two women hug. Madeleine can see that Kate loves the house while Charles does not. Madeleine promises not to steal Kate's baby. Kate invites Madeleine to Provence.

Weekend 13 : Rewriting the Ending

How will you end your novel? What will your last page look like? Feel like? Will you follow in the steps of writers like Jane Austen, shoving the characters offstage and grabbing the spotlight while the author explains what happened?

Will you dazzle your reader with a final image that pulses with symbolism, like the blinking green light that ends *The Great Gatsby*? Or will you choose a moving image: the black sables against the white snow at the end of *Gorky Park*? Will you end with your protagonist in stasis, like the wounded protagonist reading a book at the end of *The Namesake*? Will you end like *Jane Eyre*, with your protagonist at home, comfortable with herself, married to Mr. Right, with a child to assure her genetic success?

To rewrite the ending for your novel, you look at the fate of the characters: who lives, who dies, who gets married, who goes to jail, who has (or will have) genetic success. You look at core story—how your main characters made it to the end. And you check out your cast of characters to see who has possession of the resource base, the object of desire. You repeat the questions you asked when you first did your character work. What do these folks want? What do they really need? What will they die for? What will they kill for?

Getting to the End

If your protagonist does not make it to the end, follow a character who does. *Jane Eyre* makes it to the end. She starts in a cage in Act One, wearing rags. In Act Two, she climbs the economic ladder at Thornfield, her notion of a resource base. In Act Three, she inherits money and rescues Mr. Rochester. They get married. They make a baby. The baby has Rochester's eyes, proof of reproductive success.

Jay Gatsby, a male Cinderella, dies in his West Egg swimming pool a dozen pages before the end. Gatsby's death at the climax leaves the stage to the survivors: Death Crone Daisy, Tom the racist womanizer, Jordan Baker the gossip, and narrator Nick Carraway, the voice of the author. The final image in *The Great Gatsby*—Daisy's green light blinking on-off, on-off—clings to the reader's brain long after the book is done. Literary scholars who have not lifted Daisy's mask to peer at the Death Crone skull see the green light as symbolizing hope. Gatsby saw it as an invitation: Come on over, big boy; see how long you'll last on my turf. Love, Daisy.

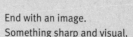

TIP FOR YOUR REWRITE

End with an image.
Something sharp and visual.

Core Story: Pathways to the End

- A Rags to Riches character ends the story with riches.
- A Grail Quest character finds the appropriate Holy Grail, tailored for genre and age. (Money, love, safety, peace, death.)
- A Revenge Quest character ends with a reward for having exacted payback.
- A Coming of Age character winds up older and wiser and often wounded.
- A female King Replacer ends up with a new king. A male King Replacer ends up with the queen and control of the resource base.
- A male Queen Replacer ends up with a new queen who is probably younger and prettier and more fertile. A female Queen Replacer ends up with the King.
- Most characters who practice Scapegoat Sacrifice wind up dead.

Who Grabs the Resource Base at the End?

Story is a competition for a resource base. Competition can be sporting, like two tennis players playing for the same trophy, or two runners who run to win. Competition can be deadly: two gunfighters shooting it out at high noon. Or two armies struggling for control of an empire. Competition adds drama to your story. When the Wicked Stepmother blocks Cinderella's path to the Royal Ball, that is competition. When Cinderella's foot fits that magic slipper, she verifies her princess genes. The resource base in Cinderella is the Royal Castle. To gain access, Cinderella barters her resource, female fertility. The king wants an heir. With the prince's help (he donates the sperm), Cinderella will produce an heir. By trading on her fertility, Cinderella ascends to Upper World. When she ascends, her Rags to Riches story ends. She has gained access to her resource base, represented by the royal castle. But it's such a good story that writers keep rewriting it, giving it a new spin. Changing the setting to fit the time; changing the resource base to entice the new audience. For Melanie Griffith (Cinderella Tess in *Working Girl*), the resource base is a job in the financial end of Big Business. Let's look at some non-Cinderella endings.

THE NAMESAKE: PROTAGONIST LOSES RESOURCE BASE

For Gogol Ganguli in *The Namesake*, the resource base is the American Woman, the fertile female who is not Bengali, who can help him escape his heavy Indian heritage, who can help Gogol cross the threshold into America. And stay there.

At the end of *The Namesake*, Gogol goes home to his mama, a full-blood 100-percent Bengali female. He's been wounded by his wife's betrayal, her insulting affair with a Frenchman of minimal resources. He has no children. His Queen Replacement story is over. Gogol's mating strategy did not bring success and this novel ends where it began, with the protagonist back home, back in exile, shut off from America. The final image shows Gogol Ganguli reading the short stories of Nikolai Gogol, the Russian writer.

This book needs a sequel.

GORKY PARK: PROTAGONIST SURRENDERS RESOURCE BASE

The resource base in *Gorky Park* is sables, those sleek producers of sable fur. The killer is the King of Fur. He steals sables from Russia, transports them to his sable farm in America. The sleuth kills the killer, a King Replacement ritual, and takes momentary possession of the sables. Instead of doing his job and returning the sables to Mother Russia, the weary sleuth opens their cages and turns them loose. A symbolic gesture, freeing the sables gets the sleuth in trouble back home. But on the aesthetic side, it provides an unforgettable final image—"black on white, black on white, black on white, and then gone"—a word-picture of Russian sables against American snow.

PRIDE AND PREJUDICE: PROTAGONIST SHARES RESOURCE BASE

Jane Austen's *Pride and Prejudice* opens with all five Bennet sisters unmarried and their aggressive mother, Mrs. Bennet, plotting to get them married before it's too late. The novel ends with three sisters married—Elizabeth, Jane, and Lydia—but a problem remains: While Elizabeth and Jane married well, their sister Lydia married badly. A half-century before Darwin, a savvy British novelist was writing about survival of the fittest based on careful mate selection and access to a life of wealth and good resources.

Instead of writing a scene at the end, Austen creates thirteen paragraphs of careful commentary, where she judges the characters on their handling of the competition for resources. The writing is a perfect example of an *expository* ending, where the author steps onstage to explain while the characters stand passive in the wings.

Bare-Bones Synopsis—*Pride and Prejudice*

There are sixty-one chapters in *Pride and Prejudice*; there are thirteen paragraphs of exposition in Chapter 61, the ending. To place Austen's judgments in context, here's a synopsis.

- Lover A resides at Longbourn, a modest English country house, with her parents (Mr. and Mrs. Bennet) and four unmarried sisters.
- Mrs. Bennet wants Lover A to marry the pompous Mr. Collins, a cousin and the designated male heir who will inherit Longbourn.
- At a country ball, Lover A challenges Lover B to a dance and he refuses.
- Lover A's sister, beautiful Jane Bennet, falls in love with Mr. Bingley, a comrade of Lover B.
- When Jane catches cold, she is invited to get well in the Bingley guest bedroom.
- Lover A walks through mud and rain to be with Jane.
- Miss Bingley, Mr. Bingley's nasty sister, turns up her nose at the mud on Lover A's dress. (Subtext: Miss Bingley is Lover A's main competition for Lover B.)
- Mr. Collins proposes to Lover A; she refuses, wounding his pride.
- Mr. Wickham, a soldier, claims that Lover B cheated him out of his inheritance.
- Mr. Collins becomes engaged to Charlotte, best friend of Lover A.

- In London, the nasty Miss Bingley is rude to Jane, snuffing out her hopes of a proposal from Mr. Bingley.
- On a visit to Charlotte, her newly married friend, Lover A reencounters Lover B.
- Lover B proposes to Lover A. She refuses for two reasons: 1) because Lover B has blocked Mr. Bingley's courtship of Jane; and 2) because Lover B has disinherited poor Mr. Wickham.
- Lover B pens a letter of conciliatory explanation: He didn't think Jane and Mr. Bingley were serious; he blocked Mr. Wickham (the soldier) from eloping with his own sister, Georgiana.
- Mr. Wickham leaves town with his regiment.
- With her aunt and uncle, Lover A encounters Lover B at Pemberley, his country estate.
- A letter arrives telling Lover A that her sister Lydia has run away with the soldier, the mendacious Mr. Wickham.
- Lover B rescues Lydia: If Wickham will marry Lydia, Lover B will provide the needy couple an annual income.
- Mr. Bingley proposes to Jane and she accepts.
- Lady Catherine, the nasty aunt of Lover B, orders Lover A to promise not to become engaged to Lover B.
- Lover A refuses.
- Lover B proposes to Lover A and she accepts.
- Both Lover A and her sister Jane find husbands.
- The author wraps up all the loose ends with a masterful summation.

Analysis—*Pride and Prejudice*

Lover A is Elizabeth Bennet, also called Lizzie. Lover B is Mr. Fitzwilliam Darcy, the nephew-ward of nasty Lady Catherine de Bourgh, who oozes with Upper World snobbery. As you probably know, either from reading the novel or from viewing a film adaptation, the subtext of *Pride and Prejudice* seethes with closed circles and intruders. The closed circle represents Society. If you have money, you are accepted in Society. If you do not have money, you are outside the walls. Without money, you are an intruder scheming to get in. The novel is a battleground between the women of Lower World and the gold-plated denizens of Upper World. When the novel opens, Elizabeth and Jane (the two oldest Bennet sisters) are both outside the circle. Their Upper World targets— Darcy and Bingley—are inside the circle. Bingley is guarded by his sister, a Death Crone named Miss Bingley. Darcy is guarded by his aunt,

Lady Catherine, another Death Crone. At the end of the novel, Elizabeth and Jane have crossed the threshold into the closed circle of Upper World society. Marriage and money have made them safe. The competition is done. Jane's good looks and Elizabeth's brains have vanquished the Death Crones. The story in microcosm is a disciplined sequence of threshold crossings, tricky, twisty pathways between Lower World and Upper World, and a competition for a scarce resource base that is tense and tight-lipped.

To make sure that the reader understands the intricacies of surviving in society, Jane Austen wrote a brilliant and ironic ending for *Pride and Prejudice*. Austen's rhetorical mode is exposition—explaining what happened to each character. The ironic tone comes from Austen's syntax, careful layers of thinly veiled nuance. The grid below contains compressed summaries of each paragraph, followed by notes on symbolism and subtext in Austen's ending.

PARAGRAPH GRID FOR CHAPTER 61, THE END OF *PRIDE AND PREJUDICE*

Paragraph	Symbol and Subtext
One: Despite having achieved her goal—three daughters out of five married—Mrs. Bennet still behaves badly.	Bad behavior from Mrs. Bennet. See paragraph three, where Mr. Bingley (he married Jane, Elizabeth's sister) moves his entire household to escape Mrs. B.
Two: Mr. Bennet visits Elizabeth at Pemberley, Darcy's estate.	Pemberley represents good resources. Marriage to Darcy brings Elizabeth into the closed circle. Her Coming of Age core story is over.
Three: To get away from Mrs. Bennet, Mr. Bingley buys an estate near Pemberley.	Mr. Bingley uses his resources to avoid the mother's bad behavior.
Four: Elizabeth and Jane train sister Kitty to be "less irritable, less ignorant, and less insipid."	Two sisters welcome a third into the closed circle of polite society, where she has a chance of catching a proper mate. To stay inside, the third sister must modify her behavior.
Five: Sister Mary stays at home with Mrs. Bennet.	No imminent escape from Lower World.

(Continued on following page)

Six: Sister Lydia's marriage to Wickham the scoundrel is not turning out well. She writes to Elizabeth.	Lydia did a lousy job of mate selection.
Seven: Lydia's letter to Elizabeth asks for three or four hundred (pounds) a year.	Lydia is the intruder trying to get inside the closed circle.
Eight: Elizabeth and the author analyze Lydia's letter. Key words: afford, economy, expenses, income, insufficient, support, cheap, discharging their bills, spending.	Elizabeth's analysis displays her brain power, a sign of good genes. She understands frugality as a way of hanging on to good resources.
Nine: Mr. Bingley, irritated by Lydia and Wickham, wants them to go away.	Bingley got away from the mother; now he's got the sister and her scoundrel husband intruding inside his tight closed circle. Life is tough for the shy guy.
Ten: Miss Bingley, who wanted Darcy for herself, decides to be cordial to Elizabeth.	With Elizabeth inside the closed circle, the antagonist sheathes her dagger.
Eleven: Elizabeth trains Georgiana (Darcy's sister) to speak up and not take any lip from men.	The protagonist turns over the Coming of Age core story to her pretty sister-in-law.
Twelve: Lady Catherine visits Elizabeth and Darcy at Pemberley.	Lady Catherine is a Death Crone with money. When she tore into Elizabeth, she revealed her core story: Scapegoat Sacrifice.
Thirteen: Elizabeth spends time with the Gardiners, who brought her closer to Darcy.	Two Mythic Helpers engineered a reunion of Lovers A (Elizabeth) and B (Darcy). The protagonist pays her dues.

HAVING FUN WITH EXPOSITION—THE RHETORICAL SCAFFOLD

Each paragraph in this final chapter is a summary of a compressed activity:

- Bingley moves his household to escape Mrs. Bennet.
- Elizabeth analyzes a letter from Lydia.
- Elizabeth trains Georgiana.
- Lady Catherine visits Elizabeth, a sign of peace.

To summarize, Austen uses exposition, an explanatory mode—the Latin root is *expositio*, meaning "to explain, to expound"—that holds the characters at a distance from the reader. Exposition stops the story. The safest place to use exposition is at the end of your novel, when the story is already stopped.

We writers love writing exposition because it sounds like our voice. Novelists, beware.

Exposition in the wrong hands is deadly stuff. If you choose an ending driven by exposition, you'll have more work when you rewrite as you craft a syntax built with weak verbs and abstract nouns. Writing good exposition is hot, sweaty work because the structure—a rhetorical scaffold—is buried and often invisible.

Paragraph four of Chapter 61 contains a good example of Austen's rhetorical scaffold. In this paragraph, she caps off sister Kitty's subplot with two carefully wrought sentences: "She [Kitty] was not of so ungovernable a temperament as Lydia and, removed from the influence of Lydia's example, she became, by proper attention and management, less irritable, less ignorant, and less insipid. From the further disadvantage of Lydia's society she was of course carefully kept; and though Mrs. Wickham [Lydia] frequently invited her to come and stay with her, with the promise of balls and young men, her father would never consent to her going."

Here's the passage separated into levels.

1She [Kitty] was not of so ungovernable a temperament as Lydia and,
    2removed from the influence of Lydia's example,
1she became,
    2by proper attention and management,
        3less irritable,
        3less ignorant, and
        3less insipid.
    2From the further disadvantage of Lydia's society
1she was of course carefully kept; and though
    2Mrs. Wickham [Lydia] frequently invited her
        3to come and
        3(to stay)
            4with her,
            4with the promise of
                5balls and
                5young men,
    2her father would never consent to her going.

Irony in the right hands is a subtle cutting tool. In this passage, Austen uses embedded clauses (see level 2, on the preceding page) to pull Kitty away from Lydia, aka Mrs. Wickham.

When you write long sentences packed with irony, you need to follow Austen's example of careful, planned repetition, evident in those three judgmental adjectives (*irritable, ignorant, insipid*) modified by *less*, in level three of the first sentence:

- less irritable,
- less ignorant, and
- less insipid.

The three repetitions of *less* suggest that sister Kitty is salvageable, but barely. Using this kind of subtle repetition (*less-less-less; to come-to stay, with-with*), Austen builds a scaffold for weak verbs like *was ungovernable*, *was kept* (passive voice), *to come; to stay* (infinitives), and *would never consent to her going* (negated subjunctive). The single action verb is *invited*, an important ritual in society. Who gets invited? Who does not? And we are back to the closed circle, inside and outside, Upper World and Lower World, winners and losers.

The nouns in this paragraph are abstract polysyllables: *attention, management, temperament, disadvantage*. Weak verbs and abstract nouns transfer power to adjectives, allowing the writer to be witty and judgmental, damning with faint praise. Is Kitty getting better? Or is she getting worse? Will she survive? Will she perish? The passage about sister Kitty climaxes in level 5 of the second sentence with biology (young men) and a proper social arena for mate selection (mixers called *balls*).

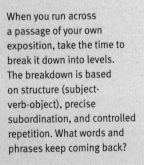

SUBTEXT

The subtext of this expository passage is a tug-of-war. The teams are Elizabeth and Jane versus their sister Lydia, also called Mrs. Wickham. Austen's use of the formal address "Mrs. Wickham" creates a chilly distance between Lydia, the daughter with no smarts, and her two smart sisters, Elizabeth and Jane, who have married money. Lydia tries to drag an unsuspecting Kitty into her web while Elizabeth and Jane want to draw Kitty into the invisible closed circle of polite society. The author's message is

TIP FOR YOUR REWRITE

When you run across a passage of your own exposition, take the time to break it down into levels. The breakdown is based on structure (subject-verb-object), precise subordination, and controlled repetition. What words and phrases keep coming back?

that Kitty is not equipped to fight hard enough to land a man of property from Upper World. Kitty is doomed.

The novel in Austen's time—after being rejected in 1797 under another title, *Pride and Prejudice* was published in 1813—was a wondrous thing because it brought theater into the drawing room. There were no screens to compete with the printed word. Audience attention spans stretched longer than a sound bite. When you write exposition for your ending, remember the shortened length of the attention span in our time.

Checklist for Rewriting Your Ending

☐ Does your protagonist make it to the end? Does your protagonist get married? Go to jail? Slink off into exile like Oedipus the King?

☐ If you have more than one protagonist, do they both (or all) make it to the end?

☐ What core stories make it to the end?

☐ If your characters were locked in a sexual triad earlier in the novel, what happens to that triad at the end?

☐ Any trace of the Three Goods (good genes, good resources, good behavior) at the end?

☐ Who takes possession of the resource base?

☐ What objects make it to the end?

☐ Does the author take over the ending with exposition?

☐ Does the author consider attention span?

☐ Is there a closed circle at the end? Who is the intruder?

☐ How long is your ending? One sentence? One paragraph? One page? One chapter?

TIP FOR YOUR REWRITE

The ending is your chance to wax rhapsodic with your prose. The action is done. The winner has won, the loser has lost, the dust of climax is gone from the air. If you're burning to write some poetic exposition, now's the time. If you're planning a series, you use the ending to hook your audience to the next book. If you're writing a mystery, you can bring your sleuth onstage in an assembly scene to explain how she solved the crime. (Agatha Christie turned the assembly scene into a set piece for crime fiction.) You can see the assembly scene at work in TV shows like *Law and Order: Criminal Intent*, where the Head Cop wraps up the crime, often with much gusto and gesticulation. Long ending or short, it's your call.

Exercises for Rewriting Your Ending

1. PARAGRAPH GRID

Using a grid with two columns, work through your ending. In column one, you summarize each paragraph. In column two, you jot notes on subtext (what's going on under the surface) and symbolism (which objects represent what).

Time for the grid: fifteen minutes

2. WRITE A SCENE

The best endings are dramatic. Even cinematic. Good action, good verbs, solid objects that are filmable. The protagonist maintains the point of view, giving your readers one last look at a good character, giving you a chance to write some memorable dialogue. At the end of *Gorky Park*, with the killer dead and the sleuth bleeding into the snow, Irina Asanova says, "For snow like this I should have felt boots you know." The Death Crone has made it to America—her reason for sleeping with the killer— where she turns back into a Siberian Cinderella thinking about her new American wardrobe. Irina exits. The sleuth releases the sables, a movable resource base. The end.

Startlines for the scene template:

- I am rewriting my ending because . . . (one minute)
- This is a scene about . . . (five minutes)
- **Setting:** The time was/the place smelled of . . . (five minutes)
- **Character A on Character B:** His/her hairdo looked like . . . (five minutes)
- **Action and Dialogue:** What are you looking at? (five minutes)
- **Intruder/Complication:** What are you guys up to? (five minutes)
- **Climax/Resolution:** Using the long sentence release (see "Weekend 8," p. 129), extend the action to a dramatic climax. (five minutes)

3. CORE STORIES AT THE END

What core stories make it to the ending?

Startline: When my protagonist (King Replacement) climbs the steps to the throne, he feels . . .

Startline: When my protagonist turns the corner and sees the place where she started (Grail Quest), she knows . . .

Writing time: twenty minutes

4. INTRUDER AND CLOSED CIRCLE

At the end of a Rags to Riches story, your protagonist should be inside the closed circle. At the end of a King Replacement story, your protagonist should sit on the throne of the old king, or sit on the throne next to the new king. At the end of a Coming of Age story, your protagonist should not only be older, but also wiser.

Startline: At the end of my novel, my protagonist finds herself . . .

Writing time: fifteen minutes

The Rewrite: Writer X Rewrites the Ending

At home in her house in Provence, Kate answers the phone. A call from Raoul. He's at the Nice airport with Molly, his new girlfriend from Pasadena. Uncle Julian calls from Pasadena. He's coming to Provence next week, to visit Kate.

Kate drives to the village of Menerbes for supplies. She's in the butcher shop settling her long-overdue bill when she hears a motorcycle outside. She goes to the door and sees Harry the Biker parking his machine. Kate rushes to him. They hug. They kiss. Kate takes Harry home to her house. They make love. Kate's divorce from Charles is almost complete. Harry takes Kate's car to Avignon, to buy tools for making house repairs. He is back, working on the stairs, when Madeleine arrives from Paris.

Madeleine smiles when she sees Harry working on her house. She introduces herself, shakes his hand, smiles at his American accent.

In the kitchen, Madeleine nods at Kate.

The two women hug.

All is well in the house in Provence.

LEARNING CURVE

As he reaches the end, X feels good. The story is clear and the structure is stable. Looking back across his work, he sees only a few holes that need filling. Rhoda advises X that those holes will get filled when he works the surface.

Etching the
Surface
of Your Rewrite

People hear the word *rewrite* and they think the word *edit*.

Edit means "cut and replace."

Cut the bad word. Replace it with the good word.

Editing is a moral act.

A morality play on the page.

What is good and what is bad?

For fiction, the answer is word-pictures.

Sharp word-pictures are good. Fuzzy word-pictures are bad. You work the surface of fiction to sharpen the word-pictures. See the black bird. A statuette the size of a football with black feathers smooth as stone. Under the slick black exterior there are jewels. To get those jewels, bad people kill other bad people. Sometimes a good person gets caught in the crossfire. Enter the sleuth to hunt down the killer of a good person. The black bird statuette is an object on the surface of a novel called *The Maltese Falcon*. On the surface means right there for the reader to see. That particular object—the black bird statuette—made the writer famous in his time. We should all be so lucky. Or so smart.

When you work the surface, you can start with line-editing, replacing bad words with good, hardworking words that make sharp word-pictures, but it's smarter to start your surface work with recurring objects.

If you repeat a single object half a dozen times across the surface of your novel, you not only tighten the book, but you also lay a path for the reader to follow.

Readers respond to repetition. Slipper enters the wardrobe scene as a lowly ash-girl dresses for a royal ball. Slipper dances on the dance floor. Slipper gets left behind on the steps of the royal castle. Slipper slides onto the foot of the ash-girl to mark her as Princess Cinderella.

On the surface, you can see the magic of repetition working. You have spent a dozen weekends on story, structure, subtext, and texture. Now it's time for surface and style. Style comes from word choice.

- On Weekend 14, you'll discover the power of repeating a single object across a span of your own choosing: page, scene, chapter, act, book.
- On Weekend 15, you'll discover the secret of ratcheting up your suspense using a simple ping-pong structure. Alternation, back and forth: action, exposition, action.
- In Weekend 16, you'll play with a powerful tool called Operation Ratio. This tool gauges the picture power of your prose. If your novel has three hundred pages, you need at least three hundred word-pictures. One word-picture per page, minimum. Operation Ratio guides you to sharper word-pictures.
- On Weekend 17, you'll make the final cuts in the surface of your manuscript. Editing at last. Because you have worked story and structure, these cuts will make but a ripple on the page.

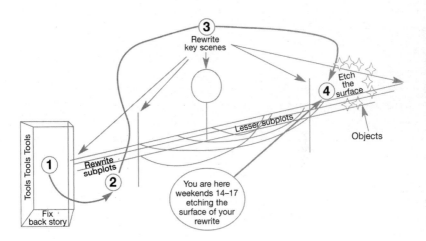

Weekend 14 : Object Lesson

Objects tell your story. When you rewrite your novel, you can tighten your story by repeating a single object: car, train, statue, slipper, harpoon, book. There's a good chance that the objects are already there, in your manuscript, waiting to be found, to be selected, to be repeated, to be laid down like neon breadcrumbs in the forest.

Readers follow breadcrumbs.

Repetition in the first draft is instinctive, reflexive, accidental. In the first draft, you're moving too fast to take time out to make strategic choices about repeating. Repetition when you rewrite, however, is a conscious act, a strategy with a clear purpose. You *choose* to bring a character back and the character grows in importance. You *choose* to bring a setting back (house, city, castle, forest, dungeon, tower, ocean liner, mother ship, alien planet) and the reader feels a sense of familiarity about the place. You *choose* to repeat a word, a phrase, a line of dialogue—and the words themselves take on more meaning.

> **TIP FOR YOUR REWRITE**
>
> Repetition has magic. It's hypnotic and powerful. Like a chant. Like a chorus in a song.

The same thing happens—more meaning, more familiarity, more power—when you repeat an object. Whether the object is a weapon (harpoon, pistol, sword, hatpin), a wardrobe item (bikini, slipper, bathrobe, white dress), a vehicle (yellow car, yellow airplane), a document (journal, diary, manuscript, CD, book), or the statuette of a black bird, the chosen object, when repeated, will cinch up your novel. Will make it feel tighter and stronger. Readers feel this strength as added value.

Repetition of an object gives you control over a span—paragraph, page, scene, chapter, act, the whole book. An object that gets repeated has a chance to grow, to blossom into a symbol.

A symbol accrues meaning. It can represent the story, all by itself. In my writing workshops, for example, I write the word *Clock* on the board. What story is this? No one knows. Then I write the words, *Sacred Tree*. A ripple out there, a gleam of light in the collective eye. I write *Party Dress/Ball Gown* and see smiles. I don't write the word *Pumpkin;* that would give the story away. So I write *Glass Slipper* because I have a point to make about structure. Hands shoot up; voices calling out "Cinderella." They know the story of Cinderella from that single object, the Object Left Behind—a single slipper made of impossible fantasy glass that represents the whole fairy tale and most of its story-clones. Working backwards from the climax, let's check the repetitions of Cinderella's slipper.

- **Climax.** The slipper appears at the climax in the Trying On scene. Our heroine tries on the slipper and it fits. The object is a measurement device. It verifies Cinderella's princess genes, certifies her for a royal marriage to a royal sperm donor. The slipper works like a charm because we have seen it before.
- **Plot Point Two.** Working backwards in the structure from the climax, we find the glass slipper on the steps of the castle at Plot Point Two.
- **Midpoint.** We find Cinderella wearing the slipper while dancing with the Prince at Midpoint.
- **Plot Point One.** We find the slipper in the Wardrobe Scene at Plot Point One.
- **Back Story.** If we plunge into the back story, we find the slipper growing from the Sacred Tree, which is rooted in the grave of Cinderella's dead mother.

With objects, we can play what-if. What would happen if you removed the slipper from the fairy tale? What would happen if you removed the harpoon from *Moby-Dick*? What would happen if you removed the letter of inheritance from *Jane Eyre*? What would happen if you removed the book from *The English Patient*? The black bird statuette from *The Maltese Falcon*? The photos from Ian McEwan's *Amsterdam*? The sable fur from *Gorky Park*? The book of Gogol's short stories from *The Namesake*? The yellow car from *The Great Gatsby*?

Remove the object and you destroy the story.

Objects are important. Repeat an object and it cinches up your story. If you believe, stop reading and start tracking objects in your manuscript. If you still need convincing, keep reading. And while you read, make sure you circle the objects in red.

Object: The Black Bird in *The Maltese Falcon*

The black bird statuette in *The Maltese Falcon* made the writer, Dashiell Hammett, a famous man. The black bird dates from the Crusades. A peace offering from the Knights of Malta, it's about the size of a leather football. Legend says the thick black paint covers a layer of precious gems cemented onto gold. The statuette is the movable resource base in Hammett's novel. It's the object of desire, what all the characters want. When a character dies, the reason is lust for the black bird. The bird surfaces fourteen times in twenty chapters, a good example of a planned repetition that made the author famous.

SYNOPSIS: *THE MALTESE FALCON*

The setting is San Francisco in the late 1920s when the sleuth meets the killer in his office. The sleuth is Sam Spade, the killer is a beautiful femme fatale Death Crone named Miss Wonderly who hires Spade to tail a man named Thursby. Spade gives the job to his partner, Miles Archer. Archer is killed, Thursby is killed, and Miss Wonderly returns to Spade's office as Brigid O'Shaughnessy. Brigid needs Spade's help. He takes her money.

Before Spade can go to work, Joel Cairo, a shadowy Levantine, pops into his office, pulls out a pistol, and says he wants the black bird statuette. Spade knocks Cairo out. Cairo, a small-time crook, is replaced by Casper Gutman, a slimy crime boss who fills in the back story on the bird, its history with the Knights of Malta, its trail of blood and death. Spade, forever irreverent and cynical, calls the bird a "dingus." When his search for the bird is unsuccessful, Spade returns to his office, where a ship's captain named Jacoby delivers the bird and then dies on Spade's office floor.

Spade sends his secretary, Effie Perrine, to stash the bird in a parcel room. With the bird in his possession, Spade barters with Gutman; he wants to trade the bird for one of his gunmen. At the climax, Gutman scrapes away the bird's black surface but finds no gold underneath. After one last kiss, Spade turns the beautiful Brigid over to the cops. She killed his partner; she deserves to die.

OBJECT IN THE SUBTEXT

Before it enters the story in a dialogue line, the bird gets two characters killed—Miles Archer and Floyd Thursby. The characters discuss the bird from Chapter 2 to Chapter 16, when it finally appears, delivered by Captain Jacoby to the sleuth's office. The bird is wrapped up. The package has the shape of a football. The captain coughs, he staggers, he dumps the football, and he dies. With the messenger dead, the sleuth takes possession of the black bird.

The bird shimmers with history, mystery, and irony. The irony pops up at the climax in Chapter 19, as Casper Gutman, the chief thief played to perfection by Sidney Greenstreet in the film noir movie adaptation, wheezes his way through a ritual scraping of black paint, removing the bird's masklike exterior. Using his little knife, Gutman tries to dig his way down through the paint to the fabled treasure horde of jewels and gold dating from the fourteenth century. The knife scrapes black paint. Shavings of black paint curl, fall to the table top. But no treasure emerges. The track on the black bird climaxes with the bleak irony of film noir. All that trouble, all those dead victims, all for nothing. The world is a wasteland with a fake falcon at dead center.

When the book was adapted for the movies, the object not only survived the journey, it provided a structure for the film: first appearance in a dialogue line in minute 37 (Act One); entrance onstage in minute 110 (Act Two); final appearance at the climax in minute 141 (Act Three). The object that controlled the structure of the novel also controlled the structure of the film adaptation—because moviemakers can film objects.

In the table below, "Office" is the office of Sam Spade. "Home" is Spade's apartment. "Lair" is the killer's apartment. "Hotel" is the hangout of the chief thief, Casper Gutman. "Room" is the shabby room of the con man. "Ch" is short for chapter. "Min" is short for minute in the film.

BOOK-FILM COMPARISON: THE MALTESE FALCON

Ch	Book	Scene	Film	Min
4	Con man wants black bird	Office	Same words	37
6	Sleuth: $5,000 for black bird	Office	Same money: $5,000	48
7	Killer barters with con man	Home	Same barter scene	56
9	Sleuth interrogates killer	Office	Same interrogation	70
10	Sleuth searches killer's lair	Lair	Killer back story	76
11	Sleuth interrogates chief thief	Hotel	Same interrogation	87
13	Chief thief: history of the bird	Hotel	History: glorious gold falcon	98
13	Sleuth: The dingus is worth $2 mil?	Hotel	Value goes up	102
14	Sleuth searches con man's room	Room	No bird	107
16	Jacoby delivers bird, dies	Office	Same dead man delivery	110
17	Effie hides bird in parcel room	Street	Same concealing technique	112

(Continued on following page)

18	Barter: bird for fall guy	Hotel	Barter: bird for fall guy	128
19	Paint scrapings: fake bird	Hotel	Gutman discovers fakery	141
20	Revenge: Killer's back story	Hotel	Spade fingers Killer	142

OBJECT LESSON FROM THE FILM ADAPTATION

The falcon is a movable resource base. A perfect example of an object of desire. The characters kill for control of the object. The writer treats the object like a character, building a back story that attaches great value to the object. The back story evokes the Knights Templar, a shadowy gang of clandestine operators from the Crusades. Chain mail, oaths of secrecy, male bonding in battle, warrior brotherhood. Before the object reaches San Francisco, it leaves a trail of dead bodies in its wake. The savvy writer extends this trail of dead bodies into Act One and links the body of Miles Archer to the sleuth. Miles Archer is the partner of Sam Spade. When Miles dies, Spade goes on a Revenge Quest for the killer. To get to the killer, he has to fight his way through a gang of killers—the white knight battling dragons and infidels—led by the clever fat man, Casper Gutman, who has the power of knowledge: Only Gutman knows the history of the bird. Gutman is a great character; he would sell his grandmother for possession of the bird.

Even before it enters the novel in a dialogue line, the falcon brings death. At the structural level, the falcon works like Cinderella's glass slipper: Each repetition of it tightens the story.

> **TIP FOR YOUR REWRITE**
>
> Conscious repetition of a recurring object, a very left-brain activity, sends the reader a message: "Confident Writer at Work." A single appearance of an object is ho-hum. So what, says the reader, another noun in a sea of nouns, no big deal. Two appearances of the object could be coincidence. But three appearances of the same object points to craft. Keep repeating objects and feel your story tighten.

Object: The Book in *The English Patient*

The object in *The English Patient* is a beat-up copy of *The Histories*, by the ancient Greek historian, Herodotus. The book enters the novel in Chapter One, when the Nurse picks up the Patient's notebook from the bedside table. The book enters the film in the first shot-sequence, when the Burned Man is pulled from the wreckage of the plane by Bedouins. The battered book makes it through the desert, through the adulterous love affair. The book is there near the end of the story, at Climax Two, when the patient dies on his bed in the Italian Villa: "His hand reaches out slowly and touches his book and returns to his dark chest."

The book is a time-travel device. When the Nurse reads to the Patient, he drops through a trapdoor into the back story, where he fell in love with Katharine Clifton, a young bride, married two weeks to her boy-husband, a British spy. In the novel, the Patient lends her the Herodotus and she reads the story of King Replacement in ancient Lydia: Gyges the spear-carrier kills King Candaules and marries his queen, Omphale. When the Patient hands Katharine the book, he also hands her his heart.

Through careful repetition, the Herodotus takes on magic. When Ondaatje's novel became a world-class film, the book survived the movie adaptation, the turbulent transition from page to screen, where it became a container for Almásy's heart. In this same book-to-film transition, Katharine Clifton grew from a minor character in the novel to a major character in the film. As her role enlarged, Katharine had more chances to invade the tight closed circle of Almásy's personal space, another example of an intruder penetrating a closed circle.

In the novel, Katharine borrows the book and reads the story of Gyges, Candaules, and Queen Omphale. In the film, she asks to borrow it and gets refused. Katharine is the antagonist; she wants to get to this guy, penetrate his closed circle. In the desert, she wants to paste her drawings onto his pages, to get her objects close to his words. Here's a scene from an early film script (you can find scripts online).

INT. SHELTER – DAY

Almásy sits alone, writing into his Herodotus, a map folded in front of him, from which he makes notes. Katharine comes across with a clutch of her sketches from the cave wall. Hands them to him. They're beautiful.

ALMÁSY

What's this?

KATHARINE
I thought you might paste them into your book.

ALMÁSY
We took several photographs, there's no need.

KATHARINE
I'd like you to have them.

> ALMÁSY
> (handing them back)
> There's really no need. This is just a scrapbook. I should feel obliged. Thank you.

> KATHARINE
> (exasperated)
> And that would be unconscionable, I suppose, to feel any obligation? Yes. Of course it would.

Katharine is already turning, walking as far from him as the cramped shelter permits. He continues with his maps.

Fast-forward: Now we fast-forward through a terrible windstorm that buries men and vehicles in deep desert sand. After the sandstorm, as they dig together in the sand, Katharine tells Almásy that her husband is a spy; he is here in the desert to make aerial maps of North Africa for British intelligence. Hearing this news, Almásy changes his mind about the book:

> ALMÁSY
> Could I ask you, please, to paste your drawings into my book?

Checklist on Objects

☐ What are the three or four really important objects in your novel?

☐ Which objects start on Page One and stretch to the end?

☐ Is each important object attached to a specific character?

☐ Do the objects change hands? When?

☐ How would you classify the recurring objects? Weapons? Money? Other treasure (gold, jewelry, bearer bonds, the family silver)? Vehicles? Toys? Machinery? Documents? Wardrobe items?

☐ What insight have you gained by inserting an object into dialogue?

☐ Are you using the close-up to describe objects?

☐ Have you used the CUT TO exercise to amplify the power of an object?

Exercises for Working Objects

1. TRACKING OBJECTS IN YOUR FAVORITE NOVEL OR FILM

Find an object that recurs at least three times in the fabric of your favorite novel or film: money, weapon, wardrobe item, vehicle, photo, precious rock, recurring tree, timepiece. Here's a list for starting out:

- Ahab's harpoon in *Moby-Dick*
- Quint's harpoon in *Jaws*
- Cinderella's slipper of glass or fur
- the magic pumpkin in "Cinderella"
- bowl of porridge in "Goldilocks and the Three Bears"
- the sniper's rifle in *The Day of the Jackal*
- the cocaine needle of Sherlock Holmes
- the morphine needle in *The English Patient*
- *The English Patient's* book of Herodotus
- the black bird statuette in *The Maltese Falcon*
- sable fur in *Gorky Park*
- the tawdry dress in *A Body in the Library*
- the yellow car in *The Great Gatsby*
- the wrist watch in *Leaving Las Vegas*
- the letter in *Jane Eyre*
- fire in *What's Eating Gilbert Grape*
- fire in *Rebecca*
- birthday cake in *What's Eating Gilbert Grape*
- nude photos in *The Big Sleep*
- the eco-boat in *Waterworld*
- the fuel truck in *The Road Warrior*
- the necklace in *The Princess and the Frog*
- the deathbed in *Evening* (Susan Minot)
- the briefcase in *Working Girl*

Writing: Choose one book or one film. Note the location of the object by chapter and act. (In films, you can note the location by the minute.) Name the scene. Lock down the setting: time, place, lighting, temperature, season. List the characters present. Summarize the action at each location. If you're working with multiple appearances of your recurring object (like the book in *The English Patient*, the sickbed in Susan Minot's *Evening*), seek help from a writing friend. Keep listing objects until you feel the book tighten. Which objects merit more attention? Which objects need more appearances?

Listing time: thirty minutes

2. REPLICATE

Exercise 1 (above) alerts your writer's brain to objects. Now you need to track objects in your manuscript. Make a list, noting locations (scenes, page numbers, etc.). When your list has fifteen to twenty objects, circle the one object that seems important to the story.

If your list shows large gaps where this key object fails to appear, use this replication exercise to ram it home.

Startline: The recurring object in my novel surfaces in Act One when . . .

Startline: The recurring object in my novel surfaces in Act Two when . . .

Startline: The recurring object in my novel surfaces in Act Three when . . .

Writing time: five minutes for each appearance

3. CUT TO

Use the CUT TO exercise to stretch your recurring object from Page One to the end. Keep each entry short; write from memory if you can. Don't use dialogue; cling to image and action. As you write the CUT TO, you will feel the book getting tighter. Repetition of a recurring object gives you control over the long span. The technique is easy because there are no penalties, only rewards. If you repeat the word, the reader's brain gets the message.

Startline: We open with the protagonist holding . . .

Writing time: one hour

4. BUILD NEW SCENES USING OBJECTS IN THE DIALOGUE

If your CUT TO exercise generated new scenes, you can start building by writing a short dialogue (five to ten minutes) that contains an object. If the dialogue hums, keep going. If the dialogue does not hum, toss in an object, something with value, and let the characters go.

Startline: What's that in your hand?

Startline: What's that in your pocket/valise/closet?

Startline: Hand over my keys, please.

Startline: Where's my money, Miles?

Startline: Damn your eyes, Madame, did you bring the thingamajig or not?

Writing time: ten minutes

The Rewrite: Writer X Rewrites Scenes for the Camera

Rhoda sets three exercises for Writer X. First, describe what the camera means to Kate. Second, draw a diagram. Place the camera in all the key scenes. Third, write thumbnail sketches for the camera in each key scene. X grabs his notebook and goes to work.

1. WHAT THE CAMERA MEANS TO KATE

Kate's camera is an old Hasselblad, 500 series. It's a gift from Uncle Julian. The camera is Kate's window on the world. It's part of her identity. By framing the world in her viewfinder, she asserts momentary control. She stops the world from moving, catches a piece before it flashes past. When she met Charles D'Amboise, Kate was shooting still shots on a TV set in Paris. Charles was a publicity agent for celebrities. He hired Kate to do a photo shoot of a rising star at the Cannes Film Festival. When Kate married Charles, he forced her to stop working. Charles hates the Hasselblad, so Kate keeps it locked away in her darkroom.

2. DIAGRAM

Writer X's diagram is a snapshot of the camera and the photos moving through the novel.

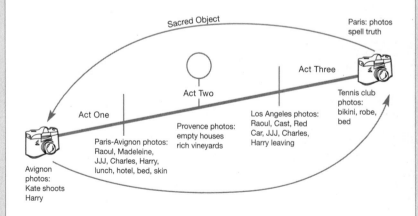

On the diagram, Writer X draws an arc from the end to the opening to remind himself how the rewrite started with a bang when he moved the camera from the beach to the square at Avignon. He draws a second arc that stretches from Avignon to the end. He shows the double arcs to Rhoda.

"That was your idea, wasn't it? Moving the camera from the end to the beginning?"

"Yes."

"How did you know what would happen?"

"I didn't know for sure."

"You seemed very sure to me," X says.

"I took a gamble, Mr. X. Recurring objects are very powerful. Now get to work on your notes."

3. THUMBNAILS: WORKING THE CAMERA IN EACH KEY SCENE

PAGE ONE AND AFTER: Avignon. Kate's camera captures Harry's image. There is magic here as Harry falls under Kate's spell. When she hurries to her car, Kate drops the lens cap, a part of Kate's camera. The lens cap is Cinderella's Object Left Behind. When he delivers the lens cap to the house, Harry connects with Kate.

PLOT POINT ONE: Kate's Paris photos foreshadow the sordid affair between Charles and the pretty blonde, Julie Jean Jardine. Kate is the Outsider; the intruder ejected from the closed circle. Back in Provence, Kate turns her camera on Harry.

MIDPOINT: Alone in the Ventoux Valley, Kate shoots photos of the empty houses. When dinner guests see her work—they are artists, like Kate—they remark on the emptiness. "Like a plague," says one guest. Enraged, Charles grabs a photo, tears it into shreds. "The neighborhood is alive and well," Charles says to Kate. "Perhaps the dead thing is you."

> **LEARNING CURVE**
>
> Charles has a secret in his subplot. He sabotages Kate's Hasselblad.

PLOT POINT TWO: When the hospital calls about Raoul's car accident, the Hasselblad is still in the repair shop. Harry Thornburg loans his Minolta to Kate. It's digital, Harry says. Just point and shoot. In Los Angeles, Kate shoots the red sports car, Charles kissing Julie Jean. She shoots April Jardine showing blueprints to Charles in a coffee shop. She returns the Minolta to Harry when he confesses.

CLIMAX: Where Kate dumps her photos and Harry's photos on the table at Madeleine's Paris apartment, revealing Charles as bad guy, transforming Madeleine from antagonist to helper, from enemy to friend.

THE END: Using her repaired Hasselblad, Kate shoots a photo of Raoul arriving at the house in Menerbes with his new girlfriend, a California girl named Molly.

LEARNING CURVE

Harry uses the returned Minolta to shoot photos of April's scale model, which he delivers to Kate at the climax.

LEARNING CURVE

With each repetition of camera and photos, the rewrite gets tighter. Writer X is surprised, pleased, and excited. To celebrate, he invites Rhoda to dinner and she accepts. With one condition: that Writer X wear a jacket and tie.

Weekend 15: Suspense

How does a small-time writer become big time?

Answer: Ratchet up the suspense.

Flashback to the 1970s. Novelist Ken Follett has written ten published novels. Moderate sales, no big hits. He tried shifting genres—crime, science fiction, children's tales—while holding down a real job at a London publishing house. Things changed for Follett at a sales conference, when a publisher suggested that he write a "chase" novel. An outdoor adventure, the publisher said, with action set against the backdrop of World War Two.

Follett responded with a memo about a German spy shipwrecked on an island somewhere off the Scottish coast. The spy carries information—something at stake—vital to the German war effort. The spy is one lone man, working alone; he's pitted against an army of British spy-catchers led by a professor of medieval studies.

The result was *Eye of the Needle*, an international best seller. A story packed with suspense that made Follett famous.

To make certain he had maximum suspense, Follett took no chances. He set up what he called a "very rigid structure" for this book: six major sections, each with six chapters, cutting between each chapter, marking the cuts with shifts in setting and point of view. Follett called his method a "ping-pong" approach.

> **TIP FOR YOUR REWRITE**
>
> With a little work, you can adapt Follett's ping-pong method to your rewrite. Your tools are the grid and the CUT TO.

Setting for Suspense

The year is 1944, the season is early summer. The place is a cottage on Storm Island. The Allies are preparing to invade France, which is held by the Germans. Henry Faber, a deadly German spy, has photos that will expose the Allied deception—empty FUSAG barracks for ten thousand men and a thousand plywood aircraft that look real from the air. (FUSAG is the military acronym for First United States Army Group, which would spearhead the Allied invasion.) As Act Two ends, Henry is waiting on Storm Island for a U-boat to take him and his photos of deception to Hitler. To reach Storm Island, Henry has killed eight people—seven British citizens and one German spy:

- **Chapter 1:** He kills Mrs. Garden (landlady).
- **Chapter 7:** He kills Major Kaldor (Nazi spy).
- **Chapter 14:** He kills Captain Langham, Corporal Lee, and three privates (five Home Guard victims).
- **Chapter 15:** He kills Billy Parkin (fellow roomer at Mrs. Garden's; now a soldier).

Payback is part of writing good suspense. Who will make Henry pay for these eight victims? Follett's answer is structural: in Chapter 17, Henry arrives at the doorstep of Lucy and David Rose on Storm Island. A short time later, in Chapter 23, Lucy climbs into Henry's bed for a heated scene of First Sex that ratchets up the suspense. Henry has killed eight people. When he kills again, will Lucy be one of his victims?

Grid for Compression

The grid that follows compresses sixty pages from *Eye of the Needle*. (Full synopsis at "Weekend 12: Rewriting Your Climax.") In structural terms, these sixty pages span the last part of Act Two and the first part of Act Three—a place of maximum thickness in the novel (all those subplots twisting together), where most rewrites get bogged down. At this point in the rewrite, you must increase the suspense in your story while not giving away the climax.

We pick up the action for the grid in Chapter 23, when Lucy climbs into Henry's bed. We feel the suspense here. Lucy thinks her husband, David, is sleeping. What happens if David is awake? What if he knows he's been replaced?

We end the action in Chapter 32, just before the climax. All the characters—minor actors and walk-ons—wait on the spy. The British spy-catchers are stuck; the German generals are stuck. The outcome of the war depends on a man and a woman on an isolated island off the Scottish coast.

GRID: SUSPENSE IN *EYE OF THE NEEDLE*

Chp	Scn	POV	Setting	Time	Characters	Content	Ping-Pong *
23	1	Henry	Jo's BR	Day	Henry	Fantasy	Expo
23	2	Lucy	Her BR	Day	Lucy & David & Jo	Fantasy	Expo
23	3	Henry	Jo's BR	Day	Henry & Lucy	Sex	Action
23	4	Lucy	Jo's BR	Day	Henry & Lucy	Sex	Action
23	5	Henry	Jo's BR	Day	Henry	Kiss	Action
24	6	Rommel	Château	Day	Rommel & Guderian	Plotting	Expo
25	7	Lucy	Kitchen	Day	Roses & Henry	Kiss	Action
25	8	Henry	Tom's	Day	Henry & David & Tom	Sheep kill	Action
25	9	Henry	Road	Day	Henry & David	Cig Toss	Action
26	10	Sid	FUSAG	Day	Sid & Bull	Watching	Expo
26	11	Spy-catcher 1	Downing St	Day	Spy-catcher 1 & Churchill	Plotting	Expo
27	12	Henry	Cliff	Day	Henry & David	Killing	Action
28	13	Spy-catcher 1	Office	Day	Spy-catchers 1 & 2	Tracking	Expo
28	14	Spy-catcher 2	Jail	Day	Cops/Thief	Q & A	Action
28	15	Spy-catcher 1	Office	Day	Spy-catchers 1 & 2	Tracking	Expo
29	16	Henry	Cliff	Day	Henry	Reflection	Expo
29	17	Lucy	Cottage	Day	Lucy & Henry	Lying/Sex	Action
29	18	Henry	Cottage	Night	Lucy & Henry	Q & A	Action
30	19	Field Marshal	Germany	Day	Generals & Hitler	Planning	Expo
31	20	Lucy	Cottage	Day	Lucy & Henry	Dressing	Action
31	21	Lucy	Cliff/Beach	Day	Lucy & Jo	Discovery	Action
31	22	Lucy	Cottage	Day	Lucy & Henry	Faking	Action
32	23	Captain	Corvette	Day	Capt & Crew	Circling	Expo
32	24	Crew	Cutter	Day	Crew	Betting	Expo
32	25	Officer	Air Base	Day	Pilots	Planning	Expo
32	26	Spy-catcher 2	Air Base	Day	Spy-catcher 2 & Pilot	First Enc	Expo
32	27	Spy-catcher 1	Map Room	Day	Spy-catcher 1 & Col	Smoking	Expo

*PING-PONG = MODE, ACTION, OR EXPOSITION

UNPACKING THE GRID

Notice how Follett paces the action by switching to scenes of exposition. Remember this technique for your rewrite.

Spy-catcher One is Professor Godliman. He runs the spy hunt from London. Spy-catcher Two is Detective Bloggs. He is Godliman's legs, his man in the field. Henry is Henry. Lucy is Lucy. David and Tom and Tom's dog add three kills to Henry's victim list. Stack up eleven bodies and you deepen the reason for revenge. The grid shows walk-ons when needed: three German generals, several policemen, a lone British soldier, a thief, and three groups of British military spy-catchers:

- In Scene 6, General Rommel chats with General Guderian at La Roche-Guyon, the German HQ near Giverny, in northern France.
- In Scene 10, a soldier called Sid watches a local bull ram a horn through a plywood tank at the restricted FUSAG staging area.
- The Thief in Scene 14 is a red herring, a Henry Faber look-alike who carries a stiletto, an object that underlines the value of fake-out objects for suspense in storytelling. Red herrings divert the spy hunt, sapping spy hunter energies.

TIP FOR YOUR REWRITE

Most of the prose in this list of scenes is expository. The characters are *chatting, watching, reporting, circling, waiting, briefing, planning.* Follett uses these expository scenes as breathers to interrupt the Henry-Lucy love story and how their twisted love leads to Henry's killing of David, Lucy's husband.

- The F-Marshal is Field Marshal Gerd von Runstedt, a member of the General Staff, who reports to Hitler about the spy as Scene 19 opens.
- The Captain in Scene 23 is a walk-on character who commands a naval corvette which is circling Storm Island, waiting for a break in the high seas.
- The Crew in Scene 24 serves on a coast-guard cutter waiting at the dock for the same high seas to subside.
- The Officer in Scene 25 is an RAF Squadron Leader briefing his pilots on their mission: to stop that German U-boat from returning to Germany.
- The Col in Scene 27 is Colonel Terry, Professor Godliman's uncle and the head of MI5, British Military Intelligence.
- Churchill is Churchill.

LESSONS FROM THE GRID: PAGE ALLOCATION

Follett devotes all ten pages of Chapter 23 to Lucy and Henry and First Sex. There are five scenes in this chapter; each scene is marked by switches in setting and point of view. In Scene 1, for example, Henry wakes up and fantasizes about Lucy. In Scene 2, Lucy wakes up and fantasizes about Henry, a balancing of male and female desires. In Scenes 3–4, their twin fantasies turn real and they mate. In Scene 5, Lucy leaves the room and Henry moves his precious FUSAG photos to the dresser, then puts them into his jacket pocket, setting up Chapter 25 (Scene 9), when David has possession of the photos. The photos are movable, like the black bird in *The Maltese Falcon*. In Chapter 27, Scene 12, Henry kills David to protect his resource.

Follett devotes all of Chapter 27 to the death struggle between David and Henry on the edge of the cliff. The fight starts when David, hoping to distract his foe, tosses his lighted cigarette in Henry's face. This amateur feint reveals David's amateur status. It guarantees victory for Henry. Victory and body number nine in the stack of corpses.

Let's probe for suspense in Scene 12. The scene opens in Henry's point of view. The jeep is stopped halfway between Lucy's cottage and Tom's cottage. Three scenes earlier, in Scene 9, David mentions the photos and tosses his lighted cigarette at Henry. After two quick CUT TO's (Spy-catcher One and Churchill, a walk-on named Sid) leave the tossed cigarette hanging in the air, Follett continues that same image to start Scene 12. David, an amateur, tosses the cigarette as a diversion. He needs time to grab the shotgun. But Henry the professional sees through the tactic. The two men scuffle. The scuffle ends with David hanging from a scraggly bush rooted to the side of the cliff while Henry, on the cliff top, interrogates him about the photos. Biology seethes in the subtext: These two alpha-male combatants have shared the same woman.

- Henry asks: How did you know?
- The photos, says David.
- Is that all? asks Henry.
- David answers with logic: The spy had sex with David's wife in David's house. No Englishman would stoop that low; therefore, Henry could not be British. If Henry is not British, then he must be a foreign agent, an enemy of the Crown.
- Henry laughs at David's schoolboy innocence. If David hands over the photos, Henry promises to pull him up. When David surrenders the photos, Henry uproots the scraggly bush and David falls to his death, no longer a cliff-hanger, as his yellow oilskin hits the water.

David's death creates two more cliff-hangers: First, how can Henry get the photos off the island, onto the U-boat, and back to Germany? Second, what will happen when Lucy discovers that Henry has killed David? The cliff-hangers generate more scenes.

LESSONS FROM THE GRID: CLIFF-HANGERS AND OTHER INGREDIENTS OF SUSPENSE

Two actions from the grid—first, Lucy climbs into bed with Henry the Spy Scenes 3 and 4) and second, Henry the Spy kills David the Husband (Scene 12)—demonstrate the mechanics of a *cliff-hanger*. What it is. How it works. To create suspense, you need other ingredients: a closed circle setting, characters playing for high stakes, a willing *suspension of disbelief* by the reader, and *cause-and-effect*.

CLIFF-HANGER ACTION. When Lucy enters Henry's bed for First Sex, she assumes that David is sleeping, that he won't hear her making sweaty love with Henry in the next room. Before David can wake up and discover the lovers, we CUT TO the next scene. The CUT TO leaves the reader hanging, as on a metaphorical cliff. In Scene 9, When David tosses the lighted cigarette at Henry, Follett suspends the action—switching the point of view to Soldier Sid at FUSAG, and then to Godliman visiting Winston Churchill—and then he picks up the cigarette in flight to open Scene 12. Henry brushes the cigarette aside and the two combatants struggle for the shotgun. In the execution scene, David uses his wife's

TIP FOR YOUR REWRITE

A rigid chapter structure does not mean that you have a rigid scene structure. In Chapter 32, for example, Follett switches the point of view four times: Henry to Lucy to Henry to Lucy and back to Henry. In Chapter 27, he stays in Henry's point of view for the fight and David's execution; the setting for the whole chapter is the cliff's edge. When you rewrite, build your structure for maximum suspense.

First Sex scene as proof that Henry is not an Englishman. Not only did Henry cuckold David; he did it under David's roof.

CLOSED CIRCLE SETTING. The bedroom setting for First Sex is a closed circle. The bed is a metaphorical island of safety. Henry's journey to Storm Island is a series of closed circle penetrations: the island of Great Britain; the FUSAG bivouac for the Cardboard Army; the ring of spy-catchers; Storm Island, isolated by geography and weather; and Lucy's cottage. To reach Lucy's body in the bedroom, the spy had to spend everything: muscle, brains, willpower.

HIGH STAKES FOR THE CHARACTERS. Henry has photographic proof that the FUSAG troop strength is a sham of cardboard and canvas. If he reaches his goal—putting that proof in the hands of Adolf Hitler—Henry will change the outcome of the war. When she enters Henry's bedroom, Lucy risks everything for a handsome stranger with all his body parts intact. If her crippled husband wakes up, she loses everything: husband, home, marriage, child, life. Until she reaches the climax of the novel, Lucy has no idea that the stakes are so high.

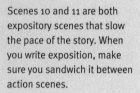

TIP FOR YOUR REWRITE

Scenes 10 and 11 are both expository scenes that slow the pace of the story. When you write exposition, make sure you sandwich it between action scenes.

SUSPENSION OF DISBELIEF. To lull your readers into suspending their disbelief, you must write enough believable, real life stuff that your readers say, *Okay, entertain us.* To write real life stuff, use everyday objects: cigarette, shotgun, jeep, photos, stiletto. To create power in the scene, make sure you have biology in the subtext. In the execution scene—a Darwinian struggle for survival—Henry is older than David, but he has all his body parts. David is younger, but he's missing both legs. David has powerful arms (good workout behavior), and Henry has the cunning of a professional (good espionage genes). David is sporting (good behavior); Henry is ruthless (bad behavior). Henry wins. In the First Sex scene, Lucy is attracted to Henry because he is handsome (good genes) and Superman strong. His climb up the cliff face is a superhuman feat. Lucy Rose, a fertile female, has the chance to mate with a god.

CAUSE-AND-EFFECT. You keep the reader inside the fictional dream with cause-and-effect. When Lucy replaces her crippled, angry husband with the superhuman spy, the reader understands. Lucy is lonely. Henry is handsome. For this moment, the mating instinct overwhelms marital propriety. Now Follett rings the bell of cause-and-effect: Once he mates with Lucy, Henry the killer spy softens; he shows us his heart. Readers like to see chinks in the armor; despite the stack of bodies, the spy is human. A glimpse of his heart, and the reader's loyalties are divided. Henry is the lone hero, after all. The one against the many. How long will his luck last? Which closed circle will turn unsafe?

LESSONS FROM THE GRID: REDUCTION TO ENHANCE DRAMATIC CONFLICT

When he wrote *Eye of the Needle*, Follett could have set the conflict as a battle between Good and Evil. Or the Allies versus the Axis. But as a professional, he knew better. Let's take one more look at the grid. Drop down to the bottom, to Chapter 32, Scenes 23–27. What's going on? Three walk-on characters (including an abstract crew) plus Godliman and Bloggs. There's some dialogue. There's lots of waiting.

The spy-catchers are stuck.

Professor Godliman, Spy-catcher One, is stuck in London. Detective Bloggs, Spy-catcher Two, is stuck on the Scottish coast. The RAF pilots are stuck on the ground, waiting for the skies to clear. The coastguard boat is moored at the pier because of the storm. The closest boat is the naval corvette, but the rough seas prohibit a landing. As the spy-catchers stall out, Follett clears the stage for Lucy Rose to save England and the world.

A lone British woman will have to stop the German spy.

Checklist for Suspense

☐ Pacing: Are you alternating fast scenes with slow scenes? Using exposition (slow) to pace your action (fast)?

☐ What's at stake in your novel? A marriage? A friendship? A house? A human being? The fate of the free world? Is there enough at stake?

☐ Have you found subtextual levels in your dramatic conflict? (Examples from Follett: Faber vs. Lucy; male vs. female; spy vs. housewife; Germany vs. Britain; Axis vs. Allies; war vs. peace.)

☐ Are you using archetypes to maximize conflict? (Examples: Faber is a Monster; Lucy changes her archetype from Virgin to Mother to Death Crone.)

☐ Have you located a section of your rewrite that needs more suspense?

☐ Have you built a grid for this section?

☐ Have you named all the scenes?

☐ How rigid is your structure? (Example from Follett: Six sections, six chapters in each section. The rigid structure allows the writer to have five scenes in one chapter and only one scene in another.)

- [ ] If you shift scenes, are you also switching either the point of view or the setting?

- [ ] Have you chosen a forty- to fifty-page section where you are planning to rewrite for more suspense?

- [ ] What happens if you run the CUT TO exercise and discover you need more scenes? Will you create a couple of new scenes? Or will you back off?

- [ ] How hard are you willing to work to create more suspense?

Exercises for Putting Suspense in Your Rewrite

1. TROUBLE SPOT

For most novelists, trouble in the rewrite surfaces near the end of Act Two. The trouble comes from all those subplots intertwining with the plot. Trouble looks like this:

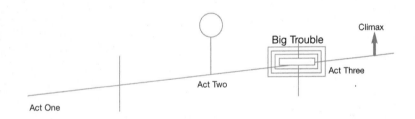

Signs of trouble: You are tired, your brain feels fuzzy, the insights fade, the action stalls, the objects get lost, and the characters lecture one another in tedious monologues. When your characters lecture each other, take a break, then step back for a longer view. Locate the troubled section and lock your scenes into a grid, using these categories: chapter, scene, point of view, setting, time, character, content, and ping-pong. In the ping-pong column, label each scene "fast" (action) or "slow" (exposition). Do you need more short scenes? Do some scenes need cutting? You stir the subtext with biology and the Three Goods. You use the CUT TO device to create cliff-hanger endings. Use the ping-pong structure to build suspense.

2. DRAMATIC CONFLICT

Dramatic conflict comes from clashing agendas. Character A wants the castle; so does Character B. To make the conflict more intense, you increase the power of Character B. Or you add lots of Character B supporters. The secret is one lone hero vs. a gang of bad guys. The director who made *High Noon*, an Oscar-winning Western starring Gary Cooper and Grace Kelly, set the hero up against a gang of bad guys. Here's the situation: The sheriff of a small Western town gets news that a gang of bad guys is coming to kill him. They want revenge. Townspeople—merchants and housewives—advise the sheriff to leave town. His support dwindles. His wife, a devout Quaker, climbs on the same train that brings the bad guys. Sweating, the sheriff faces the bad guys alone.

Startline: The dramatic conflict in my novel comes from a battle between a Monster named . . . and a Hero/ine named. . .

Writing time: ten minutes

3. WHAT'S AT STAKE?

Something at stake can be the life of the pretty damsel in the dragon's castle. It can be the Western town at high noon. It can be the courage of a wife in fear of losing her marriage. It can be buried treasure or a chunk of fertile bottomland located in the middle of a desert with a spring that gurgles all year long. Something at stake can be a house, a city, a country, or the whole free world. When politicians campaign for office, their main topic is something at stake. The enemy, my friends, is at the gates; elect me and I will deal with this problem.

Startline: My protagonist wants to save . . .

Writing time: ten minutes

4. CUT TO

The CUT TO is a structural device where you zigzag from one scene to the next, changing the point of view, trying to make enough changes to stay rhythmic. When you come back around to Character A, you produce rhythm. To use this rhythm in your rewrite, you juggle the pattern of A-B-Cs and then you come back to the same A-B-C, and then you change it on the third run to B-A-C, and then you add other perspectives from D, E, and F.

Creating suspense is a tightrope walk. It requires balance, patience, training, experience. You make a deal with the reader to suspend disbelief while you build a structure that produces excitement. Heart racing, palms wet, the audience wants to know what happens next. You switch the point of view. You advance the time, sometimes by minutes, sometimes by hours or days. You change the location, like a camera nosing into a new scene.

Startline: We open with . . . and then we cut to . . .

Writing time: twenty minutes

5. REWRITING SCENES

Make sure you compress scenes that are too long. Rewrite the scenes that need a touch-up. Use the short version of the Thirty-One-Minute Scene Template:

- The time was . . .; the room smelled of . . .
- His/her hairdo looked like . . .
- What are you looking at?
- Gripping the object, s/he lunged forward, taking her enemy by . . .

The Rewrite: Writer X Builds Suspense

X reads his rewrite. He feels the story slowing near the end of Act Two. Rhoda reads the manuscript and agrees.

"You need more suspense," Rhoda says.

"Okay. How do I get more suspense?"

"Ping-pong," Rhoda says.

"There's a table downstairs," X says. "Let's do it."

"Ping-pong structure," Rhoda says. "You rearrange the scenes to alternate between fast and slow. Between action and exposition."

"I thought we cut all the exposition."

"Draw one of your lovely diagrams," Rhoda says. "Show me where the trouble starts, and where it ends."

X sketches a diagram. It looks like this.

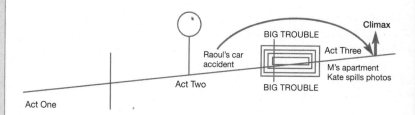

"Beautiful," Rhoda says. "Now tell me what's happening in this part of your story."

"The setting is Southern California," X says. "Kate's kid is in the hospital. Julie Jean is cheating on the kid with Charles. Kate still feels Madeleine's ice."

"Has Harry confessed?"

"Not yet."

"Has Kate discovered the business between Charles and the girl?"

"Not yet."

"There's your suspense," Rhoda says. "Releasing the secrets."

She leads X to the computer. Sits him down. Instructs him to build a grid listing the scenes between Raoul's car accident in Los Angeles and the climax in Paris. X builds a grid that spans sixty pages in his manuscript. Rhoda helps him choose column heads: scene, point of view (POV), setting, characters, action, object, and ping-pong. The "ping-pong" metaphor emphasizes the alternation between action and exposition, between story speed and slowing the story down. When X runs out of grid space, Rhoda suggests code: *C-Room* is the Conference Room. *H-Room* is the hospital room. *R-Club* is the Racquet Club. *Ap* stands for April. *JJJ* stands for Julie Jean. If there are three or more characters in a scene, then *K* is for Kate, *C* is for Charles, *M* is for Madeleine. *H-Wife (Housewife)*, which appears only once, is a walk-on character, one of Harry's tennis students. The action column compresses large actions into a single word. Raoul's auto accident becomes a *Smashup*; Julie Jean's aversive reaction to Raoul's hospital situation becomes *Boredom*. This kind of compression, squeezing a lot of words into one, is good brain exercise. The object column forces X to insert an object into each scene. "Discipline is all," Rhoda says.

GRID: SUSPENSE IN *A HOUSE IN PROVENCE*

Scene	POV	Setting	Characters	Action	Object	Ping-Pong
1	Raoul	Street	Raoul	Smashup	Car	Action
2	Charles	R-Club	Charles, April	Display	Scale Model	Expo
3	Raoul	Hospital	Raoul, Nurses	Threshold Crossing	Gurney	Expo
4	Kate	Provence	Kate, Harry	Bad News	Phone	Action
5	Madeleine	Paris, Apt	M, Kate	Shock	Phone, Ticket	Action
6	Charles	R-Club	C, JJJ	First Sex	Sheets, Tie	Action
7	Kate	H-Room	K, M, Raoul	Weeping	Leg cast	Expo
8	Kate	H-Room	K, Raoul	Whisper	Sickbed	Expo
9	Charles	Hospital	C, JJJ	Squeeze	Hot Car	Action
10	Charles	Corridor	C, K, M, JJJ	Escape	Sandals	Expo
11	Kate	Cafeteria	K, C, JJJ, Ap	Reading	Blueprints	Expo
12	Raoul	H-Room	Raoul, JJJ	Boredom	Leg Cast	Expo
13	Harry	Corridor	Harry, K	Confession	Camera	Action
14	Madeleine	Sun Room	M, C, Raoul	Arguing	Wheelchair	Action
15	Madeleine	Pasadena	M, C, K, Raoul	Pushing	Wheelchair	Expo
16	Harry	R-Club	Harry, H-Wife	Exits	Racquet	Action
17	Charles	Street	C, JJJ	C in Love	Sports Car	Expo
18	Harry	C-Room	Harry	Shooting	Scale Model	Expo

(Continued on following page)

19	Charles	Airport	C, M		Goodbye	Handbag	Expo
20	Kate	R-Club	Kate, Man		Removal	Harry's Sign	Expo
21	Charles	R-Club	C, M		Query	Money	Action
22	Kate	R-Club	K, C, Ap, JJJ		Venus Rising	Pool, Bikini	Action
23	Kate	R-Club	K, C, JJJ		Unbelting	Robe, Belt	Action
24	Harry	Paris	Harry, K		Delivery	Photos	Action
25	Kate	M's Apt	K, M, C		Dumping	Photos	Action

The grid gives X a feeling of control. After she studies the grid, Rhoda suggests that X write some CUT TO's starting with Harry walking off the tennis court to shoot the photos of April's secret scale model and ending with Kate dumping the photos in Madeleine's apartment.

X writes:

We open at the Racquet Club where Harry walks away from a bored housewife on the teaching court, walking to the main building.

CUT TO:

Charles and Julie Jean in her snazzy silver sports car with her blonde hair flying in the breeze and Charles staring at her.

CUT TO:

Harry in April's private conference room at the tennis club shooting photos of the scale model of April's resort in Provence.

CUT TO:

Kate at the Racquet Club in Santa Barbara where a man in coveralls is taking down a sign that reads harry thornburg uspta professional tennis instruction.

CUT TO:

Kate in the club restaurant watching Julie Jean rise from the water in a wet string bikini.

CUT TO:

Kate in the shadows outside Poolside Cabana Number 12 as Charles stands in the doorway wearing a white bathrobe and a woman's hand pulls him into the room.

CUT TO:

Gare du Nord in Paris where Harry hands Kate an envelope.

CUT TO:
The climax where Kate shows the photos of Club Jardine to Madeleine. [The end, with the good guys at home in Provence.]

X shows his work to Rhoda. While she reads, she jots notes in the margin. She looks up at X and smiles as she hands the pages back.

"One quick question," X says. "Some of those scenes at the pool are really short. When I rewrite a short scene, am I supposed to use that Thirty-One-Minute Scene Template?"

Rhoda shakes her head.

"Not at all," she says. "Those are miniscenes. A miniscene has fewer elements. It has a point of view, a place, and a bit of action. So there's no call for using the template."

"Why didn't you tell me this before?"

"Waiting for you, Mr. X."

"Waiting for me to what?"

Rhoda smiles at X. She gets up from her chair, crosses the room, and gives X a good long kiss.

Weekend 16: Operation Ratio

The language of fiction is word-pictures. You write word-pictures and they tell the story. Word-pictures work because the right words—concrete nouns and strong verbs—evoke responses in the reader's brain. Words strung together have their own subtext: emotion, odor, weight, substance, color, shape, nuance. When you make a sentence, or when you stack sentences to make a paragraph, you need to know what's cooking under the text.

To get at the subtext under the words, we use a sorting tool called Operation Ratio. You sort first for nouns and verbs. Nouns have substance. Verbs have action and mood. Strong verbs and concrete nouns make better pictures. To get at the subtext, you sort your verbs for strength and your nouns for weight and substance. For fiction, you want lots of concrete nouns.

Concrete nouns come in three forms: objects, body parts, and landmarks. Objects are movable, stuff you can pick up: *toothpick, watch, pencil, dagger, Glock 9mm, compact, comb, brush, powder box*. Body parts are anatomical: vertebra, throat, waist, head, face, skull, tibia, femur, finger. Landmarks are concrete nouns—you can see them, smell them, hear them rustling sometimes—that are hard to move: *house, cave, mountain, plain, river, forest, tree, hole in the ground, prairie, city, desert, garbage dump*.

Abstract nouns are mental constructs: *administration, frustration, agglutination, representation*. Abstract nouns invaded the English language in 1066, along with the conquering French army that brought the French genes that traveled with William the Conqueror.

Verbs come in three forms: weak, strong, and generic.

TIP FOR YOUR REWRITE

You can write an essay using abstract nouns, but you cannot make a sharp word-picture with them. When you rewrite your prose, cut those abstract nouns and replace with concrete nouns. Have no mercy.

There are four kinds of weak verbs: *interiors*, *infinitives*, *passives*, and *subjunctives*. An interior verb like *think* or *know* or *wonder* can be weak all by itself. The other three varieties of weakness in the verb lock onto each other with little verb-hooks to form compound verbs like "it was thought to have been considered to have [already] begun to become organized." You can smell weak verbs. They stink up your prose. They are bloated entities. They lift the language off the page, away from the hard word-magic of action and description. Some quick examples:

Interiors: *think, know, wonder, assume, decide.*

Infinitives: *to come, to see, to conquer.*

Passives: The ball *was hit* by the boy. The cornerstone *was laid.*

Subjunctives: *would, could, should, may, might, must.* If the boy only *could have hit* the ball, then the game *would* not *have been lost.*

Strong verbs express action: *hit, hammer, bop, hop, slide, glide, ride, run, sit.*

Sit and *run* are generic verbs. Generic verbs are okay—better than weak verbs—but they have zero style. That's where you go to work rewriting. That's where you make decisions, because style is word-choice. Let's practice making style decisions using Operation Ratio. Read the passage below out loud:

> *Milady sat at the dressing table, staring listlessly into the mirror. What had happened? What would become of her? She knew quite well that her husband had been deceiving her, over and over, and quite aggressively. She did not know how long this last had been. Why had he done this to her? Why had he acted so deliberately, so deceivingly? Why was he here? Why couldn't he be the one to vacate the premises? But she knew, dismayingly, that she was the one who would eventually go. Because she had to. Because she could not stay here for one minute longer. Because she could not stay in that house where she had literally spent so many happy hours so delightfully for so many years. No, she would not linger here. She would have to leave but where could she possibly go? She had no money of her own. He had always made her beg for it. If she left, she thought excitedly, she would be unable to accomplish even that tiresome task. And what about la femme, his little friend? What were they talking about? She wondered about that. What . . .*

Let's say you're working through the manuscript, working hard on your rewrite, and you encounter a passage like this. It's a limp offering, but you have an excuse: You wrote these words awhile back, when you knew nothing about story, structure, or style. A passage like this one is a place-holder. You wrote it while you were hot, while you were moving fast. You wrote it for the subtext and you moved on and all the time you were planning to come back and fix it when you rewrote.

You are here. Staring at this place-holder passage.

This woman thinking.

The passage is located near the climax, where the heroine, a married woman called Milady, must decide to fight. Fight for her freedom, fight for her identity, fight for her life. There's a husband offstage. He has the power; he controls the resource base. The husband has a mistress, a younger woman called *la femme*. Milady could lose everything if she gets uppity, so she sits in her dressing room staring into the mirror. She's thinking hard. Working up her courage to fight. The words need some work, but you can feel something in the subtext.

You have a choice here: to cut or to rewrite. The passage needs action and emotion and zip. How do you get zip into a stationary character? Where do you start? If you choose to rewrite, don't tear into the words with your editor's blue pencil. Instead, take the time to deploy Operation Ratio, packing your nouns and verbs into a grid like the one below. The *strong* and *weak* columns are verbs; the *concrete* and *abstract* columns are nouns; the numbers on the far left make counting easy.

GRID: OPERATION RATIO—"MILADY" PASSAGE

#	Strong	Weak	Weak	Concrete	Abstract
1	sat	had happened	would go	table	premises
2	beg	would become	had	mirror	minute
3	left	knew	could not stay	money	years
4		had been deceiving	could not stay	house	task
5		didn't know	would not linger		hours
6		had been	had spent		friend
7		had done	would have to leave		husband
8		had acted	could go		
9		was	had		
10		couldn't be	had made		
11		to vacate	would be unable to accomplish		
12		knew	were talking		

TIP FOR YOUR REWRITE

You use Operation Ratio to find the balance in your prose. If you're writing an essay—or a nonfiction book—your focus shifts from word-pictures to the message. In an essay, you might get away with a compound verb like *would seem to indicate.* Not if you're writing fiction. Reporters on television use phrases like *preparing to start to begin to consider withdrawing.* You can stall with verbs like that; you can't tell a story.

Operation Ratio: The grid shows more verbs than nouns, 27:11. The immediate effect of this ratio is a lack of substance and weight. The passage ripples with inference and dodges action with seven rhetorical questions.

The weak verbs (*had been deceiving, could not stay, would not linger*) outnumber the strong verbs (*sat, beg, left*). The verb ratio is 24:3, or 8:1, weak to strong. That's heavy on weakness, light on strength. There are four concrete nouns and seven abstract nouns, about a 1:2 ratio. (To make word-pictures, you need a ratio of 6:1, concrete to abstract.) So even though you write concrete nouns like *table* and *mirror,* they are canceled out by abstract nouns like *premises* and *years.* To make word-pictures, you need more concrete nouns. In specific terms, that means more objects, more body parts, and more landmarks. To make word-pictures, you also need strong verbs.

Subtext Under the Words

A close look at the language in the "Milady" paragraph gives us subtext. The verb *sat* is a generic verb of action without much movement. Milady is frozen in place. She is frozen by marriage and being under the control of her husband. Milady is a relic.

The verb beg confirms that Milady is a slave in her own household: Her husband forces her to beg for money. The verb *left* is part of Milady's if-then hypothesis, which propels her outside the resource base, the husband's money, the house in London. The verb *left* is contained by a hypothesis about thinking: "If she left, she thought excitedly . . . " No chance of action there.

The noun *la femme* refers to the Other Woman, Milady's competition. The pain of biology oozes from the French noun (*la femme* is younger than Milady; older men prefer younger women), but the passage itself still cries out for word-pictures: visuals and some kind of movement. The subtext contains a sexual triad: Milady+her husband+*la femme.* The sexual triad hints at the core story in the subtext, which is an impending Queen

Replacement. To save herself, Milady must act. Action means strong verbs.

The longest weak verb is a compound that combines the passive voice with a subjunctivized infinitive—"would be unable to accomplish"—that expresses fear by burying the emotion. Subjunctives like "would become" and "could go" clutter the passage. Verbs like "had been deceiving" and "had made" do back flips into the past. There's not enough physical detail to make a word-picture. Offstage, you can hear the sound of the reader coughing.

Instead of telling the story with word-pictures, the writer *tried to explain* Milady's motives through a series of rhetorical questions: Why did the husband betray her? What will happen if she confronts him?

TIP FOR YOUR REWRITE

Seven rhetorical questions supported by a plethora of weak verbs and *–ly* adverbs mark this passage as expository. The writer thinks he's writing narration (telling the story by compressing time), when he's really writing exposition. Exposition is easy to write, but the language of fiction is word-pictures. If you cut your expository passages, you make room for sharper word-pictures.

Because it helps you focus on words and word patterns, Operation Ratio uncovers three fragments where the writer uses *anaphora* (repetition of the same word or group of words at the beginning of three or more sentences, phrases, or fragments) beginning with *because*:

- because she had to
- because she could not stay (here)
- because she could not stay (in that house)

If we include these three fragments in our sentence count, we have a total of twenty-one sentences. If we compare sentences to nouns (twenty-one sentences with only eleven nouns), we know why the passage lacks substance. Knowing the problem allows us to find a solution: more concrete nouns. There are four objects in the Milady passage. There's a table, a mirror, a house, and some generic money. There are no body parts. Two rewrites follow. One is an example of the long sentence release, a form of syntactic flex. The second rewrite transforms the long sentence into proper prose.

The First Rewrite: Long Sentence Release

Milady's hands gripped the edges of her dressing table and her face in the mirror stared back at her a

*face of four decades the eyes still good but the dark
circles under the eyes told of trouble and then with
one hesitant finger Milady touched the mouth in the
mirror the mouth that had kissed her husband that
same mouth that had kissed her child and her lost
lovers and burning now she pulled the finger away
leaving a mark on the mirror a whorl marking her
passing and with a cry she swiveled on the stool
running a fingertip along the base of a powder box
thinking now of the twin at home at her house in
London a gift she remembered bought in Paris on
their honeymoon so long ago twenty years ago that
now seemed a thousand and now, staring hard into
the mirror, Milady looked down the years seeing
herself on her husband's arm, parading through the
Tuileries pretty dress swirling around her ankles
the ankles trim and shapely above the high-heeled
shoes and . . .*

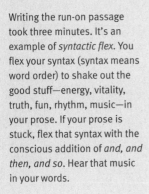

TIP FOR YOUR REWRITE

Writing the run-on passage took three minutes. It's an example of *syntactic flex*. You flex your syntax (syntax means word order) to shake out the good stuff—energy, vitality, truth, fun, rhythm, music—in your prose. If your prose is stuck, flex that syntax with the conscious addition of *and, and then, and so*. Hear that music in your words.

Writing is breathing. To sing, you must breathe. To sing for a long time—a requirement for writing worthy prose—you must exercise your muscles for writing and breathing. To check out your breath line, try reading your writing aloud. The prose in most magazines, books, and newspapers are written with average, everyday syntax. A long sentence might be forty words. A short sentence might be six words. Most of the sentences, however, run between nine and nineteen words. There are weighty forces at work in a culture dominated by screens. Readers have short attention spans; for messages, we rely on images. When you read short sentences, your breath runs short. You get into the habit of writing short. Short is acceptable. Acceptable means you mumble. Mumbling means you write tight. Mumbling means you do not sing. To sing, you must change your breath line. To change the breath line, you play with syntax, changing the length, changing the rhythm, and soon you will be singing.

Back to work.

If the run-on sentence feels too wild for your rewrite, you can make shorter sentences and retain most of the energy because your verbs are better now (gripped, stared, touched, etc.). It's easier going because you have cracked the surface. You have probed the subtext. In the Milady passage, the rhetorical questions are gone, and the nouns have glued themselves onto the word-picture: hands, face, finger, ankle, shards, mirror, powder box. Shaping the passage into shorter sentences takes five minutes.

The Second Rewrite: Proper Prose, Proper Punctuation

Milady's hands gripped the edges of her dressing table. Her face in the mirror stared back at her. Her face of four decades. The eyes were still good. The circles under the eyes told of trouble. With one hesitant finger, Milady touched the mouth in the mirror. That mouth had kissed her husband. That same mouth had kissed her child. And her lover. She pulled the finger away. A whorl remained, her mark on the mirror. Swiveling on the stool, she ran her fingertip along the base of a powder box. She had its twin, at home, her house in London. A gift bought in Paris on their honeymoon, twenty years ago that now seemed a thousand. Staring into the mirror, Milady looked down the years: saw herself on her husband's arm, parading through the Tuileries. The pretty dress swirled around her ankles. The ankles were trim above the high-heeled shoes. She was leaning into her husband, pressing her hip and breast into him and his face turns to hers, and happiness surges through her heart, and then the couple floats closer and the woman in the mirror is not herself of twenty years ago. Shock pulses through Milady's heart. Her face glows red. The woman Milady sees in the mirror is bright, supple, forever young. She has platinum hair, a platinum mouth. She has a good figure, the sleek platinum lines of an actress-starlet. Milady grips the powder box. With a sharp cry, she smashes the woman in the mirror. Smashes her past, smashes her husband, smashes his accursed mistress. Feels the sharp pain of the mirror breaking as her face

shatters, flying glass, sharp shards of mirror in her
voice as the door opens and . . .

ANALYSIS OF THE REWRITE

The place-holder passage had no body parts. This rewrite starts with *hands* gripping the table, her *face* in the mirror staring. Let's use a grid to compare the nouns in the place-holder passage with some nouns in the second rewrite:

GRID: NOUNS IN "MILADY" PASSAGE SECOND REWRITE

Place-Holder	Place-Holder	Rewrite#2	Rewrite#2	Rewrite#2
CONCRETE	**ABSTRACT**	**CONCRETE**	**CONCRETE**	**ABSTRACT**
table	premises	hands	Tuileries	decades
mirror	minute	edges	gift	husband
money	years	table	dress	child
house	task	face	ankles	lover
	hours	mirror	shoes	twin
	friend	eyes	hip	home
	husband	circles	breast	gift
		finger	heart	honeymoon
		mouth	couple	years
		whorl	woman	thousand
		mark	hair	happiness
		stool	figure	shock
		base	cry	past
		powder box	glass	pain
		arm	shards	
			door	

READING THE GRID

Objects and body parts fill the second rewrite with substance. The powder box is a relic. Milady is a relic. When she uses the powder box to smash the face in the mirror, she cracks the surface of the relic she has become. The concrete nouns dominate the passage. The abstract nouns (*honeymoon, years, happiness, shock*) are okay because they are outweighed by concrete nouns. Good verbs (*kissed, smashed, pulses*) sharpen the word-picture. We can feel the timing, sense the rhythm, a beat pulsing in the words. A beat in the language links the words to the stuff of life: Milady's breath and Milady's heartbeat. To get the beat in language, the writer repeats strong verbs. If you nail enough verbs, the writing will live on. Writers die, words stay alive.

Training Your Writer's Brain

Operation Ratio is dirt-simple Stone Age stuff. Circling, listing, counting. It trains the brain. The first grid takes time; the second grid goes faster. Once alerted, your brain will weigh and measure the prose. Once alerted, your brain will choose stronger verbs and more concrete nouns.

Operation Ratio uses numbers to cut through self-criticism, self-judgment, the carping of the internal editor, the crackly static of the left brain. You leave behind those weary, late-night mutterings—you can't write; you don't know grammar; there is no hope; all is lost; doom lurks just ahead; you'll never learn to write—because Operation Ratio transforms the knotty problem of weak prose into a mechanical solution based on counting words.

Checklist for Operation Ratio

☐ Follow the sequence in this chapter, "Weekend 16."

☐ Isolate nouns and verbs: use circles on the page, two colors.

☐ Make two lists: nouns and verbs.

☐ Sort the lists into strong and weak (verbs), concrete and abstract (nouns).

☐ Find the ratio.

☐ Suspend judgment.

☐ Rewrite the passage.

Operation Ratio works fast. You'll see big changes after the first couple of grids. You're keeping the left brain busy sorting and analyz-ing while your right brain takes a good long whiff of the words on the

TIP FOR YOUR REWRITE

Some writers balk at using Operation Ratio on their prose. Too mechanical, they say. Counting words kills creativity. But Operation Ratio is like the other writing tools in this book. If you use the tool, it works. If you don't use the tool, it won't work.

page. Keep the process simple and step by step. Once you have a ratio, pull it down to the smallest numbers possible. For example, a ratio of 12:5 becomes 2:1. A ratio of 27:10 rounds off to 27:9 and then squeezes down to 3:1. Your left brain reduces the columns of words down to a simple ratio and when you rewrite, your right brain finds better words.

It's a partnership effort between the lobes.

In rewriting, two lobes are better than one.

Exercises for Operation Ratio

1. RUNNING OPERATION RATIO

When you run Operation Ratio, you start by making little circles (flattened out circles, more like ellipses) right on the page. Be bold, not shy. Red circles for nouns, green circles for verbs. Using colors keeps your brain alert. When you have all the words circled, make lists. List of nouns, list of verbs. Don't stall around because you don't have lots of experience with parts of speech. You were born with language. Nouns name stuff. Verbs do stuff. You were born knowing parts of speech. Grammar is hard-wired in the brain. Read with a pencil. Pull your brain closer to the page. Take a close look at your style.

You divide your verb list into strong and weak. You divide your noun list into concrete and abstract. You type the words from the list into a multicolumn grid using these categories. When you run Operation Ratio, it's a good idea to start on Page One and then hit all the key scenes, for a running overview of what's cooking in your style. Do the ratios change? Do the ratios stay the same?

Time for Operation Ratio: thirty minutes

2. SYNTACTIC FLEX: SHORT SENTENCES

There are four syntactic flexes for your rewrite: short sentences, fragments, chaining, and the long sentence release we saw earlier in this chapter. When you follow Operation Ratio with a syntactic flex, your rewrite will get deeper. In the next four exercises, we will use syntactic flex to transform a line of description:

> *In the late evening of that final summer—it was*
> *actually July, I recall—we watched with trepidation*
> *from the balcony as a white limousine with Paris*
> *markings seemed to lurch, snorting and bucking, as*
> *it made its tortured, twisty ascent up the crushed*
> *stone driveway, coming to a shivery stop before my*
> *rhododendrons, giving out a bright burst of melodious*
> *song from a triple-throated horn.*

Look at the words. The verb "seemed to lurch" is weak. Time words (*late evening, final summer, late July*) locate the moment in mid-summer. The adjectives are working hard to paint a picture—*white, tortured, twisty, crushed, shivery*—and get better near the end with *bright* and *melodious*. Except for *trepidation*, the nouns (*limousine, rhododendrons, markings, burst, son, horn*) are concrete. The writer chooses to write *trepidation* instead of *fright, dread, alarm, consternation,* or *apprehension*—abstract synonyms of fear. At least, using *trepidation* shows conscious choice. Instead of cutting *trepidation* because it's abstract, let's see what happens in the examples below, when we rewrite using syntactic flex.

SHORT SENTENCES. In this exercise, you compress information into tiny units of two to five words. Short sentence writing follows the simple rule of one syntactic unit for each image or piece of information. When you use short sentences to compress your prose, you'll feel constricted. Like you want to break out. Rip off your chains and break out of the armored straitjacket. Narration compresses time. Short sentences compress narration, squeezing it down. You can hear the squeezing when you read aloud. In Greek rhetoric, this technique is called *asyndeton.* The conscious removal of conjunctions like *and, but, so.*

Sample Rewrite

> *It was 8:30 at night. The month was July. The moon*
> *just up. The car lurched up the drive. The motor*
> *snorted and belched. Character A drove. The horn*
> *tooted. A burst of melody. The horn sang its trilling*
> *song. The door opened. Character A climbed out.*
> *Stood there smiling.*

Writing: Pick a passage from your manuscript and rewrite using
short sentences.

Writing time: seven minutes

3. SYNTACTIC FLEX: FRAGMENTS

To write fragments, you toss out verbs, the beating heart of the
word-picture. In return, you explore a rhythm that can get poetic, not a
bad trade. In Greek rhetoric, this is called *ellipsis*. The conscious removal
of a particular part of speech.

Sample Rewrite

> *Evening at our house. Moon just rising. Stomach all
> a-rumble. Eyes peering ahead. Noise coming up my
> drive. Character A in his rented limo. Resplendent
> Character A. Gorgeous white limo. Gorgeous horn,
> a burst of melody. Character A the Handsome
> Prince. Singing along with the horn. Song of love. So
> gorgeous. Be still, my heart.*

Writing: Extract the verbs from the short sentences you just wrote.

Writing time: seven minutes

4. SYNTACTIC FLEX: CHAINING

Chaining forces you to start the next sentence with the word that ends
the sentence that came before. Before you have time to think. Thinking
returns you to robot prose. Prose to fill magazines and newspapers
and bad TV shows with words like elegant and unique and wonderful.
Wonderful to take a break with chaining.

When you chain, three things happen. First, you feel trapped in a
lockstep sequence not of your choosing, a forced march that obliterates
meaning. Second, your ambitious brain leaps to the end of the sentence
and that sets you free. Third, when you're set free, you start to have fun.
Planning the end of the sentence is more fun than thinking about what
you really want to say. In Greek rhetoric, this is called *anadiplosis*.

Sample Rewrite

> *The time was nine in the evening. Evening of a
> summer in Provence. Provence that bakes in the*

*heat. Heat on the stones under your feet. Feet that
keep time to the rhythm of the tootling horn on the
great white limo. Limo that has come to whisk you
away, a barefoot lady, to the royal ball at the royal
castle. Castle in the sky and Character A in his white
summer suit standing down below with the door of
the limo open. Open and beckoning you down the
steps, running like a schoolgirl, song in your heart.*

Writing: Using the chaining exercise, rewrite a passage from your
   manuscript.
Writing time: fifteen minutes

5. SYNTACTIC FLEX: LONG SENTENCE RELEASE

As we've explored earlier, the long sentence opens up to sudden release.
By writing sentences that go on for fifteen minutes or more, you unearth
sharp insights that help you see where the rewrite wants to go. Through
the conscious addition of conjunctions like *and, but,* and *so,* you spark
the language and keep the reader's attention.

Sample Rewrite

*July of a long hot expectant summer evening and the
white limo lurching up the drive bumping the rocks
of Provence and swerving to miss the rhododendron
bush the clock reading 20:32 and my stomach
churning with hunger and trepidation and the horn
toots throwing a bright burst of melody onto the
soft night air and the white door swings open and
Character A climbs out all in white like a knight in
shining armor and . . .*

Writing: Use the long sentence release after you work Operation
   Ratio.
Writing time: twenty minutes

The Rewrite: Writer X Deploys Operation Ratio

Because he is a wordsmith with a big vocabulary, Writer X resists running Operation Ratio on his style. X assures Rhoda that his style is bulletproof. "Look," he says, "at those balanced paragraphs; dig that precision dialogue." Rhoda admits that X tries to choose good strong verbs and mostly concrete nouns. Then she hands X a sample passage. "Try reading this one out loud," Rhoda says. "Just for a lark."

With great reluctance, Writer X reads aloud. The chosen passage comes from the climax of his rewrite, where Kate exposes Charles in front of his mother. The month is September. Paris is hot; Kate is pregnant, and she feels nauseous. The envelope with the photos is wet with sweat. X rereads the passage aloud, looks at Rhoda.

"Very good, Mr. X. Now it's time for Operation Ratio. Nouns in little circles; verbs in little boxes. Go."

Feeling exposed, X works the passage.

The season is hot, quite warm even for September and she does feel the warmth inside her but that could be the baby as she rings for admittance standing down below wondering what will happen. What will happen to her house? What will happen to her life? What will happen to her baby? Thinking of that, why did she happen to get pregnant when nothing happened with Charles for years and years? What if Madeleine should steal this baby the way she 'borrowed' Raoul? Look where that went. What if Madeleine should install the baby on a tennis court still wearing soiled diapers? Ugh. And then she is inside wondering where she is. Where is Madeleine's floor? And where is her door? The elevator seems to be non-functioning. Non marche pas. So she decides to ascend the terrible stairs. What if Madeleine has chosen this moment to not be at home? Could that happen after all this? And then she thinks of Harry, back there on the sidewalk, and thinking of Harry makes her cry, and she is crying, of course she would be, as she stumbles up the stairs and along the hallway wailing like a banshee and collapsing in front of a white door and looking up as the door opens to see . . .

Grumbling, Writer X builds a grid for Operation Ratio. He starts with weak verbs because he noticed a recurrence of *will happen* when he made circles. That's a weakie. He adds a column for strong verbs, more columns for abstract and concrete nouns.

GRID: OPERATION RATION IN *A HOUSE IN PROVENCE*

#	Weak Verbs	Strong Verbs	Abstract Nouns	Concrete Nouns
1	is	rings	season	September
2	does feel	stumbles	admittance	warmth
3	could be	borrowed	life	house
4	will happen	look	years	baby
5	will happen	opens	years	Charles
6	will happen		moment	Madeleine
7	will happen		home	baby
8	did happen			Raoul
9	to get pregnant			baby
10	went			diapers
11	should install			floor
12	is . . . wondering			door
13	is			elevator
14	is			stairs
15	seems to be			Harry
16	decides to ascend			sidewalk
17	has chosen			tennis court
18	to (not) be			Harry
19	could happen			stairs
20	thinks			hallway
21	Makes . . . cry			banshee
22	would be			door
23	to see			door

Analysis of the Grid

Shock rips through Writer X. His verb ratio sucks: twenty-three weak verbs to five strong verbs makes an ugly ratio of 5:1, weak to strong. The only strength comes from his unconscious repetition of *happen: will happen-did happen-could happen*. With his face burning, X defends his writing. When he wrote this passage, he wanted to show his protagonist's strong concern for the future. He is happier with his noun ratio, only seven abstract nouns to twenty-three concrete nouns, until Rhoda points out that *sidewalk* and *tennis court* and *diapers* are not in the scene—Kate climbing the stairs to Madeleine's apartment—but rather in her head.

What does X do? He does not sit down and rewrite. Instead, he goes for a run. He comes back all sweaty to find Rhoda writing her screenplay. Still burned by the grid, he assumes the corpse position on the floor, his heels propped against the wall, his arms flung wide to simulate his own crucifixion. He closes his eyes and counts down through the chakras—red, orange, yellow, green, blue, indigo, violet—and feels a sweet sense of release, and then he is breathing deep, walking beside Kate on her journey, where he sees a series of threshold crossings—door, gate, stairway, corridor, wrong door, right door, white door—that leap from the words on the grid. Emboldened by Kate's threshold crossings, X rolls to a sitting position. He grabs his laptop and starts writing.

The Rewrite

> *Her heart beats as she presses the button. The Paris sidewalk is hot on her feet, the building where Madeleine lives looms high above. Traffic crowds the street and Kate feels nauseous. She imagines the baby kicking her belly. The image makes her smile and the door clicks open and Kate is inside. Stuffy in here, hard to breathe, elevator gate cool and hard on her fingers. She closes the gate and presses the button. Madeleine lives on Three. Nothing happens. She stabs the red button. Once, twice, three times. Silence in the entryway. Trembling, Kate rakes open the metal gate, stumbles along the corridor to the stairs. At the bottom, she inhales. The air is foul with disinfectant. She presses a button and a light comes on. The lights have timers, making her hurry. Sweat pools under her arms. She feels sweat on her forehead, sweat between her breasts. An endless climb to the top, her fingers clutching the envelope, and then she pushes through the door to Étage Three and walks with heavy wooden legs along the corridor to Madeleine's door. At the end of the hallway a window burns with white light. No air in this hallway.*

She knocks on Madeleine's door.
There is talking inside, muffled
voices, secrets. A lock clicks
and the door opens and a
stranger stands there. He is
pale and fat, wearing a white
shirt and a dressing gown.
Kate smells cigarette smoke,
smoke from a stinking Gauloise.
The man speaks to her and
Kate stammers, giving him
Madeleine's name. The man's eyes cut into her skin,
collarbones, the cleft between her breasts, and she
feels his sharp desire. She hates men. His lips mouth
some words, saying the white door, Madame. Kate
shakes her head. She does not understand. He jerks
his head to the right and Kate turns away. Her legs
are heavy now, stone legs for a stone woman carrying
a stone baby. The eyes of the man are glued to her
going. She arrives at a door painted silky white and
feels nauseous. The heavy sickness pulls her down.
She reaches a hand out to steady herself and the
envelope falls from her fingers. When the white
door opens, Kate is on her knees, her head swirling,
grabbing for photos of the scale model of the resort
hotel complex that will erase her house.

> ## LEARNING CURVE
>
> As he rewrites, X can feel the
> difference in the verbs: *beats,*
> *presses, looms, imagines,*
> *stabs.* Strong verbs create
> action—Kate dizzy, Kate on
> her knees—and then the door
> opens and then . . .

Weekend 17: Final Cuts

You cut your way to a final draft. Cutting means you excise the bad prose. Bad prose blurs the word-pictures. Bad prose slows the story to explain what's going on. Bad prose is made from weak verbs and abstract nouns. Here's an example of bad prose:

> She turned fifteen, then sixteen, then seventeen.
> And then she was in college. She thought that that
> should have been wonderful, but at the end of the
> day, at the termination of her second week, she had
> begun to think somewhat differently, to consider
> options, like, well, that she could have been wrong,
> like totally. It wasn't only the faculty, the students, the
> administration, she thought fretfully, it was basically
> also the way people, like, pointedly, fixedly, stared
> at her when she changed classes, or like she wasn't
> being looked at all, and if things didn't turn around,
> if something really terrific didn't happen, like, well,
> then, she would attempt to begin to make a decision,
> strategically, to begin to start to rectify whatever it
> was she might have been feeling when she finally
> dragged herself to class only to discover . . .

This is a story about a college girl. She had high hopes for college, but now she sounds depressed. Instead of showing the character in a scene—walking to class, crossing the threshold into a hostile classroom, meeting a friend for coffee—the writer stands back and explains from a distance. The writer is working hard, but with each line the language weakens and the word-pictures blur and we are left with a confused, empty-sounding passage. This passage needs cutting. If you need proof, take a minute to circle the nouns and the verbs. Also circle any word that ends in -*ly*. (The -ly words are adverbs.)

- **verbs:** turned, was, thought, should have been, had begun to think, to consider, would attempt to begin to make, to begin to start to rectify, being looked at, didn't turn, didn't happen, should have been, could have been, might have been feeling, dragged, to discover
- **nouns:** fifteen, sixteen, seventeen, college, day, termination, week, options, faculty, students, administration, people, classes, things, something, decision, class
- **-ly adverbs:** totally, pointedly, fixedly, basically, fretfully, strategically, finally

ANALYSIS: There is one strong verb *(dragged)* trying to haul the passage through a thicket of weak verbs. The nouns are either abstract and far away *(termination, decision, administration, options)* or generic *(people, students, class)*. The writer uses *-ly* adverbs *(totally, pointedly, fixedly)* to pump emotion into the passage.

> **TIP FOR YOUR REWRITE**
>
> If you find a passage of bad prose, then cut it from the manuscript. If you need the passage, convert to a scene, starting with sense perception to lock down the point of view.

EXAMPLE: CONVERTING BAD PROSE TO A SCENE

STEP ONE: Use sense perception to lock down the point of view:

> *She entered the room and smelled wet wool.*

STEP TWO: Use action to express emotion. The emotion here is despair:

> *She sank into her seat. Took a deep breath. Her eyes felt wet. When she reached for a tissue, she raked her finger on the zipper. Red pain. She sneezed.*

STEP THREE: Put a second character into the scene. If you're writing a college novel, the other character is a teacher or another student.

> *She heard a voice. She smelled cigarette smoke. She saw a hand reaching for her. She took the hand. Warm fingers, soft skin, a silver bracelet on the wrist. She looked up to see a girl with blonde hair and blue eyes behind glasses. The girl wore a jacket that looked like silk. A red scarf swirled around her throat. Her earrings danced in the light.*

STEP FOUR: Write some dialogue.

> *"Hi. I'm Deirdre."*
> *"Terri Sue. Great scarf."*
> *"You're on my floor. Pentagon Hall."*
> *"That's right."*
> *"I know your roommate, Elise Abrams."*
> *"She send you?"*

STEP FIVE: Now lock down the object in the scene, a book, a chair, a computer for research, drawing materials.

STEP SIX: Bring on the intruder. Another student or a teacher.

STEP SEVEN: Describe the setting. Is the place a classroom? A dorm room? A library? A local pub?

STEP EIGHT: Ratchet up the suspense by adding a time limit. What if the assignment is due at midnight? What if the character who entered the scene is a mythic helper?

When You Can't Cut

Let's say you're rewriting a mystery. The protagonist is a female sleuth who gets called to a crime scene. The crime scene is a closed circle, enclosed by yellow crime scene tape. Stepping across that yellow tape is a threshold crossing, a movement from the everyday world into a world of death. The killer was here, maybe an hour ago. The sleuth is new on the job; this is only her second crime scene and the forensics people are late getting here. You've written this passage half a dozen times, but there's still something wrong. You'd like to cut the passage, finish the book, send it to your agent, sign a fat contract, and spend the advance on a flashy new sports car. But you can't cut the passage because every mystery needs a crime scene. When you start rereading the passage, you get stopped by the first sentence: "The body lay *listlessly, mournfully, terribly*, on the cold ground."

In this opening sentence, the *-ly* adverb *listlessly* modifies the verb *lay*. *Mournfully* and *terribly* are the writer's attempt to describe the sleuth's response. She felt *mournful*; she also felt *terrible*. Three *-ly* adverbs and no word-picture. There's too much distance here between the body and the reader. To rescue this passage with a rewrite, you have to chop out those adverbs and leave the body lying on the ground. You have to get that sleuth closer. You need sense perception to lock down the point of view.

Here's a sample rewrite:

> *She took two steps. The ground crunched under her boots. Her lip trembled and her knees were weak and her feet felt frozen. She stared down at the corpse. The gray hair was matted across the forehead in a splotch of dark dried blood. The eyes were open, staring up. The mouth gaped open, like the mouth of a* penitente *who had just glimpsed God. The teeth were yellow. There was a front tooth missing. The corpse wore evening clothes, a stiff white shirt with a high collar. A black bowtie hung off to one side. Something caught the sleuth's attention, a movement at the edge of her vision, and . . .*

Look what happens when you cut *-ly* adverbs. You open the sentence, letting in fresh air.

- **Action:** two steps closer to the corpse (sleuth moving, not standing still)
- **Sound:** ground crunched (sense perception locks down the point of view)
- **Object:** boots (boots suggest cold weather; winter kill)
- **Touch/kinesthesia/body parts:** (trembly lip and weak knees and frozen feet make the sleuth human)
- **Direction:** stared down (the sleuth is above; the corpse below)
- **Body parts:** gray hair, forehead, blood, eyes, teeth, front tooth (word-picture)
- **Wardrobe:** stiff white shirt, high collar, black bowtie (a party-corpse, perhaps from Upper World)
- **Intruder:** a movement at the edge of the sleuth's vision (penetration into the closed circle of the yellow-tape crime scene ratchets up dramatic tension)

Redemption

To be a writer, you must know how the language works. That includes parts of speech. If you write something like "The sleuth dressed languidly before her mirror," you are using the *-ly* adverb *languidly* to compress mood and the importance of the dressing ritual while the writer takes a breather. Try cutting the *-ly* adverb. The hole that remains when you cut is your chance for redemption with good detail. What does the sleuth see in the mirror? Where is the light? What is she wearing? How is her hair tonight? What is the state of her skin? How is her posture? Is she upright and proud? Is she stooped with sorrow and fatigue? Are there blotchy circles uner her eyes? What if the light changes? What if she hears something behind her? What if an intruder appears in the mirror? What if she sees her mother's face replacing her own?

Decision Time

At this point in the rewrite, as you cut your way to a final draft, be brave, be bold, and when you're reading over your manuscript and you come upon ten pages of thick, story-stopping explanation, give yourself a break. This prose was important to write earlier in the rough draft, as a bridge between scenes, as a place-holder, but now reading it is like slogging through thick jungle. As you circle the nouns, you sense an imbalance, an overweight of fat, Latinate abstractions, and a corresponding overweight of weak verbs. The culprit is exposition, a mode that explains, a mode that exposes subtext and secrets to the reader. When you wrote it, the passage seemed quite good. What to do now? Do you fix the pages? Or do you cut, chop, prune, and toss, making room for word-pictures that tell the story? Don't think. Don't fret about your future as a writer. Instead, stay in the here and now, the present moment, this passage, this stylistic muck, this chance to grow as a writer. These are danger signs:

TIP FOR YOUR REWRITE

If you write an -*ly* adverb, you're planting a weed in the garden of words. Weeds take up space. They steal food and water from the flowers. -Ly adverbs smother word-pictures. Bad prose needs cutting.

- Your protagonist sitting on the edge of the bed thinking.
- Your protagonist staring into the mirror thinking.
- Your protagonist thinking hard while sipping a coffee or taking a drag on a cigarette or driving to work.
- Your protagonist behind the wheel ruminating.
- Your author barging into the story to explain what's cooking.

ADMONITION
Keep the author out of the story.
If the author enters, cut the entry passage.
Cut deep and cut hard and cut without mercy.
If you cut the bad prose, your rewrite gets shorter.
Cutting the bad prose cuts the stuff that needs work.
Cutting bad prose speeds up your final draft.

Exercises for Cutting Your Way to a Final Draft

1. CUTTING -LY ADVERBS

Find the -ly adverb. Cut the adverb and make a decision. Do you need this sentence? If the answer is yes, then rewrite the sentence, starting with a sense perception: smell, sound, taste, sight, touch. -Ly adverbs keep the reader at a distance. When you cut an -ly adverb, you leave a hole. This is your chance to write better prose. Some sentences will be happier just getting rid of a slothful -ly adverb.

Cutting time: ninety minutes

2. BIG PICTURE GLOBAL SCAN

Scan your manuscript for passages of exposition. To detect exposition, look for weak verbs (subjunctives, infinitives, interiors, and passive voice), abstract nouns (*profundity, rotundity, elucidation, anticipation*), and those structural devices like *if-then* that are more useful in writing essays. Here's a quick list:

If-Then	Neither-Nor
Not Only-But Also	Some-Some Others
Either-Or	Nor Nor Nor
More-Than	Not-But

Give each expository passage a name (for example, Kate sipping coffee alone, reflecting) and a location by manuscript page number. Count the passages of exposition and estimate how much of your manuscript is devoted to explanation. Cut what you can cut. Keep going.

Cutting time: ninety minutes

3. SYNTACTIC FLEX

Voice is connected to rhythm, which is why you should read your passages aloud—to find the rhythm. Reading aloud helps you locate pauses, twists, ironic turns, peaks, valleys. Because language is so automatic, so much a reflex, most of us confine our writing to sentences of medium length, medium range, medium power, medium rhythm. It's very politically correct: Your voice sounds like the next voice sounds like the next and the next.

To break this confinement, the solo-singing writer flexes her/his syntax. Start with short sentences: "I sat there. I thought about it."

Move from short sentences to chaining, a linking device: "It was deep night. Night of my escape. Escape from . . ."

When the chaining is done, move to a long sentence. Two hundred words three hundred no punctuation and no capitals just one long sentence that speeds along in a release of insight and emotion. (Change the point of view from first person to third.)

- **Short sentence example:** *She sat there. She thought about it. The ground felt cold. She had no hope. No way to escape. They were after her. Three of them, like harpies.*
- **Chaining example:** *She sat there. There where she sat drinking coffee and thinking about tomorrow. Tomorrow when the baby would be . . .*
- **Long sentence example:** *A future without hope the horizon dark as everlasting night and the walls of her prison closing in like a matchbox made of pewter the smooth gray walls crowding her brain and . . .*

The Rewrite: Writer X Does Some Cutting

"Exposition is a disease," Rhoda says. It happens to everyone, even Writer X. The book is done and Rhoda's helping him with notes for a screenplay. He's reading pages, making tiny line-edits, when he runs across an interior passage that has Kate drinking coffee at a bakery in Menerbes and doing a lot of thinking. The writing is okay, but the passage feels juiceless. When he wrote the passage a long time back, X remembers feeling great, because he was able to enter the protagonist's head. On his second read, X circles his verbs:

Sample Passage: Kate Thinking

It was all coming to an end, she thought, but was it really? She took a sip of coffee, thinking how she would like to open an Italian coffee shop across the street, because the French coffee seemed so harsh and also because Tuscany was too far to drive for coffee when you lived in Provence. She had thought it was over several times, but now it really was, and she freely admitted to herself that she liked to win. She touched the envelope on the table. It held her photos of emptiness, empty houses, empty rooms, verification of her hard work, which she had sent to the committee way back in the summer on a whim, actually, remembering the emotion so truly, fully formed, of making a decision about something, about taking action, doing something at last after having been frozen, contained by disappointment for so long, while seeking absolution for being herself, and then she thought about California, why she had flashed on that she had absolutely no idea, but there she was in the hospital with Raoul all bruised and battered and wounded, staring at her with a glazed look and then reaching for her like a lost child who had wandered inadvertently away from home, and was now, after having been awakened, returning to the fold. And then she thought . . .

X skims the passage. He's getting faster at circling nouns and verbs. From the circled words, he sees a balance of concrete nouns (*photos, coffee, envelope*) and abstract nouns like *emotion, decision, disappointment, absolution, moment* and *verification*. Sees clumps of weak verbs and more *-ly* adverbs than he remembered writing. Reading the passage aloud, he knows why he wrote it—because it revealed Kate's character. Now it feels weak, mushy, frail. Just to make sure, X builds a grid for verbs and *-ly* adverbs. He classifies the verbs as either *neutral* (was, had), *weak*, or *strong*. The grid looks like this:

GRID: "KATE THINKING"—NOUNS AND VERBS

Neutral	Weak	Strong	-ly Adverbs
was	was coming	took	really
was	thought	liked	really
was	would like to open	lived	freely
had	had thought	touched	actually
was	admitted		truly
was	had sent		fully
	having been frozen, contained		absolutely
	thought		inadvertently
	had flashed		
	had wandered		
	having been awakened		
	thought		

When he finishes the grid, and without consulting Rhoda, X cuts the passage. Cutting makes him edgy, but this one has to go. He worked hard on this passage. Lots of careful line-edits, lots of time stolen from work and tennis and bike rides and Rhoda and drinking coffee with friends. When he cuts the passage, X leaves room for a cleaner ending, when Harry Thornburg comes back to Kate.

X shows his work to Rhoda.

"Write the ending now," Rhoda says.

"I'm beat," X says. "How about a quick beer?"

"When you cut that passage, you let in a breath of fresh air. Rewrite now, before the air turns stale again."

He sighs. He grabs his notebook, sets his timer for five minutes, and writes.

Filling the Gap Left by Cutting: Harry Returns to Menerbes

In her studio, Kate stands at the tower window
looking at the road through the stargazer telescope.
No one there. No motorcycle, no biker, no black leather
jacket. Just a dream brought on by too much sun. The
road curves, the rider comes into view. Kate's heart
hammers. She sees dark glasses, a motorcycle helmet.
The rider looks up at her, raises one hand. She hurries
to the bathroom.

In the bathroom, she studies her eyes in the mirror.
Pale blue, to match the floppy old dress.
A streak of dirt there, on her cheek. Kate splashes
water on her face. Takes a deep breath. Does she
want him to come riding back? Should she change
her dress? Should she keep him waiting? What if it's
someone else?

The child kicks the wall of her womb. The kick is
a signal. Get going, girl. Kate exits the bathroom,
walks down the corridor toward the front entry.
Through a high window, she hears the bull roar of
the motorcycle. Then silence as the engine fades. In
her mind, she pictures him raising the knocker. Is that
how love happens? A hand knocking at a door? Her
heart leaping?

Kate reaches the foyer to see
him talking to Clothilde. The
maid's back is arched, her pelvis
canted toward the visitor. The
visitor looks past the maid.
When he sees Kate, his eyes
glow. Kate feels stronger now.
She moves forward, toward the
visitor. A smile creases her face.
In her belly, the child signals
again. The kick of the baby foot.

Kate's feet move faster now.

LEARNING CURVE

Cutting the passage of
exposition makes room in X's
head for a screenplay. Writer
X is tired; Rhoda is relentless.
"Screenplays," she says, "have
all this white space. Much less
work than a novel, and the story
is there, waiting. Shall we start
with a treatment?"

Epilogue

With the novel completed, Rhoda helps X write a treatment, a film synopsis in three acts. The synopsis is seven pages long. It tells Kate's story from the First Encounter in Avignon to the closing scene where Kate is secure at last, safe in her house in Provence.

Rhoda e-mails the treatment to her agent in Los Angeles. When the agent calls, his voice is excited. He has three producers interested in a script. The very next day, Rhoda and Writer X drive into Los Angeles for three meetings.

- The first meeting is midmorning. A Chinese director famous for action films offers $20,000 for a first draft script, rewrites to be negotiated, no writers allowed on the set.
- The second meeting is lunch. An exotic lady-producer with a French accent who sees Kate's story as an art film with a seductive undercurrent of art versus business. The lady is French. Her backers are Swiss. She offers $40,000 for a first draft script. Because she makes lots of changes while shooting, the French producer wants both writers on the set in Provence.
- The third meeting is late afternoon and Writer X droops from exhaustion. The producer is a shiny-headed bald guy wearing a pricey black jacket over a black T-shirt emblazoned with gold neck chains. He wears glasses with purple lenses and flirts with Rhoda. The bald producer sees Kate's story as a romantic comedy. He has two bankable female stars panting for the script. He offers $100,000 for a first draft. He says the magic words, "Oscar-winner."

After the third meeting, Rhoda's agent offers to find a publisher for X's novel.

"Once we sell a script," the agent says, "publishers will break down your door for a chance at the manuscript."

Back home, safe in his condo, Writer X wakes to a knocking at the door. It's Rhoda, with pastries from the Wireless Café. After coffee and pastries, they discuss what happened yesterday, at those meetings. Writer X admits to being blown away. Rhoda smiles.

"It's time for Silent Movie," she says.

"Charlie Chaplin," X says. "Buster Keaton. Old stuff."

"Silent Movie," Rhoda says, "is the writer's answer to commercial chaos. We writers get confused by money and Oscar-talk. Confusion leads to inertia, then stasis, then writer's block. To break the grip of writer's block, you write a silent movie that expands the treatment with action and image. There is no dialogue. Silent Movie lays the groundwork for the finished script. You take Act One. I shall take Act Three. Then we'll unite our talents on Act Two."

Rhoda presses the start key on X's laptop. The screen comes to life. Rhoda opens his word-processing program to a new document. She tells X to write FADE IN. Under FADE IN, he writes:

EXT. AVIGNON, FRANCE–SQUARE IN THE RAIN–MORNING

Rhoda sits back, giving X room to work. X takes a deep breath. He changes the typeface to Courier 12-point. Looks more scriptlike. He stops thinking about money and fame. X is a writer. Writers write. He feels his fingers working. He is not Writer X. He is Kate in the morning in the rain. Kate alone, isolated, empty, waiting. Avignon, the square, Provence, soft rain falling. Go.

FADE IN:
EXT. AVIGNON, FRANCE–SQUARE IN THE RAIN–MORNING

Kate D'Amboise shoots photos in the rain. Empty doorways, empty streets, an empty outdoor café.

A Biker enters the Square. Kate sinks into a doorway. The Biker parks the bike, turns off his engine, walks to the sidewalk café.

Raising her camera, Kate shoots the Biker. He turns, sees her. Keeps watching as . . .

Kate walks to her station wagon. A lens cap falls from her jacket pocket. Rain flattens the hair against her head as she opens the door of the Renault, climbs behind the wheel.

INT. KATE'S WAGON–THE SQUARE–MORNING

Kate looks up to see the Biker at her window. He's holding an object, motioning for her to roll the window down.
Kate shakes her head. Her hands are jerky on the gearshift. She backs the wagon in an arc, away from the Biker.

EXT. BIKER IN THE SQUARE

Holding the lens cap, the Biker watches Kate drive off. Her wagon sputters, coughs a puff of blue exhaust. The Biker tucks the lens cap in his pocket.

INT. HOTEL BEDROOM–CHARLES IN BED SIPPING COFFEE

He watches April Jardine dressing. April moves to the bed, flips the sheet away, drops a business card on his hairy belly, then exits the room.

INT. STONE HOUSE OUTSIDE MENERBES–KATE'S STUDIO

Kate's developing photos. Hearing something, she walks to the window. The sun is out, warming the valley. Down there, curving along the road below the house, is Kate's biker.
Kate checks her reflection in the mirror. Fluffs up her hair. Takes a deep breath.

X looks up from his screen to see Rhoda across the room, typing away on her laptop. A warm feeling comes over Writer X. He feels competitive. He feels soft, pliable, vulnerable. X takes a deep breath. Rhoda looks up. Her smile makes his heart sing.

Writer X returns Rhoda's smile.

Then, filled with love, he gets back to the writing.

Appendix : Feedback

Congratulations. Your rewrite is done and you feel good about the manuscript. The story is solid, the subplots hum, the surface is smooth. Now you're smelling money, you're tasting the tang of writerly fame. You want action. So you print the manuscript, find a literary agent on Google, and then you mail the manuscript off.

ADMONITION
Before you send off your pages, get some feedback. Agents and editors are busy. The writing business is whimsical. The worst mistake you can make is sending off a half-baked product.

DEFINITION

Feedback comes when you hand your work to someone else and say, "Can you please give me some feedback?" When you ask for feedback, you give up control. Time to relax, pull out your trusty ballpoint, and take notes. Feedback opens up the manuscript, rips holes in the fabric of your prose. Better to sew up the holes now, before you send off the manuscript to an agent. There are four ways to get feedback:

SCENE PERFORMANCE. For feedback on a scene, recruit a group of friends—actors are better at scene performance than writers—and assign roles. Assign one reader for each character; assign one reader to read the narration (action and description). Keep your voice out of the scene-read. Your job is to listen, to take notes, to view your work from a perspective not your own. Use a timer on each scene. If a scene runs long, you'll know to cut. If a scene is too short, you might merge it with another scene.

Don't interrupt the reading with helpful hints to the readers. Surrender your words and see what happens. Take notes and let yourself sweat. Button your lip and learn fast.

Pay attention to your emotions—awe, horror, shame, nausea, joy, the taste of greatness, a whiff of fame—during the read. When the reading is over, ask for feedback from your cast. Author restraint is big here. Keep the lines of communication open. You asked for feedback. Write down everything and don't try to fix anything until you have your notes typed and printed. Let the notes cool. Read them over. Find a trouble spot where readers had some difficulty, where they ran into a roadblock or ran off the tracks. Find those pages in your manuscript and deploy Operation Ratio.

Don't fret about the work. Instead, use your tools. You started this rewrite with an empty toolkit. Your toolkit now bristles with writerly tools. Hang tight, keep writing. Let your left-brain editor locate the problems. Let your unconscious do the fix.

COLD READ. Read with a friend across a table. Keep the page count low—five to eight pages per session is max—and then find a neutral zone like a coffee house and sit across the table from your friend. There are two copies of the work. One for you, one for your friend. When you read, alternate paragraphs. When you come to dialogue, alternate voices. The balance is better if your friend also has pages that need reading. Take the mind off your sweat by listening to your friend's voice. Where does it hesitate? Where does it sound bored? Where does it have trouble with a word or a sentence?

When the reading is done, ask your friend for feedback. Where did it slow down? How do I fix it? Help me with that word on page 3.

SINGLE READER ALONE. Here's where you ask a reader to read your manuscript and then feed you suggestions for making it better. You hand over the pages and wait. You bite your nails when you should be doing writing practice. You wonder what's gone wrong. Is the book any good? What will my reader say? Be careful surrendering your pages. Find a reader who can see deep into structure and story.

CRITIQUE GROUP. Here's where you sit in a circle with a roomful of writers. Some groups listen while the author reads aloud. Some groups want copies of the work distributed earlier, to give people time to read and ponder. Other groups want the pages at the same time as the meeting. Reading aloud is better here. Everyone gets up to speed on the same words. Much less confusion. Some people read fast; some read slow. With an oral read, there's less focus on line editing.

Warning to the sensitive: Critique groups are really dangerous. If you are fragile, stay away. If your manuscript is unwieldy, think twice. You need rules for behavior. If the group is big—six or more—then you'll need a time limit for each critique. If there are wide gaps in skill levels, don't bite your lip. Instead, do lots of deep breathing.

To get the most from a critique group, take notes and say nothing. Keep your lips zipped. Don't try to defend your work. If it hums, most people will hear the hum. If it needs work, use the tools. Thank the group for its insight.

ADMONITION ONE: KEEP THE DISCIPLINE

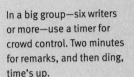

FEEDBACK TIP

In a big group—six writers or more—use a timer for crowd control. Two minutes for remarks, and then ding, time's up.

When you surrender your words, you say you want feedback but maybe what you really want is love. If you don't get love, you feel pain. If you feel pain, you back off. If you back off, make discipline your mantra. Most feedback, critique or otherwise, is structural. Most feedbackers don't know about structure, but you do. Subplot, subtext, texture, the multilayered thing under the surface of your prose. Even at this stage of the rewrite, most problems in the novel will be structural.

ADMONITION TWO: KEEP DOING YOUR WRITING PRACTICE

A novel is a product. It will fade from the shelves. Writing practice is bigger than any novel. A hot novel might make some money. But writing practice can change your life. Writing practice keeps you writing while you wait for judgment on your product. Keep the hand moving. Don't cross out.

ADMONITION THREE: PROBE THE MARKETPLACE

Agents know where the editors are. They know what the editors are buying. Agents specialize. Some do literary. Some do commercial. Some do only nonfiction, children's, celebrities, TV soaps. Do your homework.

If you have a writer friend with an agent, ask for an introduction. Get inside the loop. If you have no writing friends, go to a writing conference and meet some agents. Ask what they want. Tell them what you're doing. Don't worry about formula pitching. A good agent asks questions. Agents are human. They work hard. They get tired. They like to sell stuff. They'll take your stuff if they can sell it. You're in business now; be businesslike with your product.

For lists of agents, Google "literary agents."

Glossary

ABSTRACT NOUN

A part of speech that names abstract, non-concrete mental constructs like ideas and concepts. The word *abstract* comes from the Latin *abstractus*, meaning "removed from concrete reality." Abstractus comes from the past participle, *abstrahere*, which means "to pull away." Latin is a neat language. The Latin prefix *abs* means "away from." The suffix *trahere* means "to pull." Abstract nouns like *extraction, extrapolation, jealousy, philosophy, misconception, agglutination,* and *thought* fill up the page. They convey information by telling. They distort word-pictures. One main function of line editing is cutting abstract nouns to make room in the garden of prose for more word-pictures. *See* Operation Ratio, concrete noun, weak verb, strong verb.

ACT

A section of a play, film, opera, or novel. The word *act* comes from the Latin *agere*, meaning "to drive, to do." To control your rewrite, divide your novel into three acts.

AGENDA

Steps taken by a character to seize the resource base, or object of desire. Example: The resource base in *Cinderella* is the Royal Castle. To get the castle, Cinderella must nab the Prince. To nab the Prince, Cinderella must penetrate the royal threshold and get to the Royal Ball. To penetrate the threshold, Cinderella needs the proper costume. To access the proper costume, Cinderella calls for help. Help arrives from the Fairy Godmother, who brings the glass slippers.

ANTAGONIST

The character who opposes your protagonist. *Ante* means "against" and *agonist(es)* means "one who competes." *See* Monster, Death Crone, Subplot One.

ARCHETYPE

When we say, "The Hero stabbed the Monster," we're using archetypes to tell story. When we say, "Cinderella nabbed the Handsome Prince," we're also using archetypes. Archetype comes from the Latin, *archetypum*, which comes from the Greek, *archetupon*, meaning impression, pattern, or mold. For storytelling (writing, rewriting), we reduce a greater archetype to a lesser archetype—Hero to Warrior; Monster to Dragon—and then to a specific character: Warrior to Beowulf, Dragon to Grendel. Archetypes wield formidable power: Cinderella, a Virgin archetype, has spawned over four thousand story-clones. Jane Eyre is a Cinderella archetype; so is Tess McGill in *Working Girl*. Tess, played by Melanie Griffith, triumphs over Katharine Parker, played by Sigourney Weaver. *Working Girl* is a twentieth-century replay of the archetypal struggle between Cinderella and the Wicked Stepmother. *See* core story, Rags to Riches, King Replacement, Triple Goddess.

ARISTOTLE

The clever, farsighted, deep-peering Greek philosopher (384–322 B.C.) who gave us beginning, middle, and end, which gives us three acts and a climax, which enables the clever writer to build a stick-figure schematic that creates a visible structure for plot.

ARISTOTLE'S INCLINE

A visual schematic of a dramatic structure. A rising line depicts rising action. Vertical lines divide the line into acts. A line with an arrow tip indicates the climax, near the end.

BACK STORY

What happens to the characters before Page One. Back story is the Pandora's Box of secrets. Secrets hold the key to character motivation. Example: In the back story of *Moby-Dick*, the white whale bit off Ahab's leg. This back story trauma drives Ahab to his death at the end of the book. In the back story of *Jane Eyre*, Jane's parents die. As the book opens, she lives with nasty Aunt Reed, a Wicked Stepmom figure.

CHAINING

Writing sentences chained together by end-word first-word repetition. Example: *Repetition like the dog has fleas. Fleas leap off the dog onto my arm. Arm rhymes with charm and you forget the dog and try to get unstuck from nonsense. Nonsense with a funny rhythm.* Rhythm in chaining uses the rigid containment powers of your left brain to short circuit the left-brain editor. Paradox. When you chain your sentences, three things happen. First, you feel trapped in a lockstep sequence that obliterates meaning; second, your ambitious brain leaps to the end of the sentence and that leap sets you free; third, when you're set free, you start to have fun. Planning the end of the sentence is more fun than thinking about what you really want to say. In Greek rhetoric, chaining is called *anadiplosis*.

CHARACTER GRID

An information sorter. Standard column heads are: name, role, archetype, plot or subplot, object, fate, entry, exit, and core story. By isolating plot from subplot, the grid provides the weary writer with a snapshot of texture: subplots stacked under the plot.

CHARACTERS

The people in your story. For a novel you need to fill the three main character roles: protagonist, antagonist, and helper. To support the Big Three, you need half a dozen minor characters and two dozen walk-ons. *See* plot, subplots, Subplot One, and core story.

CHARACTER SKETCH

A brief one-page list of observed character traits—hairdo, eyes, eye makeup, jewelry, clothing—which stimulates a writer's creative guesswork about what motivates characters.

CHRONOLOGY

A ladder of key dates reaching up from the past that stretches to the end of the story. Smart writers use chronology to highlight trauma in the past, trauma that drives agenda in the present.

CLASSIC

A work of art that stands the test of time and becomes a model of the form. In the novel-world, *Jane Eyre*, published in 1847, has lasted over 150 years. Not as long as Greek sculpture, but books are paper and sculpture is stone.

CLIMAX

The high point of a designated story-span: scene, chapter, story.

CLOSED CIRCLE (INTRUDER)

A sacred space: The space can be physical, like a prison, a locked room, a confession booth, a bird sanctuary, a nation-state with borders. The space can be metaphorical, like the psychosociological unity created by two lovers, by a club or platoon or religious sect. When an intruder penetrates the sacred space, the result is drama. *See* intruder.

COMING OF AGE

Coming of age is a core story about growing up, crossing a threshold, childhood to the next stage. Coming of age works for youthful characters like Huck Finn and Margaret Atwood's teenage narrator in Cat's Eye; it also works for older (meaner) characters like Ebenezer Scrooge and Melvin, the writer played by Jack Nicholson in *As Good as It Gets*.

CONCRETE NOUN

A part of speech that helps the writer coalesce the language to make word-pictures. In the writing world, *concrete* is a metaphor for physical detail. *Physical detail* means language that grabs the reader's sense perception. If you check *concrete* in your handy desktop dictionary, you'll see entries like "specific, not general" and "a thing or group of things as opposed to an abstraction." Concrete comes from the Latin *concrescere*, meaning "to grow together, to harden." For the savvy writer, concrete nouns split into two large groups: objects (book, car, airplane, statue, hammer, tong, rock, tree, wallet) and body parts (tongue, lip, thigh, knee, ankle, toe, eyebrow). *See* sacred object, abstract noun, Operation Ratio.

CORE STORY

A power tool that untangles plot from subplot. There are seven core stories: *King Replacement, Queen Replacement, Coming of Age, Rags to Riches, Grail Quest, Revenge Quest,* and *Scapegoat Sacrifice.* Core story welds ritual to archetype, and then plugs into deep myth. Example: Cinderella's core story is Rags to Riches. The ritual buried in Rags to Riches is an ascent, a scrambling, sweaty climb up the economic ladder. The deep myth is rebirth, a phoenix rising from the ashes. Core story is the framework of the familiar. We know story; we know not how.

King Replacement	The King dies; a Stranger replaces the King.
Queen Replacement	The Queen dies; a Stranger replaces the Queen.
Coming of Age	The King grows up. The Queen grows up.
Rags to Riches	The poor peasant (girl or boy) climbs the economic ladder.
Grail Quest	The Knight hunts the Holy Grail.
Revenge Quest	The Tarnished Knight hunts the Evil Character; Society feels safe.
Scapegoat Sacrifice	The Scapegoat gets slaughtered; Society observes.

CRONE

The third aspect of the Triple Goddess archetype, Virgin-Mother-Crone. The Good Crone is the Wise Old Woman; the Bad Crone is the Death Crone. In *The Crone,* Barbara Walker says that the Crone in our time is a suppressed archetype. *See* Death Crone.

CUT TO

A power tool borrowed from screenwriting: quick cuts from one scene to another to crank up suspense. CUT TO's build a subfloor under a sequence of scenes.

DEATH CRONE

Her job is presiding over the execution of the Hero. Smart writers disguise their Death Crones, transforming them into young bodies pulsing with sex appeal and the promise of fertility. Examples: Katharine Clifton in *The English Patient,* Daisy Buchanan in *The Great Gatsby,* Nora Papadakis in *The Postman Always Rings Twice,* Sarah Leary in *The Accidental Tourist,* Brigid O'Shaughnessy in *The Maltese Falcon,* Irina Asanova in *Gorky Park,* Miss Carmen Sternwood in *The Big Sleep.* Death Crones make terrific antagonists.

DESCRIPTION

A rhetorical mode made with concrete nouns, strong verbs, and pictorial adjectives. There are three types of description: character, landscape, and object. Raymond Chandler, the detective writer, became world-famous with his descriptions of Los Angeles.

DIALOGUE

A rhetorical mode in which two characters talk.

One: I sure hope it doesn't rain.
Two: Oh, I certainly don't mind a little rain.

The best dialogue conceals subtext. The worst dialogue explains the story, expository speeches by your characters. To write good dialogue, follow the five rules:

1. one-two, one-two (Tip: Keep your dialogue lines short.)
2. echo words for glue (Tip: Repeat cool key words to bind the lines together.)
3. object in the dialogue (Tip: For focus, insert an object—jewel, money, weapon, keepsake, etc.).
4. link to the past (Tip: Have one speaker drag in something from the back story.)
5. hook to the future (Tip: Have one speaker look ahead—the next hour, tomorrow, next week, next year.)

EXPOSITION

A rhetorical mode made from mixing weak verbs with abstract nouns. Expo-expositionsition comes from *exponere*, to explain, to elucidate. Its function in the novel is stopping the story to explain the story. When you line edit, cut all exposition. Chop it out. Trash your exposition.

FRAGMENTS

To write fragments you toss out verbs, the beating heart of the word-picture. In return, you explore a rhythm that can get poetic, not a bad trade. In Greek rhetoric, this is called *ellipsis:* the conscious removal of a particular part of speech.

GENETIC SUCCESS

A burning desire to see one's genes replicated in a gene-carrier and the basis of mate selection using the Three Goods.

GRAIL QUEST

A core story based on the Wandering Knight-Errant who seeks the Holy Grail. The Quester, a low-verbal Knight Errant who cannot ask the question, quests far and wide (through Wasted Land and Blasted Desert and Mysterious Chapel Perilous) for a sacred vessel connected to the Last Supper, a Big Event in the Christian Religion. In the Grail tale from the Middle Ages, the Grail was a sacred object, a silver vessel carried by a Grail Maiden dressed in white samite. For different twists on the spine of the Grail

Quest, change the object. The quest for a weapons emplacement buried in a hillside in Greece produces a tale like *The Guns of Navarone*. The quest for a mythic jeweled bird produces *The Maltese Falcon*, a mystery based on a treasure hunt. Key elements in the Grail Quest: the Quester, his Sturdy Mount, the Grail Object, the Fisher King, the Grail Maiden, the Mysterious Castle, Chapel Perilous, the Dragon in Disguise, the Wasted Land.

GRID

A compression tool.

HELPER

One of three main roles for a character in your novel. The helper acts as a catalyst, a force for change.

INTRUDER

An alien or stranger who penetrates the closed circle to make drama. Example: In *Jane Eyre*, Jane invades Thornfield Hall, then the library, then the tower where Bertha Mason is caged, then Rochester's heart. In *The Accidental Tourist*, Muriel Pritchett invades the life of Macon Leary. Three things can happen to the intruder:

1. repelled at the threshold;
2. evicted following penetration; or
3. assimilated by the interior.

See closed circle.

KEY SCENE

A turning point or hot spot in the story where the plot collides with one or more subplots. Screenwriters name key scenes: Plot Point One marks the end of Act One; Midpoint marks the middle of the plot; Plot Point Two marks the end of Act Two.

KING REPLACEMENT

A core story based on ritual regicide and a sexual triad of King-Queen-Stranger. The King is old and the land is dying, so the Queen replaces the King with a fertile stranger. The King, a sick old man, is a scapegoat who pays for the dead land with his blood. Key figures in King

Replacement: the Sick (Rich) Old Man, the Beautiful (Young) Queen, the Handsome (Beefy) Stranger, the Wasted (Ruined) Land.

LINE EDITING

A ritual for writers in search of perfect prose. Line editing works the words on the page. The philosophical basis of line editing is this: Bad prose can get better if the writer fixes the syntax and replaces bad words with good words. Line editing works better if you have a strategy. *See* Operation Ratio, noun, verb, syntactic flex.

LIST OF SCENES

A rewriting tool. By compressing named scenes into a list, the writer gains control of sequence, the key to building dramatic intensity.

LONG SENTENCE RELEASE

An exercise for syntactic flex in which you write one long sentence and your left brain says "period here, dummy," you replace the period with speed-connectors like *and, so, but, then, when, and then, and so, and when*, and *then* at the edge of your longest known sentence, the longest sentence you never remember writing, you break through the cyclone fence of left-brain containment and you leave the closed circle of contained language and your left-brain editor goes berserk with high glee. In Greek rhetoric, the long sentence release is called *polysyndeton*. The conscious addition of conjunctions like *and, but, so*.

-LY ADVERB

A hesitation device. Adverbs can modify verbs (she said, *sorrowfully*); or adjectives (she looked *awesomely* beautiful); or other adverbs (she spoke *absolutely awesomely truthfully*). In fiction, -ly adverbs muddy the word-pictures.

MASTER SCENE

A substantial scene with the major elements: setting (time, place, temperature, season, lighting, objects); characters; dialogue; action; a stable point of view; and a high point or climax. The *two-person scene* is power-based: master-slave, prisoner-guard, officer-soldier, doctor-nurse, doctor-patient, etc. The *three-person scene* is based on the intruder and the closed circle.

MIDPOINT

A key scene at the middle of the novel.

MINISCENE

A short scene with three elements—point of view, place, and action—that appears in the controlled frenzy of the CUT TO exercise as the writer ratchets up the suspense.

MOTIVATION

The force that drives your characters. Motive comes from trauma in the back story. Example: Cinderella's mom dies. Her dad marries an evil person who cages Cinderella. Cinderella wants out. Motive creates a character agenda, steps taken by the character to satisfy her wants and needs. *See* agenda. The best source for motivation is back story.

NARRATION

A rhetorical mode that compresses time. Example: John St. John was born in 1902. He lived a long life with much hard work. He died in 1985.

NOUN

A part of speech that names persons, places, things—all graspable through the senses—and fuzzy mental constructs that are graspable only through the brain. *See* abstract noun, concrete noun, Operation Ratio.

OPERATION RATIO

A snapshot of your style. Follow this process: Select a passage of two hundred to three hundred words. Circle the nouns and make two lists: concrete nouns and abstract nouns. Concrete nouns are perceptible with at least one of the five senses. Abstract nouns are mental constructs apprehensible via the intellect. *Bird* is concrete; *administration* is abstract. You need all sorts of nouns when you write, but if you are writing fiction, where the language is word-pictures, then you need an overweighting in concrete nouns. If your concrete column numbers fifty and your abstract column numbers fifty, then your ratio is 1:1. To write good fiction, you need a ratio of 8:1, concrete to abstract. In his *Alexandria Quartet*, Laurence Durrell has some passages with ratios of 20:1, concrete to abstract. See noun, verb, concrete noun, abstract noun, weak verb, strong verb.

PARALLEL STRUCTURE

Repetition of key phrases at strategic locations in your prose. Example: "Blessed are the poor in spirit . . . Blessed are they that mourn . . . Blessed are the meek . . ."

PLOT

The path of the protagonist. What happens first and what happens next and what happens after that and how the story ends. *See* Aristotle's incline, list of scenes, sacred object, climax, resource base, and core story.

PLOT POINT ONE

A screenwriting term for the key scene that marks the end of Act One.

PLOT POINT TWO

The key scene that marks the end of Act Two.

POINT OF VIEW (POV)

Angle of perception. First person uses the pronouns *I, me, mine, myself*. Third person uses the pronouns *she, her, hers, he, him, his. Jane Eyre* is first person; *Amsterdam* is third. The key to point of view is sense perception. The character who smells, the character who hears, touches, and tastes. The character who sweats; who feels hot, cold, shivery, icy.

PROTAGONIST

The lead character in your novel. Protagonist is derived from the Greek. *Protos* means "first, foremost" and *agonist(es)* means "one who competes" for the prize. Most protago-

nists are good guys/gals, and therefore worthy of friendship with the reader. The job of the protagonist is to control the surface, what the reader sees.

QUEEN REPLACEMENT

A core story built on a sexual triad: Queen, King, Stranger. The Queen is old or no longer useful. The King replaces her with a younger female. In *The Accidental Tourist* (Anne Tyler), Macon Leary replaces wife Sarah with Muriel the magical dog-trainer. Macon, the King figure, is spiritually dead. Key figures in Queen Replacement: the Other Woman (Man), the Victim Queen, the King in Near-Death (Ticking Clock), the Rich Old Man as Death God.

RAGS TO RICHES

A core story about a threshold crossing to gain access to a resource base. The movement is up: an ascent from rags (poverty) to riches (wealth, safety, comfort). The main ritual in Rags to Riches is climbing the economic ladder. The popular archetype in Rags to Riches is Cinderella, a Virgin. Key figures in Rags to Riches: Cinderella, the Evil Stepmother, the Fairy Godmother (Mythic Helper), Villainous Helpers, the Handsome Prince, the economic resource base (wealth, castle, big house, big corporation, fat bank account, fertile land, garden, etc.), the Big Celebration (wedding, funeral, party, dance, etc.).

RESOURCE BASE

The object of desire in your story. What do the characters want? What will the characters kill for? What thing will they die for? Money? A job? A castle on the hill? A city-state in ancient Greece? A country? A planet? Gold? Buried treasure? Loot? A statuette of a black bird? A motel? Resource base is more obvious in cinema. Example: The resource base in *The Road Warrior* is the fuel depot; the resource base in *Water World* is dirt; the resource base in *Working Girl* is the House of Money. At its most basic level, story is a competition for the resource base. Resource base keeps the rewrite simple.

REVENGE QUEST

A core story that narrows the hunt for the Holy Grail into the hunt for a live creature, human, animal, alien thing. The motive for the hunt is payment. Prince Hamlet wants revenge for his father's death. Captain Ahab wants revenge for his lost leg.

RECURRING OBJECT

A concrete noun repeated numerous times in your prose. Examples: The recurring object in *The Great Gatsby* is the yellow car; the recurring object in *The English Patient* is the book of Herodotus; the recurring object in *Jane Eyre* is the letter; the recurring object in *Moby-Dick* is the harpoon. Recurring objects tighten the structure of your novel.

RITUAL

An observed action that accrues rigidity and uniformity through repetition. Jay Gatsby throws parties. His motive: He hopes the noise and the lights will attract Daisy, a married female. His repetitive party-throwing is a courtship ritual, innocent, romantic, hopeless.

SACRED OBJECT

An object in your prose becomes "sacred" through repetition. A repeated object can link to religion (ark, Holy Grail, ankh, omphalos) or to everyday life (lamp, mirror, mask, cauldron). The smartest use of a sacred object comes in *The Maltese Falcon*, where Dashiell Hammett sends his sleuth on a Grail Quest for a bird statuette that is responsible for multiple deaths. When your book gets sold to the movies, your objects will make the leap from words on the page to image on film. Gatsby's yellow car made the leap. So did the English Patient's copy of Herodotus and the monster cannon in *The Guns of Navarone*. For a full list of sacred objects, see Barbara Walker's *The Woman's Dictionary of Symbols and Sacred Objects* (HarperCollins: New York, 1988).

SCAPEGOAT SACRIFICE

A core story that involves the punishment of an innocent. When something bad happens—murder, loss, scandal, corruption, plague—society needs a scapegoat to take the blame. Example: When the kingdom of Thebes is ravaged by a plague, Oedipus the King tries to pin the blame on Tiresias, to make Tiresias a scapegoat. The pattern here is substitution of an innocent, a goat who takes the heat for the bad guy. Scapegoat Sacrifice is a staple of mystery novels. Society lusts for revenge (eye for an eye, tooth for a tooth, life for a life), so bad guys use the frame-up to make someone besides the killer pay for the crime.

SCENE

A bucket for drama. The word *scene* comes from the Greek *skaena*, meaning "tent," "stage or theater." A scene in fiction is a single action or a series of linked actions taking place in a single setting in a finite period of time. For your rewrite, *see* list of scenes, master scene, miniscene.

SCENE NAMES

Naming scenes is fun. Naming draws boxes around scenes, extracts them from the swamp of prose. Naming gives you control over a scene list or scene sequence. Scene names come from setting (the Crimson Room in *The Great Gatsby*); from action (witness interview in a mystery); from ritual (near-death, rebirth, party, wedding, funeral); and from structure (Midpoint, Plot Point One).

SCENE TEMPLATE

A structure for rewriting a scene—warm-up, overview, setting, character description, action and dialogue, intruder and closed circle, and climax—in thirty-one minutes.

SHORT SENTENCES

One component of the syntactic flex exercise. Compressing into short sentences ("See Spot run." "I want my cookie." "The grass was short.") constricts your narration.

Narration compresses time. Short sentences compress narration, squeezing it down. You can hear the squeezing when you read aloud. In Greek rhetoric, this technique is called *asyndeton*. Writing short sentences takes you back to childhood. Simple syntax, no room for puffy polysyllables.

STAGE SETUP

A term borrowed from theater: time, place, temperature, season, lighting, props, objects in the landscape. In a novel, stage setup alerts the reader not only about time and place, but also about mood, atmosphere, and depth of scene. Stage setup contains symbols, adding dimension to the writing. Smart writers build solid stages. Place precedes character.

STORYLINE

A bare-bones description of plot or subplot. To find the storyline, write for ten minutes using this startline: "This is a story about . . ."

STRONG VERB

A part of speech that helps the writer make word-pictures. Strong verbs come from concrete nouns like *hammer* and *smash* and *lob*. Example: "The boy hammers the baseball." When you write fiction, you need to overweight strong verbs to weak. *See* weak verb, Operation Ratio.

STRUCTURE

An arrangement of parts. Novels have a plot and two or more subplots. Plot runs on the surface; subplots run under the plot. A story has three parts: beginning, middle, and end. Novels and films have three acts. Act One is the beginning, Act Two is the middle, Act Three is the end. To mark each act, the screenwriters create "plot points." Act One ends with Plot Point One; Act Two ends with Plot Point Two. Because Act Two is often overlong, screenwriters created Midpoint. Acts are built with scenes. To see the structure of an act, we use a scene list.

SUBPLOT

A secondary story running under the plot. *Sub* is a Latin prefix. It means "under, below, beneath, down there."

SUBPLOT ONE

Home of the antagonist. Key to dramatic conflict. Key to your rewrite. A story can have two, three, four, or more subplots, but the most important subplot is Subplot One.

SUBPLOTS TWO, THREE, FOUR, FIVE, ETC.

Secondary storylines attached to major characters in a piece of dramatic literature. Multiple subplots create a thick texture, tough to handle in a rewrite. *Jane Eyre* has five subplots; *The English Patient* has five subplots; *The Great Gatsby* has six subplots. *See* Monster, Death Crone.

SUBTEXT

The unsaid, not-said, semivisible, opaque stuff that lurks below the word surface. The stuff of subtext is emotion: anger, despair, hate, greed, love. When we rewrite, we work the subtext.

SYNTACTIC FLEX

An exercise that uses syntax to put more rhythm in your prose. The process uses timed writing, moving the writer through four syntactic patterns. *See* short sentences, fragments, chaining, and long sentence release.

THIRTY-ONE-MINUTE SCENE TEMPLATE

See scene template.

THREE GOODS, THE

Good genes, good resources, good behavior. The key to mate selection, a standard ritual in storytelling, which ties character motivation to genetic success. In fiction, a *baby* becomes the gene-carrier, thrusting parental genes into the future. Example: If Character A has good genes and good behavior and bad resources, your story is how she hooks up with Character B, who has good genes, good resources, and bad behavior. (See *The Red Queen* by Matt Ridley; see *Madame Bovary's Ovaries*, by David and Nanelle Barash.)

TRIPLE GODDESS

Virgin-Mother-Crone, three aspects of the major female archetype. The Virgin is a young female. Her color is white. The Mother is a child-bearing female. Her color is red. The Crone is an ancient female. Her color is black. (See the "Trinity" in Barbara Walker's *The Woman's Encylopedia of Myths and Secrets*.) *See* Death Crone and Rags to Riches.

WEAK VERB

A part of speech that kills your chances of writing word-pictures. There are four kinds of weak verbs: subjunctives, passives, infinitives, and interiors.

Subjunctives: would, could, should, may, might, must.

Passives: The ball was hammered by the boy. It has often been thought that . . .

Infinitives: In order to get downtown, it is necessary to ride the bus.

Interiors: think, know, understand, allege, assume, opine, realize.

See Operation Ratio, strong verb.

WORD-PICTURE

The language of fiction. Jack Kerouac, in *Spontaneous Prose*, has thirty rules for writers. Rule 26: "Bookmovie is the movie in words, the visual American form." And Rule 22: "Don't think of words when you stop but to see picture better."

WRITING PRACTICE

Writing like an athlete trains; writing every day, whether you feel like it or not; writing under the clock, timing yourself to distract the internal editor; writing with these rules: keep the hand moving, don't cross out, don't edit, go for the jugular, go for first thoughts, don't think, lose control, spend it all. (See *Writing Down the Bones*, by Natalie Goldberg.)

Index

About the Author

Robert J. Ray, Ph.D., is the author of more than a dozen books, including five in the Matt Murdock PI series; three in the Weekend Novelist series; a cop-novel, a tennis novel, a thriller, a reading-for-writing book, and a how-to on small business entrepreneurship that is now in its 6th edition.

During his quarter-century teaching career—Texas, Wisconsin, California, Seattle—he has coached hundreds of writers in fiction and nonfiction. Ray's credo: With focus, a weak writer can get stronger; a strong writer can reach for perfection.

This book, *The Weekend Novelist Rewrites the Novel*, combines Ray's love of teaching and a life–long fascination with word and story, sentence and rhetorical device, and the often invisible structure of the novel.

Ray's personal writing breakthrough came when he learned the power of writing practice from Natalie Goldberg's workshop in Taos: Write with a kitchen timer, keep the hand moving, and don't listen to the ruthless internal critic.

Ray lives in Seattle with his wife, Margot, and a yellow tabby cat named Hugo.